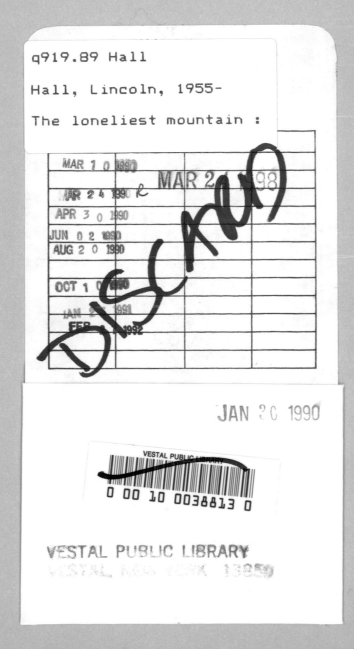

THE
LONELIEST
MOUNTAIN

THE
LONELIEST
MOUNTAIN

The Dramatic Story of the First Expedition to
Climb Mt Minto, Antarctica

Text by LINCOLN HALL
Photographs by JONATHAN CHESTER

THE MOUNTAINEERS
Seattle

Acknowledgements

Books, like expeditions, are a team effort and *The Loneliest Mountain* is no exception. We would like to thank the editorial staff at Simon and Schuster Australia, particularly the Publisher, Kirsty Melville, who supported the expedition and the book even before we left Australia, and our editor, Susan Morris-Yates.

For *The Loneliest Mountain's* visual style we are most grateful to designer Deborah Brash, who created the book under pressure of difficult deadlines, and to Alistair Barnard, who produced the elegant maps.

Many of the expedition members, as well as friends and family also contributed greatly during the preparation of the manuscript. Simon Grimes, Lyle Closs, Greg Mortimer, Chris Hilton, Barbara Scanlon and Margaret Werner made invaluable comments about the text, while Greg, Margaret, Chris, Lyle, Peter Gill, Glenn Singleman, Don Richards and Colin Putt helped add depth to the book with their appendices. Colin also provided the diagrams of the *Alan And Vi Thistlethwayte*.

To Dylan Arjuna Hall and Narayan Shresta

AND

To Kay Gordon

The Mountaineers: Organised 1906 '. . . to explore,
study, preserve and enjoy the natural beauty . . .'

© 1989 Text, Lincoln Hall
© 1989 Photographs, Jonathan Chester

Published by The Mountaineers
306 Second Avenue West, Seattle, WA 98119, USA

Published simultaneously in Australia
by Simon & Schuster Australia
7 Grosvenor Place, Brookvale NSW 2100

A Division of Gulf + Western

Designed by Deborah Brash/Brash design
Maps by Alistair Barnard
Typeset in Hong Kong by Setrite Typesetters Ltd
Produced by Mandarin Offset
Printed and bound in Hong Kong

Foreword

Thomas Keneally

'In the tracks of Sisyphus, we haul the weight
of our ambitions in our sleds.'

I REMEMBER a day when Lincoln Hall was sitting at his ease on the sundeck of my house in Sydney and chatting about his experiences as a member of the first Australian party ever to climb Everest. All of us there on the sundeck were dressed for a summer's day. I noticed the damage which several seasons of Himalayan frostbite had done to Lincoln's feet and hands. As non-climbers always do, I wondered about the compulsion which makes an Australian, born in the sun in a country of ancient, worn-down mountains, seek the transcendent cold and height of the highest mountains of all. Yet it was obvious from the way Lincoln talked that mountaineering was the focus for his view of the world and for a certain mysticism to do with the earth.

This book is an account of an extraordinary Antarctic trek to the highest mountain in North Victoria Land, Mt Minto. Minto itself would not necessarily be the problem. The fiercest challenge seemed to be to get the party of six men through the Antarctic ice on a small boat endearingly named the *Thistlethwayte* and then inland on skis to the base of the mountain. The six wanted to prove that small non-official parties of dedicated people were appropriate for the exploration of Antarctica. When and if this party — led by the calm, gangling Greg Mortimer — reached the top of Mt Minto, they intended to dedicate it 'as the cornerstone in an Antarctic World Park.'

Lincoln Hall's tale is one of the two or three best and most engrossing accounts ever written about travel in Antarctica. The writings of Scott, Shackleton, Mawson have an enormous grandeur, but they suffer from two great deficiencies. You find them running out of adjectives and insights to convey the awesomeness of Antarctica's great mountains and the spaces between them, to convey what all this and the withering cold do to the human spirit in its threatened little sheaf of flesh. Secondly, they were sometimes less than frank about the conflicts and variations of personality which occur even amongst the bravest parties. So they failed to give their work its full human dimension.

Lincoln Hall can write very well about the unspeakable aspects of Antarctica. 'The spirituality is here too, but it is raw and awaiting an interpretation.' And in matters of humanity and potential conflict he is equally gifted and frank.

This book will go a long way towards explaining why some humans drag themselves through a landscape of frightening dimensions and hellish cold, all for the sake of some revelation which is almost impossible to pass on to others in words.

Besides that, I'm pleased to say this is an old-fashioned ripping yarn. Simply what befell the party on its 21-metre vessel going to and returning from Antarctica is all to do with survival by centimetres and luck and courage. And in the spirit of the best Antarctic literature, the party faces a situation where even to reach Minto, even to spend an extra day climbing it, could mean becoming trapped in Antarctica for the whole winter of total darkness.

Because of its force and narrative energy, I hope this story reaches thousands of readers.

Contents

Prologue

THE night is dark enough to disguise the huge drop beneath me while I concentrate on lifting my foot up to the small metal plate clamping the two cables together. I grunt with the effort. If it was not for these intersections in the web of structural cables the climb would be easy. I straighten my leg as I lean back and the action pushes my body up. Now I can reach above the overlap of the cables and place the second loop of high-strength cord around the thick bundle of woven steel. I clip the loose of the cord into my harness and enjoy the feeling of relief. One length of cord is strong enough to hold my weight but up here it is good to have another as a safeguard.

I tilt my head back and look up. Greg is climbing strongly and is already far above me, as if he has been dragged upwards by the angels who protect the earth. Two cables to my right, Andy matches my slow pace. The cables run diagonally at an angle of about 15 degrees from the vertical. Gravity forces us to hang beneath them as if we were climbing a continuous overhang. The difference is that instead of the comforting feel of a rock wall in front of me there is only air.

How strange it is to be here. I look out over the night lights of Sydney rather than across to sandstone buttresses rising out of a green carpet of eucalypts. The act of climbing always traps my mind in the present as I concentrate upon the slow-motion acrobatics I perform. And when I rest, I contemplate the scene below me. The jazz club's serenade ceased two hours ago. Only taxis prowl the streets beneath us. The huge cylinder of the MLC building rising across Market Street is silhouetted by the full moon. The heart of Sydney no longer feels like a madhouse full of cars battling traffic-lights and air-conditioned office-workers fighting telephones between cigarettes. Instead of deploring the loneliness of the concrete jungle, I marvel at the imagination of the person who designed Centrepoint Tower, and of the society which spawned the fantastic skyline of this city. Sydney will never seem the same after this climb.

Three o'clock in the morning; two hours above the roof of the building and 100 metres above the city streets. I glance up at the base of the giant flowerpot-shaped restaurant perched on top of the metal column. The cables which stablise the structure disappear above me in the darkness. We will get a better view of the whole construction when daylight comes. By then, our huge banner of protest will be stretched between the cables, and we shall hang there suspended, waiting for the world to notice us. For a few hours or a day, depending on the initiative of the police, Centrepoint Tower will become Sydney's highest billboard. Our advertisement is not brand specific; simply a blanket ban on all nuclear warships.

I turn my concentration to the mechanical movements of sliding the cord up the cable, transferring my weight to it, and then sliding the second cord up beneath it. When I concentrate I can stretch a few centimetres more. Those increments add up when spread over a 200-metre climb.

The city is expanding beneath us now. From up here neon lights are no longer heavenly messages floating above freeways and intersections. They remind me of the reflections of an evening rainbow on a wet asphalt road. The builders of roads never intended such accidental beauty, just as the makers of

Greg Mortimer, Lincoln Hall and Andy Henderson suspend a banner from the cables of Sydney's Centrepoint Tower as a protest against nuclear ships.

signs did not have this viewpoint in mind. Climbs always give me a different perspective on the world.

I look across 5 metres of air and realise that Andy is drawing ahead. There is no race, but I remember our sense of urgency. Darkness protects us now but with the coming of dawn we will be seen. By that time we have to be well above the tiny half-way platform which can be reached by a trapdoor from inside the tower. I speed up the routine of sliding the upper cord, transferring my weight, sliding the lower cord, transferring my weight. The next intersection of the cables draws slowly closer and my heart beats more quickly with the adrenalin of anticipation. Put it out of your mind, I tell myself. Concentrate on the action of climbing and worry about the hard parts when you reach them.

It is much cooler here than on the roofs where we slept for a few hours while waiting for the floodlights to go out at midnight. As the wind begins to blow I am glad that I wore extra clothes. The nylon webbing stirrups attached to the cord around the cables flutter in the breeze and remind me again that only air lies between me and streets below. I smile to myself in the darkness, and dismiss what I was about to think of as the cold.

How different is this climb from the next major expedition Greg and I shall undertake. This climb will be over in a few hours; then there will be hours of waiting while we bargain with police. The quiet satisfaction that follows other climbs will be followed by handcuffs and the bright lights of television cameras. What a strange world we humans create for ourselves. Nowhere on earth is further away from here than Antarctica.

ANTARCTICA

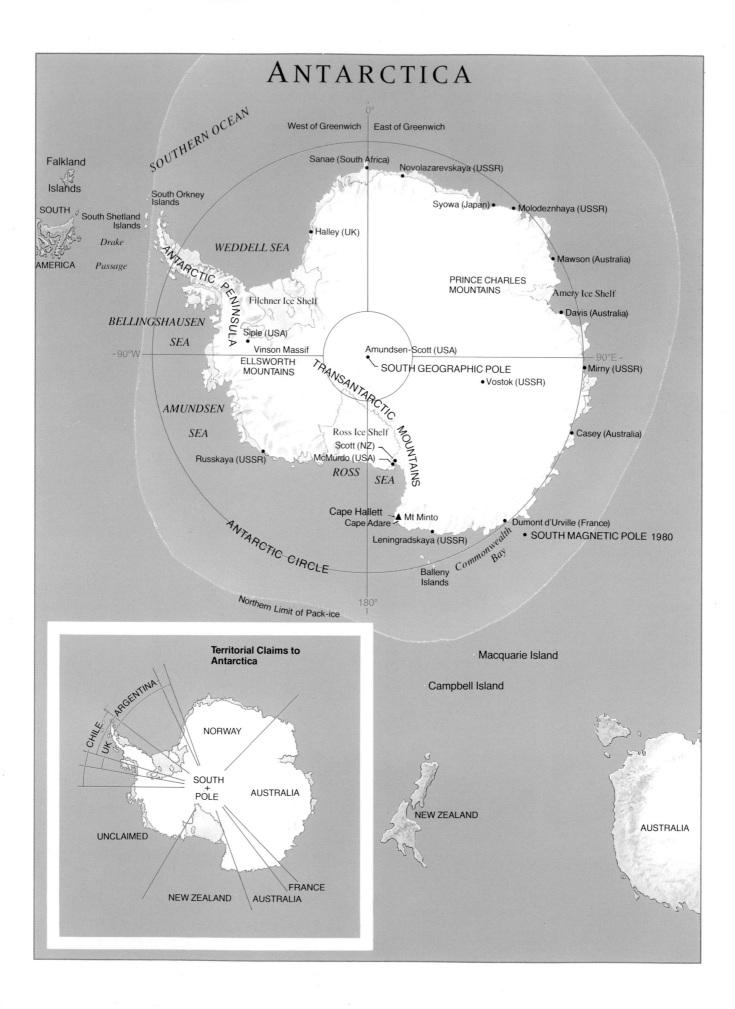

SOUTHERN OCEAN

West of Greenwich | East of Greenwich

0°

Falkland Islands

SOUTH

South Orkney Islands

South Shetland Islands

AMERICA

Drake

Passage

Sanae (South Africa)

Novolazarevskaya (USSR)

Syowa (Japan)

Molodeznhaya (USSR)

Halley (UK)

WEDDELL SEA

Mawson (Australia)

PRINCE CHARLES MOUNTAINS

Amery Ice Shelf

Davis (Australia)

BELLINGSHAUSEN SEA

Filchner Ice Shelf

ANTARCTIC PENINSULA

Siple (USA)

Vinson Massif

− 90°W

ELLSWORTH MOUNTAINS

Amundsen-Scott (USA)

SOUTH GEOGRAPHIC POLE

90°E −

Mirny (USSR)

TRANSANTARCTIC MOUNTAINS

Vostok (USSR)

AMUNDSEN SEA

Casey (Australia)

Russkaya (USSR)

Ross Ice Shelf

Scott (NZ)

McMurdo (USA)

ROSS SEA

Cape Hallett
Cape Adare ▲ Mt Minto

Dumont d'Urville (France)

SOUTH MAGNETIC POLE 1980

Leningradskaya (USSR)

Commonwealth Bay

ANTARCTIC CIRCLE

Balleny Islands

180°

Northern Limit of Pack-ice

Territorial Claims to Antarctica

CHILE

ARGENTINA

UK

NORWAY

SOUTH + POLE

AUSTRALIA

UNCLAIMED

NEW ZEALAND

FRANCE

AUSTRALIA

Macquarie Island

Campbell Island

NEW ZEALAND

AUSTRALIA

Introduction

ANTARCTICA is a land of contradictions. It is the coldest place on earth and yet in summer the sun circles the sky twenty-four hours each day. Seventy per cent of the earth's fresh water lies frozen on this highest and driest continent. The world's largest mammals swim in waters colder than 0°C. Rocky shelves around the coast are homes for huge rookeries of black and white birds whose very appearance is a caricature. From the South Pole everywhere is north. Each spring the coast gives birth to icebergs — majestic floating ambassadors which sink *Titanic*s, *Endurance*s, *Southern Quest*s and all ideas of human omnipotence.

Mountaineering is just as contradictory. Every year dozens of people die in the Himalaya attempting to climb the mountain of their dreams. To the outsider, they appear like moths throwing themselves at a candle flame — their ambition seems pointless, misdirected. But to the climbers the mountains offer intense beauty, a struggle against fear and hardship, a mirror for the soul. To its most dedicated practitioners climbing has become a religion.

It was inevitable that mountaineers would turn their eyes to Antarctica — the sport of contradictions in a land of paradoxes. The continent itself is inaccessible enough to allow true pioneering. The Transantarctic Mountains form one of the longest mountain ranges on earth, containing thousands of mountain valleys which have never been visited.

Many of the more accessible peaks have been climbed but most of the early explorers were kept busy with the enormous tasks of mapping the land and pushing back the borders of the unknown. Their adventures have no equal in terms of commitment and isolation. More recently, exploration has been conducted by helicopters and well-supplied tractor trains. The harsh environment and vast scale of Antarctica make these excursions seem daunting, but they bear no comparison to the journeys of Shackleton, Amundsen, and Mawson.

The modern world has lost sight of the precedents set by those early adventurers. Polar expeditions have become huge national or international affairs, and the earth a giant laboratory full of resources to be used when appropriate technology is discovered. The dry and inaccessible documents produced by science and bureaucracy capture nothing of Antarctica's magic.

The continent remains remote and aloof but, like every wild place on earth, it is threatened with destruction. Private adventures into the wilderness would be indulgent if they did not, at least sometimes generate public concern. Our aim was to climb a mountain, but the size and style of our expedition was actually more important than the goal itself. Given enough resources, anything can be achieved. The challenge is to meet our world on its own ground, because then one has no choice but to understand it.

The task we set ourselves was to climb Mt Minto, the highest peak in the mountainous country along the western shore of the Ross Sea, known as North Victoria Land. Only three or four peaks in the whole range had been climbed, and the highest remained untouched. Mt Minto had defeated four previous teams, only one of which was able to reach the base of the mountain. We soon discovered why.

Greg Mortimer and I first planned the expedition for the summer of 1986–87. I looked into the possibilities of sponsorship while Greg investigated a method of getting to Antarctica. Air transport seemed out of the question because the only aircraft capable of landing there could not carry enough fuel for the return journey. The only ship available to sail from Australian or New Zealand waters was a Norwegian icebreaker with a charter price of $600,000. On top of this, we would have to add the costs of food, equipment, and the enormous job of raising the money to pay for it all.

While we debated our chances of being able to do this in time for departure at the end of 1986, we learned of an Austrian expedition, funded by its government, which was ready to go. The Austrians had already made one attempt the previous season but their ship, the *Southern Quest,* was crushed by pack-ice before the mountaineers were able to get ashore. No-one was killed but all their equipment and supplies went to the bottom of the Ross Sea.

We did not wish to race for Mt Minto in the manner of Amundsen and Scott, nor did we like the idea of being the second party to climb the peak, so we planned our departure for the following season. Hopefully by that time a less expensive ship would be available. If the Austrians did manage the ascent before us, we would congratulate them, then find another objective, even though we knew anything else would be second best. Mt Minto is the highest peak in the Admiralty Range, and to make the first ascent would be on a par with being the first to climb Mont Blanc, Mt Cook or Mt McKinley. That was the reason it had attracted attention from as far afield as Austria, a country with a long history of mountain exploration.

Early in 1987 we heard that once again the Austrians had failed. This time they did not even set foot on ice. Instead, they waited in New Zealand for the ship they had chartered to break free from pack-ice and come north to collect them from Christchurch. By the time the ship arrived, the short Antarctic summer was past its zenith, and even if the mountaineers had been able to reach the continent it was certain the freezing of the sea would trap them there for the winter. Greg commiserated with them by telephone, and they told him they would try again in two years' time. We heard that some New Zealanders were also making plans for Mt Minto that year. Our only opportunity would be the summer of 1987–88.

We stepped up our preparations. Lyle Closs and Jonathan Chester joined our team. Lyle had long nursed the ambition of an Antarctic adventure, so it was a logical step to combine his talents and resources with ours. Jonathan, an experienced Antarctic expeditioner, did not hesitate to accept Greg's invitation, even though it meant giving up his position on the Bicentennial Mt Everest Expedition. There was great deal for each of us to do. We had to assemble all the necessary food and specialised equipment, find a ship as well as the money to charter it with, and interest a film crew in our project. The four of us spent many nights planning everything from the best way to reach the continent and approach the mountain, to the number of tents to take with us.

By mid-1987 our plans had become more concrete. After exploring every option we settled upon chartering a ship from the Oceanic Research Foundation, a non-profit organisation created to service the needs of ventures such as ours. Not only was there work to be done on the boat, but also in collecting and stowing supplies, which began to take up more and more space in our storeroom. Greg and Lyle devoted all their spare time to scheduling deadlines for the delivery of equipment, and to other fine details.

Mt Minto was going to be climbed – and we were determined to be the first to stand on its summit.

The Climbers

LINCOLN HALL, 33, is originally from Canberra, ACT, where he first began rockclimbing at the age of 15. Although he intended to pursue a career as a herpetologist, his enthusiasm for mountaineering led him to work as a climbing and trekking guide in Nepal, India and South America. While based in the Himalaya, Lincoln climbed Ama Dablam, Annapurna II by a new route on the south face, and many lesser peaks. In 1984, Lincoln was part of the successful Australian expedition to the north face of Mt Everest, about which he wrote his first book *White Limbo* (1985).

JONATHAN CHESTER, 38, grew up in Adelaide, where he learned to climb and first worked as a climbing instructor. Although he studied biogeography, Jonathan, works as a freelance photojournalist. His memorable climbs are the Caroline Face of Mt Cook, the second ascent of Big Ben on Heard Island, Broad Peak in Pakistan and Annapurna III in Nepal. Jonathan has made five journeys to Antarctica, including Project Blizzard. He is the author of *Going to Extremes* (1986) about Australia's Antarctic heritage, and *The Himalayan Experience* (1989).

GREG MORTIMER, 36, is from Sydney, NSW, and, as a teenager, learned to climb in the nearby Blue Mountains. After completing his degree, Greg initially worked as a geologist in some of the remotest parts of Australia, New Zealand and Antarctica. In recent years he has also worked as a climbing instructor and mountain guide in those countries and in Nepal. His most notable climbs have included the first ascents of the south face of Annapurna II, Nepal, in 1983, and of the Grand Couloir, on the north face of Mt Everest without oxygen in 1984; and the first Australian ascent of Vinson Massif, Antarctica, after the Mt Minto expedition in 1988.

LYLE CLOSS, 35, grew up in Tasmania where, as a teenager, he learned to climb. He pioneered many new routes on cliffs throughout Tasmania, including the first ascent of the west face of Federation Peak. As his career in journalism and public relations progressed, Lyle moved to Sydney and continued to rockclimb regularly, both in Victoria and New South Wales, where he opened up new routes on isolated cliffs in the Blue Mountains. Lyle has long been fascinated by Antarctica: he discovered his university's collection of books on Antarctic exploration — and nothing was ever quite the same again.

GLENN SINGLEMAN, 30, grew up in Sydney and studied to be a doctor. As well as this, Glenn has always had a great interest in film-making and went to film school for three years. He made his first documentary with Chris Hilton in 1987, recording Chris's ascent of the Sydney Tower. Through Chris, Glenn became interested in rockclimbing and subsequently he has climbed around the Sydney region and was the first Australian to climb Carstensz Pyramid (Puncak Jaya) in Irian Jaya. His latest documentary, again with Chris Hilton, recorded the Mt Minto expedition.

CHRIS HILTON, 27, grew up among the Snowy Mountains of Australia where he learned to ski and to climb. Before undertaking a degree in engineering, Chris worked as an instructor at the Australian Outward Bound School. Any free time from studying was spent mountaineering, skiing and rockclimbing. Rather than work as an engineer, Chris preferred to become involved in film-making. With Glenn Singleman he made a documentary about his ascent of the Sydney Tower. Chris and Glenn's next film was the documentary of the Bicenntenial Antarctic Expedition — also called *The Loneliest Mountain*.

The Crew

DON RICHARDS, 67, was born and brought up in Sydney, and was an engineer until he retired. A licenced radio amateur, Don was ship's mate to Dr David Lewis and radio operator for the Oceanic Research Foundation's (ORF) Mawson Anniversary Expedition to Cape Denison, Antarctica, in 1981. He was skipper and radio operator of the ORF's ship *Allan And Vi Thistlethwayte* (previously the *Dick Smith Explorer)* for Antarctic expeditions in 1985 and the Mt Minto voyage. As well, Don has been skipper/radio operator on numerous other observation and scientific voyages of the New South Wales coast and Tasmania.

COLIN PUTT, 62, was born in New Zealand but later moved to Sydney where he worked as a chemical engineer, but spent much of his spare time bushwalking, rockclimbing and sailing. Colin has been engineer and ship's mate on many expeditions, and has climbed in many countries including New Zealand, Australia, Norway, Greenland and England. He was a member of the party that made the first ascent of Big Ben on Heard Island. Colin was instrumental in developing the Scientific Expedition Group and is President of the Oceanic Research Foundation. In 1987 he was named 'Adventurer of the Year' by *Australian Geographic.*

KEN SCOTT, 35, was born in northern Queensland. He is an ex-navy diver and has also worked as security guard and as a builder. His great love has always been 'messing about in boats'. He has taken part in ocean yacht races and has also frequently worked delivering boats around the country. Ken's involvement with the expedition to Mt Minto initially arose because he himself was building a yacht in which to sail to Antarctica. Ken is currently studying for his ship's master's ticket.

PETER GILL, 38, grew up in Singleton, NSW, and is a descendant of James Clark Ross, who discovered the Ross Sea — and named Mt Minto. After a series of outdoor jobs he decided to study zoology at university. Peter became involved with the Oceanic Research Foundation in 1982 and has undertaken many expeditions with them. In 1983 he began research into the Humpback whale, which continues to this day. In 1985, in what later seemed to be an invaluable rehearsal for the Mt Minto expedition, Peter took part in an expedition to Cape Hallett in the tiny 15-metre yawl, *Riquita.*

MARGARET WERNER was born in Melbourne and spent most of her early life in Victoria. In 1973 she moved with her husband and daughters to the Blue Mountains, west of Sydney, NSW, to run a motel at Blackheath. Margaret later bought The Bay Tree Tea Shop at Mt Victoria, the centre of rockclimbing for Sydney climbers. Surrounded by such enthusiasm, Margaret took up climbing, too, and has undertaken many first ascents in the region. Margaret has trekked to Gaumukh, the holy source of the Ganges, and from Nepal into Tibet. After the Mt Minto expedition she voyaged as a cook on the *Bounty.*

To Hell
For A
Pastime

TO HELL FOR A PASTIME

'Of course you've heard the old saying, a man who'd go to sea for pleasure would go to hell for a pastime.'

COLIN PUTT

Wednesday, 31 December 1987

A scene of confusion greets me when I arrive back at Pier Eight, Walsh Bay, after only three hours' sleep. Dozens of friends, family and media people crowd the wharf above the *Allan And Vi Thistlethwayte*. Low tide makes our 21-metre schooner seem even smaller than usual. I climb down onto the cluttered deck. Our snow machine is strapped to the deck mid-ships, and jerry cans are tied at the base of the foremast. Behind the wheelhouse the inflated Zodiac surf-rescue boat lies on top of bags of onions and parsnips.

We six mountaineers, plus crew members Pete Gill and Margaret Werner, worked through until 4.30 am, loading the hold with climbing equipment, small fibreglass sleds, skis and enough food for a year. Skipper Don Richards, engineer Colin Putt and seaman Ken Scott finished their struggle a few hours earlier, exhausted by a week-long battle with an ancient gearbox which had chosen to die on Christmas Eve, the day before our planned departure. Today is New Year's Eve, which means we are leaving Sydney seven days behind schedule. It was a week of uncertainty, a time when we doubted the wisdom of choosing the twenty-one-year old *Allan And Vi Thistlethwayte* as the boat to take us to Antarctica. On this sunny summer's day I need to present a positive face to my family and friends, and to Barbara who is carrying our child.

I climb down the steep stairs into what used to be the hold when this ship was a fishing trawler, and throw the last of my luggage on my bunk. I try not to notice how little space there is for six of us to share. Our three-month journey to the ice will be the first sailing voyage for Greg Mortimer, Lyle Closs, Margaret Werner and myself. Chris Hilton and Glenn Singleman, film-makers, are also virtually novices at sea. Jonathan Chester is the only member of the climbing party who knows what lies ahead of us, since he has already sailed to Antarctica and back on this boat. There will be much for the rest of us to learn from Jonathan and the four experienced sailors on board.

The eleven of us stand on the edge of the wharf with our backs to the water. Greg makes a short speech of thanks to the many people who have helped us. His voice is full of relief and joy that his dream is at last becoming a reality. Allan Thistlethwayte, our patron, wishes us luck, and then we all smile for the cameras.

Allan and his wife Vi lead the way on board. They will sail the length of Sydney Harbour and leave us at the Customs Wharf at Watson's Bay. A short joyride is the very least we can do for the man whose generous

Dr Glenn Singlemann surveys his reference texts and the mountain of medical equipment prior to departure.

Previous Page: The warm light of sunset shines on the masts of the *Allan And Vi Thistlethwayte* as we head across the Southern Ocean towards Antarctica.

Margaret Werner farewells the crowd and the Australian mainland as we motor out into Sydney Harbour.

intervention only two months earlier prevented our Bicentennial Antarctic Expedition from being abandoned due to lack of funds.

With my attention centred on the crowded wharf, I miss the moment we cast off. Streamers are thrown, and as they stretch I realise that yes, we are underway at last. Emotion, usually so intangible and private, fills the air with a charge which is almost electric. The thin streamer which runs from Barbara's hand into mine unravels and draws tight. In the instant before it snaps I feel the power of this last physical connection between us. I look down at the loose blue coil in my fingers. It will be three months before we can share more than these shreds of paper.

I turn to Lyle who is standing beside me on the roof of the wheelhouse. He looks up at his wife and son and daughter, totally bewildered and almost in tears. This is his first expedition, one he has lived and breathed for the last year and a half, and one which was in doubt until the day we left. I reach out and touch his shoulder. When he turns, his eyes look straight through me. He knows that I cannot understand the value of what he is leaving behind.

I look for Greg and see him standing on the handrail, his weight on one bare foot, and his arms wrapped around one of the mainmast shrouds. The pressures of organising the expedition have left him exhausted. Only the day before yesterday we six climbers agreed to cancel the trip if the gearbox was not repaired within twenty-four hours. Yesterday when the motor was tested and all the gears worked, we shouted in triumph. Now Greg's tired face is full of happiness.

Jonathan is taking photographs of us, of the boat, and of the people on the wharf. The royal blue walls of the cabins are plastered with the logos of some of the sponsors who provided us with their products—Nikon, Duracell, Kodak, Codan. Above them in the shrouds flutter the flags of the

Australian Geographic Society, Sigma Data Corporation and Johnson Outboards. Jonathan set up most of these flags and stickers, and at least one appears in each photo he takes. He is ever mindful of our obligations to our sponsors and of his role as expedition photographer.

Glenn holds his 16 mm movie camera to his eye and swears when Chris lets the long microphone appear in the frame he is shooting. I smile at the energetic duo, and anticipate the entertainment their aggressive fashion of working together is bound to bring the rest of us.

Margaret stands with her feet on the lower of the two port rails. Nothing can contain her excitement. Her cheeks are wet with the tears of farewelling her three teenage daughters, but her eyes are almost forced closed by the width of her joyous smile. All of us feel sorrow and joy, but Margaret manages to express both without conflict.

As sailors, Pete Gill and Ken Scott should be more accustomed to these departures than the rest of us on deck, but they stare back at the wharf with the same intensity. Meanwhile, Colin disappears into the engine room and Don steers us between the ferries and other small craft on the harbour. Old hands at the game of sailing and the game of life, neither Colin nor Don appear at all excited. Whooping it up is left to the younger generation. Meanwhile there is work to be done.

Jonathan lets his cameras dangle from his neck long enough for him to open a bottle of champagne. I am too tired and confused to join in the toasting. I stand apart from the others and watch Sydney Harbour slip by. The Manly ferry travels much faster than this, I think to myself. It will take us a long time to reach Antarctica.

We drop anchor in Watson's Bay and watch the customs' boat pull up alongside. The three blue-suited officers go into the galley to sort out the paperwork. We have to do no more than fill out one form. Allan and Vi leave with the customs' boat, and shouts of 'Wish we were coming all the way.'

Now there are just the eleven of us. Before raising the anchor and motoring out of the Heads Don, as captain, gives a brief explanation of life at sea. Before now, we have had no time to consider such a simple matter as the seafaring routine. I am surprised at how little Don has to say, but I

Left: Don Richards worries about the gear box; *Centre:* Helper John Chancellor, Lyle Closs and Glenn Singleman stow the film equipment; and *Right:* Pete Gill adds a final coat of paint during the last frantic days before departure.

We anchor in Watson's Bay and while waiting for custom's clearance, serve drinks to our patrons Allan and Vi Thistlewayle.

suppose he expects each of the experienced watch-masters to continue our education. Certainly our skipper is no Captain Bligh. He explains that there will be four watches: himself with Jonathan and Lyle; Ken with Chris; Pete with Greg; and Colin with Glenn and me. Margaret will be left free to concentrate all her energy on her duties as cook. Each watch will last four hours, apart from two two-hour 'dog' watches at 4 pm and 6 pm. It sounds like a good system, with plenty of time to sleep between turns of duty.

Out of the Heads, the ship leans to port under a gentle wind while the engine helps to push us along. The cliffs of Sydney's coast form a dark band between the water and the glare of the afternoon sun. Already I feel cut off from the rest of humanity. Within an hour I am seasick over the side, then I feel instantly better. Someone sights a dolphin. I wash my mouth with a handful of seawater and hurry forward. The continual movement of the boat is disconcerting enough to make me keep one hand on the rail even in these gentle seas. Four dolphins dart across the bow and play in the wave of water pushed aside by our hull, welcoming us to a different world.

Pete turns towards me, smiling now that he is at sea again. Of the eleven people on the *Allan And Vi Thistlethwayte*, Pete is the only one who has already been to Cape Hallett, our destination. Two years earlier, he and four companions sailed the 15-metre *Riquita* further south than any small yacht had been before. They spent only two hours at Cape Hallett, the southernmost point of their voyage, before rough conditions forced them to sail out into the Ross Sea. Pete is a solidly built but softly spoken man whose gentleness can be seen in his eyes and his easy smile. He is a biologist because he loves life in all its forms, though his anarchic streak has led him to shun academia.

Early in the evening, Margaret presents us with a pre-cooked dinner which we all hope is an indication of the feasts to come. She is glad to have the relatively simple task of heating food while she adjusts to the constant but irregular rocking motion of the ship. The cramped galley offers very different challenges from her busy teashop in the Blue Mountains west of Sydney.

The galley, and Don and Margaret's bunks, occupy the aft-most section of the ship's metal hull. Above their bunks is the wheelhouse, with stairs leading down into the galley. Entirely separate and accessible only from above decks is the old fish hold. Now called the Fish Cabin, it has been converted into a central sleeping cabin as quarters for the climbing party. Forward again is the engine room, which is reached through the forecastle where Colin, Pete and Ken are to sleep. In emergencies, the engine room can also be reached through the floor of the Pleasure Dome. This compact squarish structure belies its fancy name. It is no more than a windowed metal box which is bolted over the engine room hatchway to give extra cabin space above deck.

Because the galley is too cramped to seat all eleven crew, some of us overflow up the stairs into the wheelhouse. Surprisingly, I find that eating settles my stomach so that I feel almost healthy by 8 pm when my first watch begins. Colin, Glenn and I take responsibility for the ship for the next four hours. At Colin's suggestion we decide to have two rounds of forty minutes apiece at the wheel.

During the frantic weeks before departure, the problems with the engine and the gearbox weighed heavily upon Colin and left him showing a gruff and rude face to the world. Tonight his gentler side appears as he mutters about sailing and unaffectedly slips lessons from his own adventures into the conversation. The breadth of his knowledge begins to show.

Standing watch involves keeping an eye on a range of navigational gadgets. Don has suspended his radios from the roof of the wheelhouse, above the stairs leading down into the galley. Above the chart table against the aft wall, the Satnav is bolted in place. This device converts satellite signals into readings of latitude and longitude. On the port side of the wheel is the radar screen. The radar dome itself is mounted on the mizzen mast behind the wheelhouse. Next to the radar screen is the gyrocompass, and beside it, directly in front of the wheel, is the magnetic compass. To the right of the wheel and bolted to the roof is the log, a device with a digital readout of our water speed in knots and the distance we have travelled in nautical miles.

The main job is to keep the boat pointed in the right direction. It takes some practice before I can keep the ship moving in a straight line. Colin takes over the helm from me for the last part of our watch. A few minutes before midnight Glenn goes to rouse Ken and Chris from their bunks. Colin and I sing 'Auld Lang Syne' to bring in the New Year. Colin's voice is deep and rich, but mine is ruined from singing too many Bob Dylan songs. The quiet confines of this ship are a long way from the revelry which I know is taking place ashore.

Friday, 1 January 1988

Already we have been at sea for twenty-four hours. When I awoke this morning there was no land to be seen: for the next three weeks our universe will be this—the ocean, the boat, and the eleven of us on board. I wonder how I will cope with the overcrowding. The boat is narrow for its 21-metre length and, because none of the cabins are connected, each of the downstairs cabins has a claustrophobic feel. While we sail through the Australian summer, the fresh air is welcome when we move from cabin to cabin above decks. Once we reach Antarctic regions and the rigging is coated in ice and the decks are awash with freezing water I am sure we shall all curse the poor design of the ship. The ceilings in the galley and the wheelhouse are too low for me to stand upright, but this is not as big a problem as I expected because the pitch and roll of the ship forces me to balance with my feet well apart.

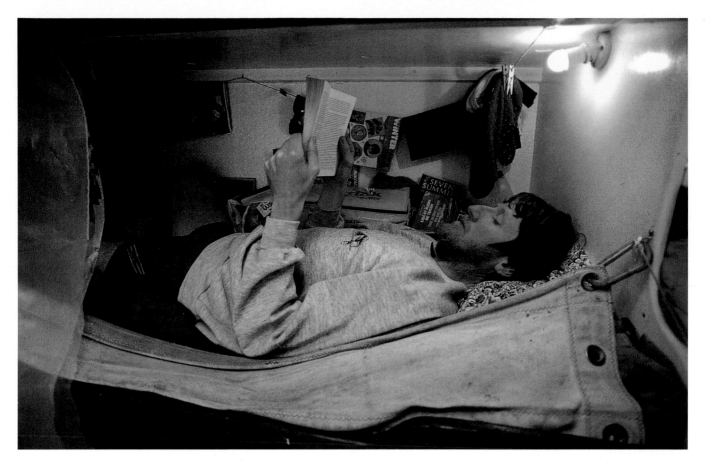

Lyle Closs soon takes to his bunk, where he will spend most of the voyage incapacitated by seasickness.

Don, Peter, Ken and Colin seem to think nothing of the discomforts of life on board, although I know our journey across the Southern Ocean aboard this small vessel will test all of us. I have heard stories of 30-metre waves swallowing boats and tumbling them like dice. The sailors seem to have no qualms, and they certainly share no death wish. As a novice at sea, I am excited by the prospect of coping with new dangers because I do not know how I will respond. Our crew's concern is with the ability of the boat to withstand whatever the ocean has to offer. Under the name of *Dick Smith Explorer* the ship has made three journeys to Antarctica. The toughest of these was when David Lewis deliberately froze the ship into the ice for a whole winter. This track record is reassuring, but provides no relief for Ken and Lyle who have been seasick since we left the Heads. It surprises me that Ken is sick, because he has spent years at sea as a navy seaman. Lyle lies in his bunk between bouts of dry-retching over the side. Ken seems to be better off because he can sleep.

Sunday, 3 January

My alarm wakes me at 3.50 am so I pull on my clothes, stagger upstairs into the cool morning air and hurry into the wheelhouse. I take the helm from Pete and steer the ship into a southerly headwind. The sea is choppy but gentle, and occasionally a bird swoops by half a metre or so above the waves. I wonder how life will be in two weeks time when we hit the big storms which circle the tail end of the world unhindered by any land mass.

Towards the end of our watch, Don emerges from his bunk beneath the wheelhouse. A few minutes later Margaret appears from the opposite side and immediately begins organising things for breakfast. Don calls this sleeping area beneath the wheelhouse the Executive Suite. It has the

virtues of relatively fresh air and ease of access to the galley, and the disadvantages of very little headroom above the bunks and of opening directly onto the noisy common space of the galley. Margaret definitely deserves to be as comfortable as possible on this small ship. As cook she is working harder than anybody else.

By 11 am the ocean is virtually calm: Lyle feels well enough to turn on his computer and play a few games. He teaches me the rudiments of the word-processing program but my mind is too dopey from the ship's motion to absorb much. I leave him clinging to the roof of the Pleasure Dome with the computer lashed in place, typing a few words of a press release each time the pitch of the boat allows him to. The games are forgotten as he concentrates on composition. He is a strange sight with his state-of-the-art lap-top computer — barefooted, a bottle of sunblock jutting out of the back pocket of his shorts, and the traditional lines of his broad-brimmed hat modified by a square of tea towel sewn on to protect his neck from the sun.

Monday, 4 January

Most of us seem to have relaxed into life at sea, though Lyle and Ken continue to be sick. I feel some tension in Greg's manner as well, and I attribute that to the difficulties we are having with the engine. Yesterday Colin announced that he will not run the engine until he has worked out why it is overheating. Once again we feel the shortage of time, as we wait for Colin's verdict. The Antarctic coast is free of ice for only a few months each year, so by early March we must be sailing north out of the Ross Sea. That gives us a mere ten weeks to sail 2500 nautical miles, find a route through the pack-ice so that we can land on the continent, and then make a journey totalling 300 kilometres along glaciers and over passes to and from Mt Minto. In the middle of that trek we must find time to climb our 4000-metre-high mountain. It was an ambitious schedule even before mechanical problems began to beset us.

I am aware that the success of this expedition is more important to Greg than to anyone else because he has put so much effort into considering every factor which might affect our journey. He has been to Antarctica twice before: once as a mountaineering guide and field assistant for the New Zealand base at McMurdo Sound, and once with a German geological team studying North Victoria Land. It was from the decks of the German ship, the *Polar Queen*, that Greg first saw Mt Minto. For those of us who have not visited Antarctica, any time we spend on the continent will be new and exciting, but I know that Greg needs much more than a successful landfall.

I have learnt how stubborn he can be once he has made up his mind that something can be achieved. It might be a climb, the organisation of an expedition such as this, or the resolution of a personal crisis, but only rarely does his manner betray his tensions. Greg has many friends who never see more than his warmth, his gentleness and his delight to be alive. He can smile and behave as if everything is all right, while his eyes reveal a mind desperately juggling alternatives. His quiet manner disguises his tendency to bite off huge chunks of life which are sometimes too big for him to swallow.

The climb we made of Everest in 1984 has influenced him greatly. From being a man who quietly pursued the esoteric goals of mountaineering in the furthest corners of the earth, Greg, as one of the summiteers, was thrust into the limelight as a national hero: lunch with the Prime Minister, the Medal of the Order of Australia, television and radio stations begging for interviews. Suddenly he was respected by people who had dismissed climbing as frivolous and self-indulgent. Standing on the highest point on the earth's surface was an achievement everyone could appreciate. He learnt that actions did indeed speak louder than words, but that sometimes words were needed to emphasise connections which had long been obvious to him. He used his new-found voice to expound the worth of wilderness areas and to inspire others with the spirit of adventure. Now, at the real beginning of an expedition which he expects to be as demanding as Mt Everest, Greg is starting to worry that this old ship will not be strong enough or fast enough to meet our deadlines.

My writing in the Pleasure Dome is distracted by a cry outside.

'Come back here, you bastard! There's nothing else to look at!'

I peer out the small door of the Pleasure Dome and see Lyle knitting a scarf as he stands by the wheelhouse. I follow his gaze to an albatross disappearing across the waves.

Lyle is by no means the man he seems. About a year and a half ago he visited me at a friend's ramshackle flat in Coogee, where I was staying while recovering from a broken arm. The plaster had been removed the day before, and when I returned from my first swim of the season, Lyle was sitting on the doorstep. I had not seen him in a dozen years. My memories of him were of a wild Tasmanian climber, uncouth and independent, with a ragged beard and long brown hair. That day in October his beard was trimmed and his hair was the short, sensible length that allows a business suit to be worn with no pretence to individuality. To the outward world he had become conventional. I was surprised to learn that he was the marketing manager for a leading software company, and that he was

very happily married with two kids in the heart of Sydney suburbia. In 1974 the climbing scene in Australia was so small that everyone knew each other by name if not personally. Interstate rivalry was keen, but the one uniting belief of our sport was a rejection of the rest of the world. We were an arrogant cult with no time for the mundane, the materialistic, and the suburban. Despite the fact that I had mellowed considerably, I was surprised to see that Lyle, once the epitome of the 1970s rockclimber, had slipped into the sheep's clothing so completely that I almost believed he had put himself out to pasture. Upstairs while drinking tea and slouching against the wall to offset the sloping floor of the flat, I soon understood that Lyle's wild streak was merely well disguised.

He pulled out a folder with Bicentennial Antarctic Expedition written across the front. The thickness of the file surprised me, considering it was only a few days since Greg had mentioned Lyle's keenness to join our expedition to climb Mt Minto. Lyle had nursed a passion to visit Antarctica for years, ever since he worked at Fisher Library, at the University of Sydney, pasting call numbers on the spines of books. He stumbled across the section on Antarctica and read almost every volume. Inspired to organise an expedition to the Antarctic he soon realised the prohibitive cost of a private venture to the frozen land. He attempted to list the reasons why companies might like to sponsor him and ended up with a blank page—eighteen years of rockclimbing was not enough. Then he decided the solution lay with people who had a record of successful mountaineering expeditions, and who had signed and fulfilled sponsorship deals in the past. He heard about the Mt Minto climb from Tim Macartney-Snape, and on Tim's advice rang Greg and offered to organise the trip in return for a place in the team.

At the time, I had other preoccupations. I had recently fallen in love. As well, my head was full of the scenarios I was trying to weave into my half-finished novel. After doing the bulk of the organisation for the First Australian Mt Everest Expedition I knew exactly how much work was involved. I was more than happy to renounce the chore of the organisation. Lyle's deal sounded fine to me.

Tuesday, 5 January

I wake up at 9 am to the sound of the boom slamming back and forth above the entrance to the Fish Cabin. When I climb up the ladder there is no-one at the wheel. Becalmed. I go out to the foredeck where Colin is attaching the hand-powered bilge pump to the deck.

'It's unwise not to have an operational bilge pump,' he says. 'And with the engine in pieces it's a good idea to get the hand-pump working.'

'Sure,' I say, not welcoming the reminder that the engine is dismantled.

Already the timing is overtime. In early March the surface of the Ross Sea will begin to freeze, and within days the ice could be thick enough to lock our ship in place for the winter. In two months' time we must be back on board, sailing away from the continent. Every day is precious.

In the galley Margaret is busy fossicking in the cupboards for the ingredients for bread. The ship's motion is so gentle that the large plastic bottles containing muesli, bran, and sugar sit on the table without sliding.

Greg calls out, 'Dolphins!', but by the time we are on deck they are almost out of sight to the west.

I go back to my breakfast. Ken appears and Margaret tells him about the dolphins. He nods. 'I saw a 2-metre shark yesterday, right out here by the wheelhouse door. Reckon it might have been a baby whale shark.'

Left: Dressed in his homemade 'dreadnought' suit, ship's engineer Colin Putt greases the gears of the anchor winch.

'Why?' I ask.

'Because of its shape.'

Ken takes events as they come, and does not seem to get excited about anything. I sense that this reliability will last even in the toughest conditions.

Colin, Glenn and I sleep for a few hours before our midnight to 4 am watch. Colin takes first turn at the wheel then disappears into the engine room to continue working on the engine, but before leaving he relates his understanding of Jewish history according to Joseph Flavius, then quotes some poetry.

Outside the ocean is dark but alive with waves made choppy by the wind. Behind us, the full moon rises and sends golden reflections across the water to our ship. The tiny pricks of starlight are dimmed by the full moon, as if the stars are resigning their astrological importance. I consider the peace of the ocean and wonder about the majesty of the world above and beneath us—the sky, the water, and our small boat in between. Rather than being disturbed by our isolation, I feel security at the smallness of our worries.

Pete returns from the Pleasure Dome where he has been writing his diary. 'Too beautiful a night to sleep through,' he says. We talk for a while and I mention the extraordinary amount of information tucked away in Colin's head.

Pete agrees. 'He knows a little bit and has an opinion on just about everything.'

'I wonder what keeps him going away on trips like this one,' muses Glenn.

I remember that this is Glenn's first expedition, which means he has not yet asked himself this question. Perhaps after this trip he will find that he, too, develops the need to live beyond social restrictions in places where the environment makes the rules. Expeditions may become a part of his life as they have for Greg, Jonathan, Colin and myself.

Thursday, 7 January

At midday I do a few laps of the deck, and the fresh air stirs my appetite. Greg is in the galley talking to Colin.

'Now that I've cooled down a bit I can go back to work,' Colin says, climbing the steps up into the wheelhouse. 'The engine room is hotter than hell on a summer's day.'

'What's the latest with the engine?' I ask Greg, who is beginning to prepare lunch after insisting that Margaret take a day off.

He shrugs. 'They still don't know. And it sounds complicated. More complicated than it ought to be.'

The ship is at 41°S now, which puts 7° behind us and 30-odd to go. We have been at sea for six days now, and at this rate our journey to the continent will take another month.

'If we run out of time, we might have to settle for a smaller peak.'

'We'll be all right,' he says with a smile. 'We've still got five or six days up our sleeve.'

The glint in his eyes tells me we shall be cutting our margins very fine. It is typical of him to allow no consideration of alternatives until the main chance is given away.

'It's a strange feeling,' I say. 'All this.'

'Yeah. Frustrating because we can do nothing about it.'

'That's right. And we've got two weeks to do it in.'

He laughs. So far the frustration is not getting the better of him. Yet I know that one more day might be all it takes to reduce him to the tight-lipped moodiness which sometimes possesses him.

As the radio is our only connection to the world beyond the horizon, the extra talents of skipper Don Richards as a radio operator prove invaluable.

Jonathan seems very depressed today. He has not complained but the frustration and boredom show in the set of his face and the angle of his thick bushy eyebrows. He has a wash to improve his mood.

'How do you feel now that you're clean, Jonathan?' Margaret asks.

He shrugs and munches a biscuit. 'Terrible,' he says. 'I feel like going out somewhere.'

Margaret laughs. 'So did I yesterday after a wash. I felt like going to the movies.'

Jonathan nods glumly.

'You could go up to the bow,' I suggest. 'Or to the stern.'

'I've been to the bow.' He helps himself to a piece of cake and goes back to the wheelhouse.

Our voyage holds few surprises for Jonathan. Three years earlier he sailed to Commonwealth Bay on this ship with Don as skipper and Colin as engineer. At that time the vessel was named *Dick Smith Explorer* and the purpose of the expedition was to try to conserve the huts built by Douglas Mawson and his team between 1911 and 1914. There were twelve on board and conditions were equally uncomfortable. Mechanical problems were much less of an event because more time and energy was put into preparing the ship. Even so, after one week's sail south of Hobart a bearing in the drive shaft collapsed. Though Colin was able to make repairs, the motor was reserved for emergencies. Jonathan also sailed to Heard Island in 1983 on board *Anaconda* to make the second ascent of the 2746-metre Big Ben, a volcano in the middle of the island.

Jonathan regards sailing as little more than the means to very desirable ends, an attitude which has the unfortunate side-effect of encouraging him to live in the past or the future while he is on board. 'By nature he is energetic, almost hyperactive, a valuable quality on any expedition that excludes sailing. He continually surprises the rest of us by the degree of his organisation. Whenever anyone remembers they have forgotten something, or is clumsy enough to break a piece of equipment or drop it overboard, Jonathan reveals that he has a spare. Most of the time he tries to ignore his depression by sleeping or reading a book. This strange form of hibernation is interrupted only by eating, watch-keeping and regular morale-boosting stints of photography. His happiest times are when he sits in the Pleasure Dome and lovingly blows away every speck of dust and every salt crystal from his seven cameras and numerous lenses.

After lunch I wash some clothes in a bucket of water and hang them to dry from the ratlines on the aft shrouds. Greg is leaning over the rails at the bow watching the sea, so I walk over to him.

'There's some big waves out there now,' he says. 'But they're not steep enough to make things too rough.'

'It's like crossing the Heads to Manly on a stormy day.'

He laughs. 'Just keep telling yourself that.'

I have a vision of lying in my bunk muttering the phrase like a mantra as a hurricane smashes our boat to pieces.

'It's really good we got this wind today,' Greg comments, 'because at last we're going somewhere, not just drifting. We're moving along at a good pace now. If we weren't, we'd all be climbing the walls.'

'If we could find some walls to climb.'

An ominous band of cloud appears across the sky. When we are almost beneath it, a strong gust of wind hits us from the south and the cry goes up to change the sails. Fighting the wind is invigorating, and it is good to learn how quickly sail changes can be made.

We stare out across the endless blue waves for a few minutes.

He says, 'I was sitting on top of the wheelhouse this morning and I thought about how it must have been before charts and Satnavs and radars. Imagine discovering an island. It must have been really exciting—sailing along without a clue as to where you were going. Not a clue. It would have been a real buzz.'

'Yep. Sea monsters and who knows what hiding over the horizon.' I try to imagine an ocean unexplained by maps and stories. The waters surrounding us seem so vast that I can imagine anything, even an ocean leading to new worlds, perhaps to the edge of the earth.

During Chris and Ken's watch an ominous band of cloud appears across the sky. When we are almost beneath it, a strong gust of wind hits us from the south, and the cry goes up to change the sails. Glenn and I pull down the mainsail while Greg downs the jib. Pete and Chris trim the foresail. Fighting the wind is invigorating, and it is good to learn how quickly sail changes can be made. The boat sails slowly across the wind as Ken follows the best course he can into the squall.

While we tidy the sails I am called in to the radio because Don has made radio contact with an amateur radio operator in Mt Victoria. First Don and Colin discuss the problems of the engine with friends who have tracked down the motor's specifications from other engineers. Then Barbara comes on air from Mt Victoria and we swap a few stilted sentences. Don takes over the microphone and lapses into his radio codes and call signs.

A week away from the woman I love, and yet I have just talked to her. I have never been in this situation before. On other expeditions, communication has been limited to irregular letters where the time lag is apparent even as I write, and the answers come many weeks later from what seems like a different planet. Our radio contact is special because it is our only connection with the world beyond the sea and the sky.

Friday, 8 January

During the night the seas stayed rough which meant the ship continually pitched from side to side. Glenn and I discovered the disadvantage of the bunks running the width of the boat. Rather than being rocked from side to side like everyone else, we slide from end to end, and every time we change tack we need to swing around so our heads are uphill.

'A lot of rocking and rolling for not much grooving along,' says Greg as he leaves the wheelhouse after breakfast. 'We should get into the *Guinness Book of Records* for the slowest trip across the Southern Ocean.'

The sky is overcast and the sea is choppy on top of a big swell. Dark clouds threaten a storm.

Ken appears with a cheery 'Morning all.' He checks the latest plots on the charts then looks up suddenly with surprise and says, 'I think I'm going to be sick.'

He manages to get his head out the door for his first vomit, then he steps outside in case more is to follow. A big wave breaks over the side and fills his gumboots with water. He steps back inside, cursing, and his nose begins to bleed.

'This is not fair,' he says. 'I'm going back to bed.'

Instead he goes below to the galley where I hear him relate this series of misfortunes to Margaret. 'You must have got out of the wrong side of your bunk this morning,' she says.

Glenn, at the wheel, turns his head and smiles at me wryly. We both know that the bunks in the forecastle have so little space that there is scarcely room to roll over, let alone choose a different side to get out of.

Sunday, 10 January

I awake sometime after daybreak with the feeling that the ship is out of control. There is shouting and feet running around on deck and sounds of the mainsail being pulled down and a return to the normal noises of sailing. Over breakfast, Margaret tells me that we sailed seventy-three nautical miles during the night and the boat reached 8.8 knots with Lyle at the wheel. That is too fast for safety, so the sail area was reduced and we continued more sedately. It is foggy and drizzling all morning, but the dismal mood of such weather is broken when we sight a young fur seal, who swims alongside the boat for an hour. Completely at ease in the sea, this creature emphasises our remoteness from our proper environment. Colin, Don, Ken and Pete feel at home out here, but there is no denying that we are guests of the ocean.

After lunch the skies clear and the day becomes beautifully sunny. I sit on the roof of the Pleasure Dome and look out over the waves. Pete joins me and begins to talk.

'In the galley just now Greg said to Margaret and me that if the engine doesn't work today he wants to turn around and head back to Sydney because you guys just won't have time to climb Mt Minto.'

'Well, he has a point. Eventually we would get there by sail alone but we can't afford to wait that long.'

'Even if we have no engine, it seems silly to be out here with a boat-load of food and go nowhere.'

'It does, but I think we have to look at our obligations to our sponsors. Probably it would be best to turn back and keep what we can until next year.' Deferring the expedition at this stage would be an organisational nightmare, and the thought makes me shudder.

We both look out across the waves.

'I guess we'll decide tomorrow.'

Tuesday, 12 January

Early morning watch today. A touch of orange in the clouds announces the passing of the night, but this dash of colour fades into the greyness of the sea and the sky. As the day dawns the sea turns blue, somehow reflecting the colour of the sky above the clouds. The ocean seems more self-contained on a day like this. Four-metre waves roll underneath the boat and head determinedly eastwards. Next stop, South America, as Colin said yesterday. The ship rocks from side to side as the waves go by, yet our 100-square metres of 6.5-millimetre-thick steel feels secure.

Occasionally crests are sharpened by the wind, and when they break water slaps hard against the boat. On the biggest rolls the port side of the deck goes under, and water threatens to come in the wheelhouse door half a metre above the deck. We have been on a port tack for a day and a half now and at last we are sailing south at good speed. Margaret prefers a starboard lean because it raises the sink and allows the water to escape down the plughole.

We crossed 49°S during our watch, and with luck we shall break 50 today. Tasmania and New Zealand are well behind us now, and every day the air gets cooler, the water colder and the nights shorter. The water

temperature has dropped from 16°C to 11.5°C. It is dark at 10 pm and light at 4 am. Albatrosses draw casual remarks now instead of the excited flurry for cameras at the first few sightings. These giant birds seem so much at home as they sweep around the boat in huge circles, disappearing into the troughs between the waves and reappearing with their wings only centimetres above the water. Storm-petrels seem more remarkable to me because they use so much more energy. They remind me of swallows as they dart amongst the waves. Somehow they find enough to eat to keep warm in the cold air of the Southern Ocean.

In the afternoon Chris and Glenn film Greg, Jonathan, Lyle and me sitting in the Pleasure Dome talking about the expedition—its conception, organisation and objectives. Greg does most of the talking with occasional comments from Jonathan and me. Lyle can do nothing but sit in the corner looking miserable from seasickness.

It is good to turn our minds towards the continent. Colin ran the engine for an hour today and all seems to be well. Greg has bounced back, full of enthusiasm because engine and wind are both working for us now. Our various delays have amounted to a total of two weeks which means that timing has become even more critical.

Eight pm to midnight watch. It is raining gently and under the heavily overcast sky visibility is almost zero. After everyone has gone to bed I stand by the rail and look at the black water sparkling with phosphorescent plankton as the roll of the hull breaks the waves into foam. Occasionally a larger greenish shape flashes by, but each one disappears before I have time to form an image of its outline. Two thousand fathoms of water. I wonder what sort of strange creatures exist down there.

Engine problems encourage us to set the sails to make the most efficient use of the wind.

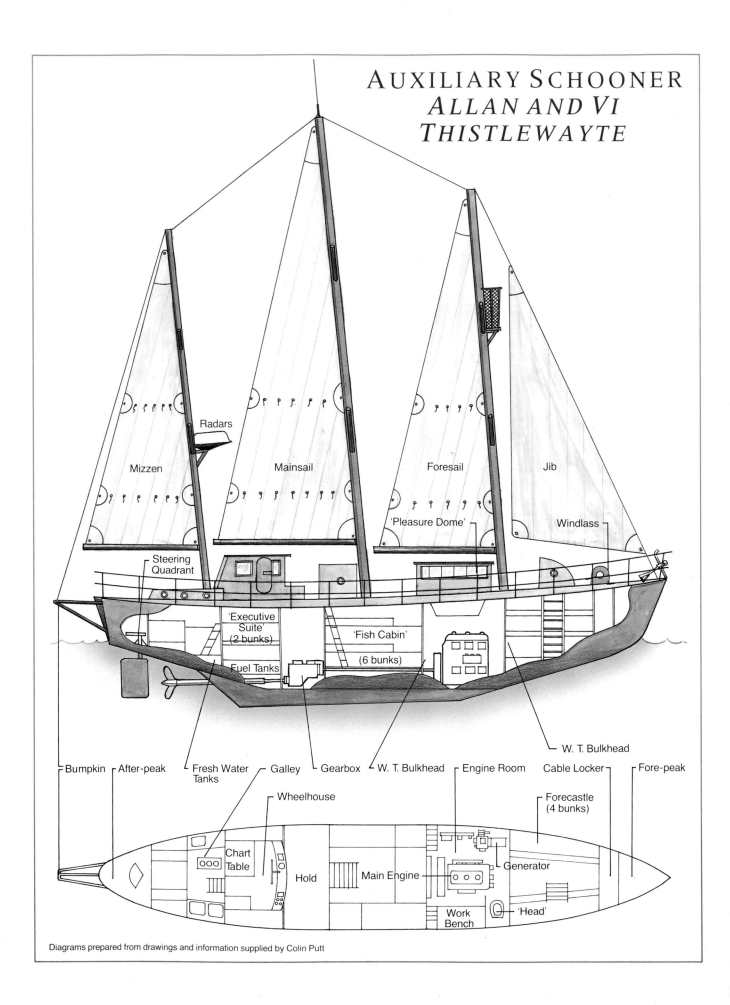

AUXILIARY SCHOONER
ALLAN AND VI THISTLEWAYTE

Radars

Mizzen

Mainsail

Foresail

Jib

'Pleasure Dome'

Windlass

Steering Quadrant

'Executive Suite' (2 bunks)

'Fish Cabin'

(6 bunks)

Fuel Tanks

W. T. Bulkhead

Bumpkin — After-peak — Fresh Water Tanks — Galley — Gearbox — W. T. Bulkhead — Engine Room — Cable Locker — Fore-peak

Wheelhouse

Forecastle (4 bunks)

Chart Table

Hold

Main Engine

Generator

Work Bench

'Head'

Diagrams prepared from drawings and information supplied by Colin Putt

Wednesday, 13 January

Lyle and I sit reading in the Pleasure Dome while Chris and Glenn shoot a sequence out on deck. They film one take, then discuss how they can improve it. Two more takes and the discussion becomes an argument.

Lyle chuckles and says, 'They're a real Laurel and Hardy pair. We need a film crew to film the film crew filming.'

I smile but keep my nose in my book. Glenn stoops through the low door, sits down, and grabs one of the computers. Chris appears in the doorway and begins to talk calmly about the need to hurry less. 'If I'd had more time to organise it, I could have eliminated all the wind noise.' Glenn is dismissive, saying, 'We haven't got enough time.'

'What do you mean? There's still an hour of sunlight and you're sitting here playing computer games!'

Glenn replies, 'The sunlight's not strong enough now.'

I hold up my hand in an exaggerated gesture of conciliation. 'What you boys need is a director.'

Chris glances across at me, smiling in an attempt to show that he is not taking any of this too seriously. 'We are both directors.'

'Ah,' I say. 'There is your problem.'

Chris ignores me, and sees that Glenn is concentrating upon the computer. He gives up the pretence of being calm. He pulls away from the door and says loudly, 'You know what they're going to say? "Great visuals, pity about the sound."'

He stomps away down the deck.

'Don't you worry about that,' says Glenn, but Chris is already gone. I smile at Lyle who is managing to contain his laughter. Glenn is absorbed by the computer game. Electronic pings and buzzes are the only noises in the Pleasure Dome.

I wonder how their teamwork will be when we reach the ice. A great deal will be happening, and Glenn will not have time to think up complicated arty shots—or at least if he does, we will not have time to pose for him—and Chris will have to record each sound or conversation when it happens. My limited experience with film making has shown me that the task is difficult in the best conditions, and Antarctica will probably turn on the worst.

My first meeting with Chris and Glenn was last year, during the planning of our Centrepoint Tower climb. Several months earlier Chris had climbed the tower and escaped. Unlike Greg, Andy Henderson and myself who stopped halfway up with our banner, Chris had climbed right up to the restaurant, swung out underneath on a jig he had made for the purpose, then continued up the overhanging outside walls, much to the surprise of the cleaners inside. On the man-made summit, he coiled his ropes, watched the police cars arrive in the streets far below, and waited for the inevitable arrest. When no-one arrived after fifteen minutes he found an unlocked door which led to the top of a huge spiral staircase. While he scampered down the stairs and emerged into the Centrepoint shopping complex, police were riding elevators to the top. Chris walked out into the street and caught a cab home. His nine-hour climb was the culmination of months of careful planning and research. He gave Greg, Andy and me vital information concerning the dimensions of the cables we would have to climb and the location of the alarms we would have to avoid, then suggested that he and Glenn, who had filmed his climb, should come to Antarctica with us.

A few nights later we saw the video of Chris's climb. Not only was the whole project and its execution audacious, but the camerawork was bril-

THE VOYAGE TO ANTARCTICA

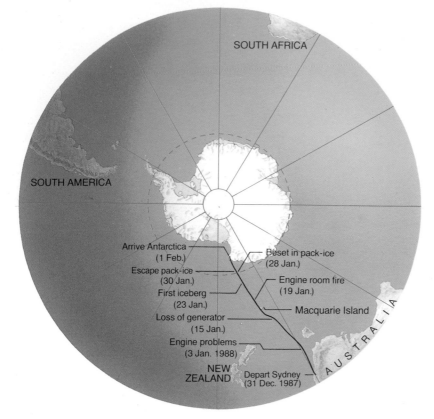

liant. Chris was a competent rockclimber who had done only a small amount of mountaineering in New Zealand. Glenn had only recently discovered rockclimbing and was a complete novice on snow and ice. His second profession was medicine, so we joked that if he fell he would at least be able to work out what damage he had done. Their relative lack of experience was offset by nerve and dedication, and so they joined the team.

I leave Glenn to his computer games and Lyle to his book and go outside to sit on the roof of the Pleasure Dome. I brace my green gumboots on the handrail and feel the cold air chilling my fingers and face. The sun is only a few degrees above the horizon, sending its yellow light dancing straight across the water to meet me. An albatross soars across the reflection, a silhouette against the golden waters. The sun is unique in its ability to make everyone who feels its rays imagine they are its focus. As I think this, the sun vanishes behind a low bank of clouds. In the softer light, a sense of space pervades everything, making the ocean seem bottomless and re-establishing the sky as eternal. The rest of the earth lies everywhere beyond the horizon. Alone on the decks I watch the sky slowly blacken until it blends into the same dark shade which fills the sea.

Thursday, 14 January

'Do you see them, Margaret?' Greg's cry interrupts my reading.

Moments later Glenn appears and begins to rummage for one of his movie cameras. 'There's a school of black and white dolphins playing at the bow.'

They must be hourglass dolphins, I think, remembering an illustration from one of Pete's books. Moments later I am dressed and scrambling up the ladder with my camera securely zipped inside my waterproof jacket. Pete and Margaret are at the bow. Margaret squeals with delight.

'Look! Look!' she shouts to me, pointing at some shapes thirty yards away and just below the surface. Seconds later the animals burst into the air. The white flashes on their sides contrast sharply with their black bodies, and the effect reminds me of photographs I have seen of killer whales.

'Hourglass dolphins,' says Pete. 'My favourite kind.'

The animals break the crest in unison and surf down the face of the wave towards us. I see how the white shape on their sides narrows in the middle to form the shape of an hourglass. They use the momentum of their ride to dive underneath the boat.

'There's about seven of them,' says Pete. 'I think one of them has a young one.'

The dolphins stay with us for two hours. They dart across the bows of the ship and surf the water pushed aside as the bow smashes down with every swell. The young one stops and snorts through its breathing hole for a few seconds and I cannot help but feel it is playing to its audience.

'Of course it is,' says Pete.

The highlight of the afternoon is the making of Margaret's chocolate cake. Despite the violent tossing of the boat, she manages to mix the ingredients without incident. The problems start only when the two cake tins are in the oven. A particularly violent roll slams the trays into the oven door and the mixture sloshes over. Margaret asks me for an orange and, while Chris holds the door open, she uses it to wedge the tins in place. At that moment the boat rolls again and another big dollop of cake mix sloshes out over her hands, over the tea towel she holds the tray with, and over the orange. Chris shuts the door before anything else can happen, and we all laugh.

I say, 'I'll bet you are the first person to bake an orange in the Southern Ocean.'

The afternoon passes easily as I lie in my bunk reading. Storm noises — the slap of waves on deck and on the skylight, the flapping of sails and the banging of rigging — make me realise I had fallen asleep. I dress, don my waterproof overalls and jacket, then climb up the ladder. A wild scene greets me. The sky is grey above huge and choppy seas. Waves break against the starboard side and are carried across the boat by the wind. The spray is like a heavy rain falling sideways. White caps top every wave. For the first time I feel the flimsiness of our craft compared to the forces which besiege us, and yet it is an exciting feeling.

Pete, Lyle and Glenn haul down the foresail and furl it, then replace the jib with the smaller and stronger storm jib. Pete watches the boat's response to the wind and the seas and decides to set the mainsail again with two reefs. Colin appears en route to his bunk from the galley and the five of us tie the reefs and haul the ropes. The halyard is hooked around one of the ladder rungs rivetted to the mast, and because of the strong wind it takes a few minutes to free it. All the while the ship pitches sharply from side to side. Everything outside is wet and I have to be very careful not to slip and be tossed into the ocean. Pete and Colin are wearing harnesses with a length of rope attached and clipped to a shroud or a railing — essential equipment in these conditions, I decide. Until now it has seemed to be just one more piece of equipment to put on, even though Colin habitually advises wearing them. Wet hands are chilled to numbness by the wind, but it is not a desperate situation. Both Colin and Pete have a very clear idea of

what to do. Every adjustment is considered and carefully executed, but for the first time we are shown the darker moods of the roughest ocean in the world.

The sea is all-powerful, heaving around us like an angry monster from a surrealistic dream. Sydney is a long way away, more than the two weeks and 1500 nautical miles plotted on the chart. Our world has narrowed to just the ship and the endless ocean around us. Our minds can escape along the mental planes of books or daydreams but the ocean is always with us, continually rocking the ship and making everything echo with the slap and rush of waves.

Left and above: The social agenda on board is very limited, so meal times are a highlight every day. Despite the cramped galley, Margaret's skill and imagination produces food which not only keeps us fit but manages to boost our morale.

Friday, 15 January

The storm continues through the night and the next day. In the afternoon, Pete and I move one of the sheets tied to the storm jib because it is chafing against the corner of the Pleasure Dome.

'I love gales,' Pete has to shout from only two metres away.

'Yeah, it's great, isn't it?' I notice a pair of small grey birds swooping close to the waves.

'Prions,' shouts Pete.

Back inside the wheelhouse, I relieve Colin at the helm as big swells come rolling through like trains. They lift the boat and then we plunge down the face of the wave. At times it feels almost as though we are surfing. The swell is confused by the choppiness of the sea. Everywhere there is white water swirling in troughs or breaking on crests. Sometimes we catch the edge of a swell, or a wave slaps us from the side, and the boat rolls sharply and the pull on the wheel is strong as I attempt to hold our course. It is exciting stuff, and my efforts to control the ship only leave me more in awe of the forces.

Over dinner Colin explains that not only is the engine playing up again, but now the generator is out of action. He and Don have deduced that the fault

The two four-hour watches which punctuate the day for each crew member help to keep us occupied. At the helm, Greg Mortimer tries to hold the ship on course.

is a broken wire in the coil, and the coil is accessible only if the generator is unbolted from the floor and moved away from the forward water-proof bulkhead. This is not possible unless the huge engine is moved — clearly impossible while at sea. The conclusion is that we shall be without 240-volt power for the rest of voyage. No oven, no refrigerator, no electric jug, no fluorescent lights, no fan to ventilate our sleeping cabin. We are allowed limited use of the 24-volt lights while the engine is running, but until the engine is fixed we must manage with torches. It seems that no sooner is one thing fixed in this ship than another goes wrong, and that is a ludicrous situation when undertaking such a major journey.

A faint rainbow heralds a magnificent evening. Margaret and Pete come out on deck to enjoy it. Yellow light shines through the clouds behind us to the west. A few broad rays stand out like searchlight beams against the dark storm clouds behind. The choppiness of the sea has died down a little since this morning and the distance between the swells has increased. The swells themselves have grown tremendously. We look up at a huge wave bearing down upon us but as it nears the ship, we ride up and over it. Im-mediately the boat tips towards the trough, and though we stand upright relative to the deck, Margaret and I now stare directly into the water. Because a trough follows the wave we seem to be sliding down beneath the next crest. Margaret screams as this one towers above us until it seems impossible that our ship can scale this wall of water. But this wave passes beneath us as well, and only the lip of the crest breaks across the deck.

'This is more frightening than grade 18,' says Margaret, referring to the limit of her rockclimbing ability.

'We'll get used to it.'

Greg comes down the stairs and pulls off his waterproofs. He laughs when he notices the plastic stalk with a tiny torch on the end of it which

Jonathan has clipped to the book he is reading.

'What's that?' Greg decides to draw attention to the newest of Jonathan's endless parade of gadgets. He resists the teasing with a smile, but Greg continues his jovial sarcasm. 'You make me realise I forgot to bring mine.'

Jonathan deflects the criticism, 'And they forgot to bring a 240-volt generator that works.'

'Amazing, isn't it?' I say. 'All these things going wrong. It's like a conspiracy.'

Greg slips into his sleeping bag, looks up at the condensation around the hatch cover, then says, 'Every day it becomes more and more like going to sea in an ice-cave.'

I laugh. My amusement refuses to be dampened by the truth of the comparison. Jonathan is once again lost in the world of his book.

I lie on my bunk and look up at the skylight. On each of the four white walls of the skylight recess a pair of Buddhist eyes have been painted. The design is taken from the Tibetan Buddhist stupas of Kathmandu. Blue-rimmed ellipses, dipping slightly at the top to partially hood the blue iris and its darker pupil, are spaced either side of a serpent-like symbol. Above this stylized nose is a circle in four colours which denotes the third eye. In Nepal and Tibet, these faces are painted on the four sides of the tower which tops the huge dome-shaped stupa. The eyes stare out across the houses and the countryside which circle the temples. They symbolise a world view and the universality of Buddha's teachings.

Here, in the skylight of the Fish Cabin, the four faces stare at each other. The thought occurs to me that this positioning of the eyes is indeed appropriate, symbolic of the hours of introspection indulged by the six of us as we lie in our bunks below, and of the consideration we are forced to show each other because of our cramped quarters.

Saturday, 16 January

I come up from below decks and find that the storm has died completely. The transformation from yesterday is almost unbelievable. Colin is working on the engine, so the boat is almost motionless, and Pete sets the sails while Greg lashes the wheel in place. Music blares out of the cassette player.

Greg shakes his head and says, 'It's amazing how many songs mention sailing.'

Jonathan leans against the chart table while writing his diary. 'That's because people have such a romantic notion about sailing,' he says. 'Until they do it. It's a much better thing to have done than to be doing.'

I climb up onto the roof of the Pleasure Dome and sit ready to meditate. When I complete my practice and open my eyes Greg is walking away from me along the deck. A Mintie has been carefully placed in front of me. I smile, pocket the sweet, and stretch my legs.

I stroll back along the gently pitching deck to where Pete and Greg sit on top of the wheelhouse.

'How was it?' asks Greg.

'Great,' I say, then pause to consider. 'The motion's a bit distracting, but it's good to tune into your breath and your body for a change, rather than to the problems of the boat or seasickness. It shows you how much it's in your mind.'

'Not for Lyle and Ken,' he says.

'No.'

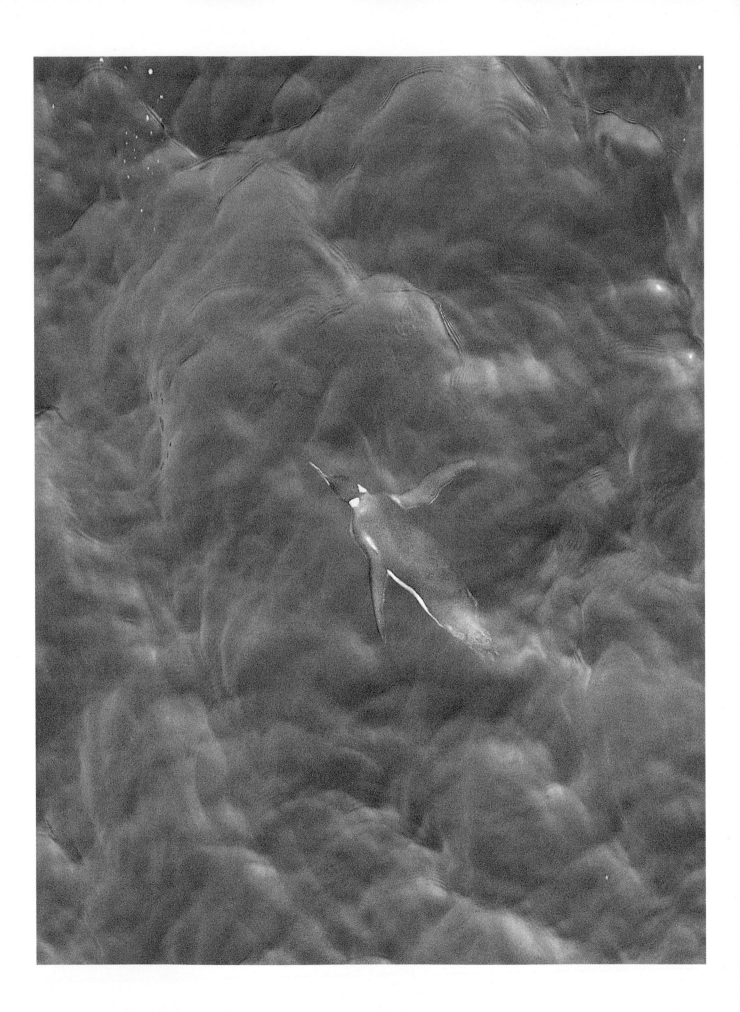

'One time, when I was in Nepal in the mountains,' begins Greg, 'trekking somewhere or other on a nice day with nothing to worry about, I told one of the Sherpas about Antarctica. I explained that it was twice the size of India: nobody lived there—only ice and mountains and strange animals around the coast.' Greg looks at me now so he can watch my reaction. 'Dawa said it sounded like the perfect place for a temple.'

I laugh at the reminder of the Nepalese perspective. As a Tibetan Buddhist, Dawa considered an unspoilt region ideal for the worship of existence. I think about how strange it is to embark upon a major mountaineering expedition without the company of a few Nepali friends as cooks or fellow climbers.

I remember our return to life after the climb of Annapurna 2 which Greg and I made with Andy Henderson and Tim Macartney-Snape in 1983. Our descent from the 7967-metre summit was a desperate struggle to avoid avalanches in the face of a blizzard which kept dumping metre after metre of snow. We ran out of food, our fixed ropes were swept away, and for several days we were unsure whether we would survive until nightfall. When we finally approached our advance base camp we found, to our horror, that there was only snow-covered ground where our tents had been. Our Nepali friends must have concluded that because we were nine days overdue we were dead. But as we hobbled the last few metres to where the kitchen tent had been, we saw the edges of a tarp sticking out of the snow. We burrowed like frenzied animals, pulled the tarp aside, and found the makings of dinner. Inside a small pot was a cake Tenzing had baked. The next day, when we struggled down into the zone of green where other life began, we met our friends climbing up through the steep bamboo jungle. All they had done was complete the first stage of striking camp, and now they were returning to wait for us with the latest batch of mail from Kathmandu. They were demonstrating more faith in our ability to survive than we had felt ourselves.

The single most joyous time of my life began that evening at the small village of Hoga. The villagers saw our emaciated bodies and gave us food and shelter without a word. Through the mild night we slept in the bamboo shed which was home for the water buffalos in winter. We woke to warm sunshine and the smell of fresh potato curry on the fire. As we relaxed in the sun eating yoghurt and flat bread the villagers passed by and thanked us. Even today I do not understand why. Perhaps they were thanking the gods for sparing our lives, or thanking us for daring to offer ourselves to the inhabitants of heaven.

After a difficult climb, my senses are heightened and my prejudices are shed in favour of the needs of the moment. The emptiness of Antarctica is one of its exciting aspects, but at the moment part of me regrets the absence of a new human culture to learn to respect.

Lyle must be finding his sea-legs at last because he stands watch at dinner time. He and Jonathan sing in the wheelhouse while the rest of us sit in the galley and eat. Margaret dishes out seconds, and says, 'I have to save a little for Lyle.' Thinking aloud is her way of making mental notes. 'He's eating after the radio sched.'

'Why?' I ask.

'He's worked out that if he eats and then lies down immediately, he has a good chance of digesting the food.' She puts a big dollop of pasta into the bowl which Glenn holds out to her. 'If he ate now it would be over the side before the end of his watch.'

'And you've spent so long cooking it,' I say.

Left: A lone King Penguin, possibly from Macquarie Island, 100 nautical miles to the west, spent an hour swimming around the ship.

A smile plays on her lips despite her reproving glance. Lyle's suffering should not be made the source of jokes.

In the wheelhouse, Jonathan has run out of words but Lyle's fine voice reverberates through the galley. '"Midnight special..."'

'I think it's better when he's sick,' says Don.

'Nonsense,' I say, enjoying the song.

'"...Shine your light on me."'

'Let him have fun while he's feeling well,' says Chris.

'"Midnight special..."'

'That's right,' I say. 'It's only five minutes a day.'

'"...Shine your ever-loving light on me."'

Monday, 18 January

When I wake late in the morning, I see through the skylight that a piece of ribbon tied to a halyard flutters listlessly, indicating that there is no wind. The sky beyond is pale blue and a faint sunshine beams down the stairwell. Green gumboots appear at the top of the stairs, followed by blue long johns, a grey windcheater and the stubbled face of Glenn.

'Nothing happening?' I ask.

Glenn shakes his head. 'Absolutely nothing — 0.0 knots and the main sheet just broke.'

'What about the engine?' Chris asks. 'Can Colin get that going?'

'I think Colin is mending the boom for the main. It's unusable at the moment.' He shakes his head again. 'What else can go wrong with this ship?'

I do not let myself think about the question for fear of tempting fate. Chris rolls over and goes back to sleep. Glenn slides into the bunk below me.

The boredom of being motionless is broken by a king penguin, presumably a visitor from Macquarie Island, 100 nautical miles to our west. The bird stays with us for few hours and even surfaces less than a metre away when I rinse my washing over the side.

Early in the afternoon Colin connects the propeller to the drive shaft, starts the engine and we begin to run at seven knots. As I write my diary in the galley, Greg computes our average speed as eighty-three nautical miles per day, with 956 to go. Twelve more days at this speed. We now have no time up our sleeve.

Jonathan is in a good mood at dinner time, as if his spirits are governed by the state of the engine. He entertains us with stories of climbing in Alaska — his tale of having the pick of his ice-axe driven through the palm of his hand when he was caught in an avalanche, and the terrors of photographing grizzly bears.

Pete at the wheel spots some fins so I rush out on deck. Five hourglass dolphins cavort around the bow. Greg, without his waterproofs to protect him from the wind, shouts out, 'Good to see you, but it's too bloody cold to hang around,' and then he scampers below.

Pete says, 'They don't feel the cold, except when they stick their fins out of the water. That's why they don't do it very often.'

'They must think we're crazy.'

Pete nods. I leave him watching his beloved dolphins and flee to the wheelhouse. Exceptionally clear radio signals from Sydney and Springwood tonight, but garbled noises from operators in the northern hemisphere.

Left: The 'Pleasure Dome' provides a change from our stuffy sleeping cabin. It's a place to read, play computer games, listen to Pete play his guitar, or just to sleep.

Tuesday, 19 January

I look forward to dinner at the end of an uneventful day. In the galley I sit at the table and watch the steam rush out of the huge pot on the stove whenever Margaret lifts the lid to stir the soup. When the others arrive I am jammed in against the wall and my appetite is automatically regulated by the compression of my stomach. Dinner is a thick, vegetable soup. Most of us have a second helping, even though Margaret reminds us that there is steamed pudding to follow.

Silence falls as the last of us finishes slurping. As if to punctuate the pause, a buzzing sound comes from somewhere. Brows wrinkle and ears are cocked around the table.

'The stove,' I suggest, imagining the kerosene jet has developed an extra whine.

'The oil pressure light,' says someone else.

Ken at the wheel cuts the engine and says, 'It's the telephone.'

We burst out laughing because the telephone which has not worked all voyage now seems to have a mind of its own. Colin is already on his way to the engine room. Jonathan follows him and the rest of us ease into the extra space around the table.

Seconds later Jonathan's voice comes down the wheelhouse stairs, 'Fire in the engine room!'

There is a mad scramble as we all try to get out from behind the table, past the stoves and up the stairs. Both wheelhouse doors are flung open as we rush out on deck.

'I'll take the wheel!' cries Margaret, noticing that Ken has abandoned it. 'What's the course?'

'One thirty,' I tell her, thinking as I speak that it is ludicrous to worry about our direction while the ship is burning.

Grey smoke is pouring from the forecastle door and out of the trombone-shaped ventilator above the engine room. We run along the deck. Greg, Jonathan and I stand by the entrance above the forecastle stairs as Colin's face appears in the doorway. 'It's out now, but it's so full of smoke I came up for a breather.'

'Which fire extinguisher d'you use?' asks Greg.

'The one in the forecastle'.

'Small one?'

'Big one.'

'So there's plenty left if it flares up again?'

'Yes.' This makes Colin think. He asks, 'Can someone look through the hatch-cover?'

I crawl into the Pleasure Dome and stare through the windows beside the hatch-cover. Jonathan hands me a torch. All I can see is the beam reflecting back from thick brown smoke.

'Nothing!' I shout, and crawl out again. 'Only smoke.'

Colin disappears, muttering about putting on the electric light for a second to check.

Jonathan turns to me, his eyes still wide with amazement. 'I opened the door,' he nods at the Pleasure Dome, 'and I could see all these orange flames along the wall, lapping right up under the bench. Then Colin got them with the fire extinguisher.'

Chris and Glenn appear with their camera and tape recorder but they have missed the action. Colin reappears and confirms that the fire is out.

'I don't believe it,' I say. 'The bloody telephone rings to let us know the engine room is on fire.'

'And those phones haven't worked for three years,' says Jonathan. 'The lines must have shorted out.'

'Definitive proof of God,' I begin, but Jonathan moves away and ducks into the Pleasure Dome to help Greg remove the emergency hatch in the floor. Smoke pours out of there now as well.

Nothing important remains to be done, except the post mortem. I return to the wheelhouse as Chris and Glenn begin to film Don using the radio.

I turn to Pete who was asleep in his bunk when the fire was discovered. He was woken by the smoke when Colin yanked open the door into the engine room. Fully clothed now, after escaping from the smoke in only a T-shirt and long johns, he stands by me shaking his head.

'What's the damage?' I ask, fearing the worst, imagining that we may have to abandon the expedition.

'Couldn't be better.'

I raise my eyebrows.

He grimaces and rephrases his answer. 'If you've got to have a fire in the engine room in the middle of the Southern Ocean, you couldn't have had a better one.'

This reply is more satisfactory. Nuisance value only: a tool box burned, the partition between the engine and the toilet badly charred.
Greg comes to bed with a faint smile on his face.

'The question on everyone's lips,' I say, as he climbs up into his bunk, 'is what's going to be next?'

'No, I disagree,' he says. 'Plain sailing now, I reckon, because our luck's changed. We were so bloody lucky.'

'Really?'

'Yeah. For sure. The batteries stored under the toilet were really bloody hot—so hot you couldn't touch them. They were ready to explode. And

Above: In the aftermath of the engine-room fire, Colin considers the culprit: a wooden toolbox which slid underneath the overheating engine exhaust pipe, began to smoulder and then caught alight.

Following page: Our vessel is of interest to the many species of birds which hunt for food in the Southern Ocean. Soaring black-browed albatrosses are a magnificent counterpoint to the irregular crash and roll of the waves.

the neoprene fuel lines were almost melted through. With 6000 litres of diesel in the tanks, and the cocks to turn off the flow at the bottom of the hold, think what would have happened if the telephone wires had not short-circuited from the heat...'

'Could have cooked the engine...could have cooked the lot of us.' I think for a moment. 'As soon as I heard, "Fire in the engine room", I thought, "That's it, about turn, back to Sydney in three weeks."'

Greg flashes a smile at me, but the serious look in his eyes lets me know he is not joking.

'Take longer than that in the inflatable rafts,' he says.

For the first time I consider the possibility that we could have sunk. I smile at my naivety, then I reach out and toussle his hair. So close, I think, so close...

Wednesday, 20 January

The early morning watch is slow until Glenn and I begin swapping stories about South America. Afterwards I return to my bunk and sleep until midday. Chris comes down the stairs and says to Glenn and me, 'Guess what, boys? The engine's playing up, using twice as much fuel and oil as it should, making noises, and we're going to have to shut it down for two days.'

We stare at him, unable to say anything.

'It's true, I tell you, it's true. And Colin apologised to Greg about it.'

'It's unbelievable.'

I lie back in my bunk and sigh. Everything seemed to be going so well at last. As if to dismiss any thoughts I might have that Chris was joking, the engine loses revs, hovers at a lower level for a minute, then shudders to a stop.

I go on deck. There is no wind.

Over lunch I learn that Colin and Ken have traced the problem to the second cylinder. They start the motor and run it on two cylinders. First indications support their diagnosis because the motor runs well and no grey smoke billows out of the exhaust. Colin is optimistic and the rest of us live in hope.

Tonight's radio session is special because Barbara is waiting to talk to me at Mt Victoria. When I take the mike I have trouble getting clear signals, so I feel frustrated. After a few minutes of experimentation we receive each other clearly. Barbara says she is very well, busy with the teashop and seeing friends. She says she is getting much fatter. This news of her pregnancy immediately makes me want to turn around and go home. I say that I hope she is not overworking. I want to be with her and talk to her more, but instead I tell her I love her and miss her, and that I'll see her in a couple of months.

Margaret takes over and talks to Tanya, her youngest daughter, then reads the letter she has written to her family and friends because she says that she gets tongue tied and forgets to say what is in her heart. Emotions run close to the surface out here in the middle of nowhere.

Friday, 22 January

Though the sky was heavily overcast throughout our midnight to 2 am watch, the darkness was not complete. By two o'clock the sky was noticeably lighter. It is strange to think that when the clouds clear, the sun will be

shining for more than twenty hours a day. It is unusual to get this far south with only one storm, but no-one has remarked upon our luck in this respect, perhaps out of superstition that such a comment will provoke a hurricane.

The days blend into one another. If it was not for my diary I would have lost track of time. We left Sydney three weeks ago yesterday. The time has passed quickly, which paradoxically makes the journey seem much longer. The days are randomly mixed into a routine of eating, sleeping, talking, reading and writing, and lying on my bunk. Watch-keeping is the only regular punctuation. Despite our impatience to arrive at the continent, time no longer seems to matter.

Glenn and I take the noon to 4 pm watch so that Colin can permanently disconnect the No. 2 cylinder. Hopefully our engine problems are over, but with the 240-volt out of action and the fire damage to the batteries for the 12-volt system, I wonder what will be next.

Sometimes I lose my ability to concentrate upon the present, and I feel bored and frustrated, especially over the delays we have had to accept. We six mountaineers feel impotent because the ship's problems are entirely beyond our control, yet timing is critical for us. None of us want to be stranded for the winter, but I feel particularly desperate, because I want to be present at the birth of my child.

There is a really good atmosphere at dinner tonight. For the first time Lyle is wedged in against the wall at the galley table. The boat has now sailed past all our guesses of the latitude of the first iceberg sighting. A second piece of paper is handed around for another try. After dinner, Glenn and Greg manage to convince Margaret to break into the chocolate ration. Our fruit supply is healthy; although the apples are beginning to lose their crispness, the oranges seem to taste better as each day goes by. We may have lost our fitness after a month at sea, but Margaret keeps us very well fed so that it should only take a few days to get our muscles back in trim.

We cross 63°S this evening and, according to the Satnav, there are only 508 nautical miles between us and Cape Adare, the northernmost point of North Victoria Land, and our second preference for a landing site if we cannot reach Cape Hallett. If we can maintain this average we shall arrive in another four or five days. The ship has become home for all of us, so much so that it will be strange to go ashore again—especially in a land devoid of people. I imagine that after our confinement the overriding feeling will be one of space and emptiness. We shall find out soon enough. For all its problems and peculiar social demands, I suspect we may find boat life hard to give up. Above all else it signifies security and our passage back to Australia.

Left: **On deck in the fresh air, Lincoln, rugged well against the cold, takes time to write in his diary.**

A FROZEN WORLD

A FROZEN WORLD

'When time slows to a mountain's run,
Night's dark curtain stays unfurled,
Or the sky is circled by the sun,
Both prisoners of a frozen world.'

from *'Mirrors of Ice'*

Saturday, 23 January 1988

Waves crash across the deck when I poke my head out of the Fish Cabin, but I manage to reach the wheelhouse without getting soaked. In the galley Pete is finishing his breakfast and Colin relaxes by the table. Margaret is in her usual position by the stove. Last night's bread-baking on the kerosene stoves was a success, so the toaster sits on one burner and the kettle on another. On the third burner is a pot with the lukewarm remains of the morning's porridge.

'Iceberg,' announces Don at the wheel.

'Where?' screams Margaret. 'Where?'

'On the radar.'

I run up the steps and see the small solid patch highlighted by the rotating arm of green light.

'It's still three or four nautical miles away,' says Don.

Margaret rushes out on deck and then back inside to look at the radar. Already almost everyone is on deck. Jonathan is at the bow with a camera to his eye.

'Straight ahead,' says Greg. 'A touch to the starboard. It's moving really fast.'

I peer into the sleet, expecting to see a bump somewhere near the horizon. Instead there is a huge square-cut castle of ice looming out of the water. Margaret exclaims with such enthusiasm that the rest of us laugh.

'It's big.' My surprise prompts me to state the obvious.

'Remember it's three miles away,' says Greg. 'It's so powerful. The whole thing's just peeled off the front of a glacier somewhere, and here it is cruising by at quite a few knots as if it knows where it's going. Amazing.'

The apparition gives me the feeling that we are no longer alone on this vast ocean. The power Greg speaks of is more than a physical equation of mass and wind. Tall cliffs of blue ice stand out of the mist. On its flat top a pinnacle juts up, and to the right at water level are some other square shapes, perhaps connected, perhaps being bulldozed along in front of the huge mass of the berg.

Despite a hand raised in protection, the sleet is making my glasses impossible to see through. I turn away when a wave smashes against the hull. Most of the wave misses me but two metres away Glenn is drenched.

Sunlight breaks through the storm-clouds and reflects from the ocean and the pack-ice.

Previous page: Mt Herschel, at the head of Moubray Bay, is a formidable backdrop to the icebergs and Adelie penguins of Cape Hellett.

Rough seas during a storm keep everyone below decks or in the wheelhouse.

Even so, he films the path of the wave across the deck until it hits Peter by the mainmast boom. I smile at his dedication. Pete is well covered by his waterproofs but he retreats to the wheelhouse. I decide to photograph icebergs on a day when there is not so much sleet and seawater in the air.

When I come up on deck several hours later we are hove to with the wheel lashed in place. It is bitterly cold. A few snowflakes swirl around, melting as soon as they touch the wet deck or rigging. Diffuse sunshine breaks through the clouds but without enough strength to raise the temperature; the only effect is to create a silver reflection on the waves. Our iceberg has long since disappeared, so once again we face empty seas. As the hours pass the swell increases in size. We might be steering towards a storm, but with luck these big waves are the remnants of someone else's gale.

Sunday, 24 January

We are rewarded on our early morning watch by the sight of another magnificent iceberg. It grows from a small triangle on the horizon at about 5 am to a huge pyramid drifting past a nautical mile from the starboard side, four hours later. Against the pale grey sky it looks like the material of dreams, a floating mountain of neither land nor sea, and yet solid enough to reflect the sunlight more brightly than the sky. The pen and ink drawings of the early explorers no longer seem exaggerated.

By the time of our evening watch the weather is bleak again and the seas are rough. Everyone crams into the wheelhouse to hear the radio sched. The air becomes so fuggy that queasiness forces me outside. No sooner am

I out on deck than a huge wave breaks over the wheelhouse and drenches me. My waterproof bib-and-brace keep my lower half dry but the rest of me is soaked. At least I am refreshed enough to resume my place at the wheel. Lyle reads another story for the *Australian* newspaper over the radio to Camille, who tapes it. He is in much better health than when he spoke to her a week or two back, and she is obviously delighted to hear more spirit and life in his voice.

Betty, the radio operator at Mt Victoria, comes on air with an urgent message for Margaret. I guess the news before anything is said, as does Margaret, who is already crying. An old family friend died of cancer yesterday morning. Margaret can scarcely speak. She needs to be with her family and her friend's family, but our five-year friendship and journeys together to India and Nepal make me the next best thing. Chris offers to take the wheel, so I go below. Greg is already trying to comfort her. I squeeze onto the seat beside them and join their embrace, though I can think of nothing to say.

And now, as I lie in my bunk, I remember how the news of other deaths reached us while we were climbing Annapurna and Mt Everest. During expeditions such as these I try to come to terms with the possibility of dying, but though the fragile nature of mortality becomes more apparent, it gets no easier to accept. I fumble for the Gita amongst the books jammed in the narrow shelf beside my bunk and hunt for a passage I read this morning in this ancient Hindu scripture: 'That which is not, shall never be, that which is shall never cease to be. To the wise these truths are self-evident. The Spirit which pervades all that we see is imperishable. Nothing can destroy the Spirit.'

Monday, 25 January

Today we cross the Antarctic circle, and by dinner time we are a little over 67°S. Margaret decides we should celebrate with a feast. The menu is Curried Eggs in Coconut Milk, Mashed Pommes de Terre, and Crepes à la Chris. Morale is high as the end of our sea voyage draws near. I am reluctant to predict that in two days we shall see the continent because a storm or a problem with the engine may delay us — I do not want to tempt fate.

Outside on the horizon is a giant cowboy hat. The white top of an iceberg seems to float above the water because its rim of ice-cliffs blends into the sea. I go below into the Fish Cabin to where Greg lies reading in his bunk. 'Maybe we're in a post-apocalyptic novel,' he says. 'Who wrote us into this?'

As I pull off my gumboots and waterproofs and climb into my bunk I ponder the urge for adventure which has brought us here. Lyle, sprawled on top of his sleeping bag and obviously suffering, must constantly be asking himself the same question.

'It seems hard to believe that we are nearly there,' I say, hoping Lyle will find some sort of comfort in the comment.

He groans. 'Sometimes it feels like it will never end. And people reckon hell is a furnace.'

Greg watches him for a few moments then looks at me. 'It can't be good for you these sea voyages,' he says. 'We're all starting to look drawn around the eyes.'

He leans out from his bunk to peer at the discoloured mirror on the wall. 'It's happening to me, too.'

'There'll be some horrified faces on the wharf when we get back,' I say.

'Hmm,' he muses. 'Just like the return of every other expedition.' I wonder what it is that shows on our faces.

I look at the photo of Barbara which is stuck to the wall by my bunk. This picture is so firmly burnt into my mind—her impossibly blue eyes and hair blacker than the ink of my poetry—lines which capture her no more effectively than the photograph. My memories are only part of her as well—incomplete images, each of which carries some of her essence.

Greg sits opposite Lincoln and Glenn (right) during a lunchtime which lasts for hours. Boards screwed to the table decrease the rate at which bowls and plates leap onto the floor when the boat pitches and rolls.

Tuesday, 26 January

One in the morning, and yet there is plenty of light for me to write by on the chart table in the wheelhouse. During our whole journey south we have been heading east as well, and so the real time is more like 2 am. The measuring of time does not mean much, for nothing can hide the fact that there is no longer any night. Now only a prolonged dusk marks the quietest part of the day. Colin, in his dark green oilskins, seems to be dancing with the wheel, adrift in memories of old dancehall days. Of course, all he is doing is keeping his feet warm.

When it is my turn at the wheel I pass the time by watching a distant iceberg move relative to the ship on the radar screen. After handing the helm over to Glenn, I step outside. The seas are calm, as befits this part of the day. Snow falls steadily and forms a white coating on everything. The deck is as slippery as ice when I walk up to stand at the bow. The snowflakes swirl around me and melt into the dark blue sea. Nothing can be seen in the water and yet I am content to stand here, gently shuffling my feet to fight the cold, my arms crossed around the forestays for security and my fingers stuffed up opposite sleeves.

The only breeze is from the rush of air as we motor forward, but even this is freezing. Despite the cold and the chore of getting up at all hours to stand watch, the routine of boat life is simple, so simple that it allows the mind to go into a type of limbo. It is hard to comprehend that soon we must be ready for a new set of rigours. The first few days away from an expedition base camp are always hard. It is a time of doubt when I wonder where I shall find the strength to push myself to the top of mountains which tower impossibly high above me. Our approach to this peak will be especially difficult, and yet I relish the thought of the effort. My body cries out for something more than eating, standing by the wheel for hours, taking the air out on deck for a few minutes, and the eternal quest for a comfortable position in my pitching bunk. Even so, life on board has been easier to tolerate than I expected. Despite our cramped quarters, the limitless ocean gives a feeling of freedom and hence of peace, and it is in this that I find my satisfaction.

Australia Day. Last summer was my first January in Australia for nine years. Now I am absent again, this time to experience some of the worst weather in the world. When I was out on deck, the air temperature was just high enough for the snowflakes to clump together in sodden lumps which immediately wetted and cooled everything they settled upon. I think of the sun on Sydney beaches, a far saner and more controlled meeting of people and ocean than ours. Next summer will be my next chance to admire suntanned bodies smelling of coconut oil. For the moment I shall have to tolerate the less sensuous smells of salt and stale sweat.

The thick air of the Fish Cabin is hit with a blast of fresh air when Chris opens the door and announces dinner. There are stirrings in all the bunks apart from Glenn's, for he is asleep in Chris's bunk to avoid the sideways

The wind continues to blow from the south-east which, unfortunately, is the direction we wish to head. So we remain hove-to, with the wheel lashed in place to stop the rudder from swinging wildly.

motion of his own. Everyone mutters and curses. Greg glances at Lyle who lies on his back slowly shaking his head.

'Yes, Lyle,' says Greg. 'It's all true. It's all really happening.'

Lyle groans. 'I know it's true. The problem is it just keeps on being true.'

For the last few hours we have been hove to while a gale blasts us from the south-east, and before that we were motoring into the wind at 2.5 knots against a 2-knot current. These conditions guarantee that Lyle will not be vying for a place at the crowded table.

Margaret has baked an Australia Day apple pie and we listen to the radio sched. while eating this specialty. At the end of the sched. with Australia, the Greenpeace boat, en route to their Antarctic base, calls in from just south of Campbell Island. They have an ice report which is only five days old, and we learn to our joy that there is very little ice around Cape Adare, though we are likely to meet a band of pack-ice some time before then. Don arranges another sched. for tomorrow then reads out our latitude and longitude.

'Our position is 68°S by 168°E. Are you able to give us a weather report, please? Over.'

There is silence for a few moments before an answer comes back.

'A low pressure system is centred...' then a pause, 'Just about where you are. It will probably hang around for another twenty-four hours or so.'

We have to laugh. Here we sit in the eye of the storm. Outside the scene certainly fits the prediction. Snow and sleet are blowing across the boat at 20 knots, fast enough to sting exposed skin not already numbed by the cold. Big waves pass underneath the boat, tipping us wildly from side to side as they go by. The wind blows the crests off the waves so there is water as well as snow in the air. Visibility is only about 400 metres. After that, the ocean blends with the dark greyness of the sky.

Wednesday, 27 January

On watch at 2 am. It is light but still overcast and stormy. The wind continues to blow from the south-east, which is the direction we wish to head, so we remain hove to. The wheel is lashed in place to stop the rudder from swinging wildly. Colin and Glenn share the seat so I slouch in the starboard corner by the wheel.

'Why don't we rotate at forty-minute intervals?' suggests Colin. 'Then each of us gets to sit down.'

'Okay.'

'Since our last watch we haven't lost much ground,' he continues. 'In fact, we've made some east.'

'It all helps, I suppose.'

Glenn and I swap stories about India to pass the time. Colin slips in appropriate jokes or anecdotes. He opens the door a couple of times to check for ice. Our body heat in the damp confines of the wheelhouse makes the windows fog over. I wipe them occasionally but the effort is wasted because enough snow is plastered on the outside to make vision indistinct anyway. Shortly before 3 am we swap positions, but instead of sitting down I open the door and step out into the gale. I glance to the bow and see huge icebergs looming out of the mist directly ahead of us. Immediately I swing around and shout through the door, 'Icebergs ahead.'

Glenn stares at me in disbelief.

'I'm not joking.'

He comes outside to check. 'Hell. They're bloody close.'

Colin pokes his head through the door then quickly withdraws it. I scamper along the icy deck to get a view unobstructed by the reefed sails and the rigging. There are three icebergs, sharp pyramids nestled together or perhaps frozen into one piece beneath the water line. At first I think they are only 100 metres away from us but I realise from the size of the waves breaking against them that we must be at least four or five times that distance.

I go back to the wheelhouse and report that no ice fragments threaten the ship. Colin is at the wheel sailing the boat north-east. We make only 2.5 knots, but this is sufficient for us to draw away from the bergs. We relax again, warm our hands, and joke about the perfect way to snap into wakefulness on an early morning watch. After a few minutes Glenn sticks his head out of the door.

'There's another one! Right in front of us!'

'It's like looking at North Head from South Head,' says Colin, reminding us of our departure from Sydney Harbour. 'It's enormous. Much further away than it looks.'

No need for panic yet. I take the wheel and obey Colin's instructions. His course points us directly at the berg but he insists that the monster will slip by well to the starboard. Twenty minutes later he is proven right. I go on deck to take some quick photographs. Haste is necessary because of the cold and the need to keep my camera out of the falling snow. Waves smash a long way up the sides of the berg, and occasionally one breaks over the top from behind it. The sight reminds me of the power contained in these big seas. Until now we have accepted them without fear as the normal condition of the Southern Ocean. I think of the mess these waves would make of Sydney's beaches, and try to imagine how our small ship would appear from the berg: out of place and insecure.

Glenn scrapes the snow away from the windows then we go back into the shelter of the wheelhouse. Once again I think of Pete's previous journey south in the *Riquita*, when the wheel was on the small aft deck and open to the elements. With only five of them to share the watches, it must have been a gruelling journey.

Soon it is time to call Ken and Chris and to retire to the warmth of our bunks. The air in the Fish Cabin is stuffy and foul, but the seas are too wild to allow even one door to be tied open. I light a stick of musk-scented incense and quickly drift off to sleep.

When I come back on deck we are motoring on a course of due east by the magnetic compass. Because we are close to the South Magnetic Pole, almost due west of us now, a correction factor of 80° must be added to the magnetic compass reading. Our true course is a little east of south.

Don and Jonathan are on watch. Don is at the wheel and Jonathan, ever-needful of something to do, is tuning into a weak signal on the radio.

He abandons the radio, and says to me, 'Things are getting pretty low when you resort to listening to some guy talking to his sweetheart.'

'Why?' I ask. 'What are you tuned into?'

'Some guy at Mawson Antarctic Station talking to his girlfriend in Melbourne.'

'Well, what's she saying? What's happening in Melbourne?'

'I don't know. I can only copy his voice and she's doing all the talking.'

We pass a few more icebergs today. Don contacts Greenpeace again, and they are able to give us a more recent ice report. If we can get through the band of pack-ice somewhere to the south of us, it sounds as though we will be able to sail right into Cape Hallett. In the cramped quarters of the galley

From the crow's-nest, Lincoln watches the way ahead carefully. From that height he can see the edge of the pack-ice — a white line stretching along the horizon to the south.

Greg dances around overjoyed, while I warm my feet on the bread pot.

'Our boat is its own tiny world, and the small contact we have via the radio does not extend it much,' says Lyle, lying down after talking to Camille on the radio. 'It's hard to visualise other people's lives because we have seen no-one else for a month. Just sailing is all-absorbing, especially for me, flat on my back most of the time.' He stares silently at Jonathan's bunk above him. 'The rest of world seems so far away.'

'Only because it is,' says Glenn.

Thursday, 28 January

Colin, Glenn and I are up early for the 4 am to 8 am watch. Above decks, the sky is already bright from the sun shining weakly through thin cloud. We motor across a bitterly cold easterly breeze. Almost as soon as Greg and Pete hand over the helm and head for their bunks, we spot a car-sized lump of ice which we must steer around. Within minutes we change course again to avoid another one. The seas are slight but the surface is made choppy by the wind, and so it is difficult to predict the course of these wayward pieces of ice. Before long the sea is dotted with specks of white which do not vanish like the familiar flash of breaking waves. Colin assures us that most of these fragments are too small to be a danger, but large blocks start to become more frequent. The three of us rotate between the duties of standing at the wheel, keeping watch on deck, and warming up in the wheelhouse.

While Colin is at the bow, Glenn and I agree that these scattered bits of ice must be the tail end of the pack. When the density of the floating ice increases we become more certain of our verdict. The smaller lumps are soon too numerous to dodge so we slow down the motor and push through. We are forced to steer within a dozen metres of the larger pieces. These are weathered into fantastic shapes by the sun, the wind and the water. We see families of gargoyles and garden gnomes frozen in place and disguised by snow, as well as three-headed sea monsters, ducks, camels, car bodies, and a treacherous piece whose dome, half a metre above the water, is an eighth of the diameter of the mass concealed just below the surface. With so much open water around the ship there is plenty of margin for error, but that fact does not stem our excitement.

At the wheel Glenn adopts the melodramatic tone of a sports commentator. 'Remember: you saw it first on the Big Watch.' He glances down at the compass. 'Zero seven zero on your dial.'

I relieve Colin at the bow and take over the task of directing Glenn. During this fine manoeuvring the helmsman's view is obscured by the length of the ship and by the rigging, so I extend an arm in the direction we need to steer and wave my hand vigorously if the response is not fast enough. The light snow which has been falling all morning is made vicious by the wind. My glasses protect my eyes but the snow melts on the lenses. Luckily the wind comes from the port side so we are not forced to look directly into it. Glenn comes out on deck so I return to the wheelhouse to warm my numb hands. After an hour we are through to open water where there is only an occasional block to avoid.

Soon it is time to rouse the next watch. Very little ice is visible when Ken and then Chris arrive and so they do not share our excitement. As if to mark the end of our watch, the snow stops falling and the sun dissolves the thin cloud. I head for the warmth of my bunk via a climb up to the crow's-nest. From there I can see the edge of the pack, a white line stretching along the horizon to the south. Greenpeace told us it was 100

We steer the boat carefully through fragmented ice-floes.

nautical miles long, so we have to find a way through if we are to reach the continent in time. I go back down to the Fish Cabin and sleep for a couple of hours. Chris and Glenn wake me as they rummage amongst their film equipment.

'We've been motoring parallel to the pack but they think they've found a lead and we're going into it.'

My feet are still cold so I rub life back into them. Gumboots are good at keeping feet warm only until a wave pours down the top of them.

Chris returns to fetch something. 'We are cruising past big blocks only 3 metres from the boat,' he says. 'It's really impressive out there.'

Worth getting out of bed for, I decide. Up on deck, the world is different from when I went below. The air is still bitterly cold but the sun is shining brightly on calmer seas. Paradoxically, travel through the higher density pack-ice is safer because the ice is barely moving. Around us the blocks of ice dampen the movement of the waves, so that now the water is almost calm. Though we steer much closer to the big chunks, there is no concern that the pieces will drift against the hull.

I climb up to the crow's-nest where Greg stands shuffling his feet. He is calling directions down to Pete, who gives hand signals to Don at the wheel. Thirteen metres above the deck it is much easier to appreciate the nature of the maze we must find our way through. Ahead the ice looks impenetrable, and I ask Greg which way he thinks we can go.

'I'm just taking it 100 metres at a time in this thick stuff. Look, you can see across to the left there's a place we might be able to squeeze through.'

He calls out an instruction to Pete.

'You soon work out that the leads between the floes are obscured ahead of us, but that doesn't mean there's no way through. A path becomes obvious as we get closer. The pack isn't close enough together to stop us yet.'

'Where are you trying to get to?'

'See that big berg on the horizon?' He points slightly to the right of our course. 'I think there's blue water beyond that. If you look carefully you can see a dark line on the horizon, not a white one. That might be the other side of the pack or it might be a wide lead. It's a good place to head for, either way.'

'A lot of ice between us and there.'

I have no feeling for what is possible and what is not in this strange world of pack-ice. I remember Don and Colin's paranoia about running into ice, and yet below they are concentrating on steering the boat through calmly enough. I turn and look back at our wake. Our course is very much a zigzag one, and yet we are able to maintain our southerly direction. Frequently we turn sharply to skirt a large floe. I feel reassured by the amount of pack which is already behind us.

Our course takes us towards some storm clouds, but Greg tells me they are being quickly blown west.

'If the clouds weren't there, we could probably see Mt Minto.'

'Really? We're that close?'

'It's a big mountain.'

I stare ahead in silence.

'Interesting,' he says.

I follow his gaze down to the bow. 'What is?'

'Our bow wave is pushing aside pieces of ice the size of a car.'

It is much colder up here and so my fingers quickly go numb when I take a photograph. I could shoot roll after roll of film in the attempt to capture the nature of this scene, but the cold helps me to economise. It is a

Left: Reaching the pack-ice is exciting proof that Antarctica lies not far beyond the horizon. We crowd the mast and the roof of the Pleasure Dome to get the best possible view of what lies ahead.

joy to look out over a seascape which is more than water. I realise that my eyes have been starved for another dimension. Most of the floes are flat sections of frozen sea which were once joined together to form a huge platform of ice around the continent. We steer away from the big chunky fragments of icebergs trapped in the pack. Their shape is less regular than the floes and from our vantage point in the crow's-nest we can see the dark mass of the ice below the water. If the ship runs into one of these we might hole the hull, so we cautiously motor by them with plenty of room to spare. Occasionally we pass floes with a surface area the size of a tennis court, but which appear to be no more than 2 metres thick. How good it would be to get off and run around on one of these.

Time to go down, I decide, but I have to wait until my fingers warm up inside their thick woollen mittens so I can grip the rungs rivetted to the mast. I climb down past Pete who is standing on the yard arm because three in the crow's-nest is definitely a crowd. It feels much warmer on the deck because there is almost no wind down here. I remember Pete's comments about those-who-know seeking shelter from a storm in pack-ice. I look around me and decide that such bold sailors certainly must be in the know because much stronger ships than ours can be crushed if errors of judgement are made.

I sit in the Pleasure Dome and write in my diary. In search of a word, I lift my head and see a 20-metre piece of ice slide past only a few metres from the side of the ship. It is flat topped and unmarked. I suppose the sun, the wind and the waves will slowly weather furrows and channels in its surface until it breaks up and becomes a series of multi-towered masses like those outriders of the pack we saw this morning. Yesterday Greenpeace told us that supply planes headed for McMurdo Station sighted one berg which is 90 nautical miles long. If it was blown our way, it is possible we would not be able to motor out of its path before we were run down, but luckily it is a long way to the east.

Chris calls out that lunch is ready. I crawl out of the Pleasure Dome and go into the wheelhouse. Jonathan is at the wheel with Colin and Don standing by. In the galley Margaret fills bowls of soup from a big pot simmering on the stove. She explains that it was a long time coming because the water pipes were frozen and had to be wrapped with hot tea towels. Only Chris sits at the table. Everyone is so enchanted by the world of the pack-ice that they have forgotten their hunger.

'Amazing out there, isn't it?' I ask, not expecting an answer.

He nods. 'It's other-wordly. First of all you don't see the sun for two weeks, but meanwhile above the clouds the days slowly change into twenty-four hours of light. And the next thing, we're sailing past all these weird ice creatures, frozen into the strangest shapes. We're surrounded by them.' He spreads margarine on a biscuit. 'It's like something is preparing us for our epic journey. We'll be ready for anything after this.'

Chris's idea of our voyage becoming a kind of Pilgrim's Progress enchants me. I think of the different ways each of us is responding to this new world. Don, Pete and Jonathan have seen something of this before, while Greg and Colin know it well. To the rest of us it is like visiting another planet in a rusty antique spacecraft.

I eat greedily and try to convince Margaret to leave the soup for people to dish out for themselves. Sometimes she feels the call of duty too strongly.

'Go on deck and look at it all. You'll see why even your cooking hasn't enticed them down here.'

Pete descends the stairs and chases Margaret out of the galley. With

biscuits in my hand I am not far behind her because I do not want to miss any of this incredible scene.

Throughout the afternoon we motor slowly through the pack-ice. After a month of open sea, it is a delight to feast the eye on more than an expanse of water. We are all excited by the prospect of sighting land tomorrow, though the strangeness and beauty of the pack absorbs our attention now. Jonathan swaps lenses and photographs the ice and the ship. Chris and Glenn wedge themselves in the bow railings and film everyone's reactions. Margaret sits on the deck in front of the Pleasure Dome with her sketch pad, frustrated by how quickly the floating jigsaw around us changes. Lyle spends most of the day standing on the roof of the Pleasure Dome pointing out the course to Don or Colin at the wheel, and watching his dream of Antarctic adventure come true. He is obviously delighted to be of some use after spending most of the voyage sick in his bunk. For hours on end, Greg gives directions from the crow's-nest. It is much colder up there and he eats virtually nothing all day, but he is determined to find a route through the pack.

Late in the evening Greg thinks he can see open water a few hundred metres in front of us, but we come to a dead end. We hurriedly eat dinner while Don makes short work of the radio sched., then we try to work our way across to the east. Greg shouts directions confidently from above, and we manage to squeeze into another lead. We follow this to its end and try to push our way through to another narrow stretch of water. The floe ahead of us refuses to move and we realise that it is much deeper than the other floes we have been pushing past, and that its momentum could quite easily crush the hull. We go into reverse, but already another floe has drifted in behind us. Ken pushes at it with the boathook and I jump over

Above: With the open waters of the Ross Sea only a few hundred metres away, we try to push our way through dense pack-ice.

Following page: After hours of tight manoeuvring and carefully pushing aside ice-floes, we find that we can go no further. Nor can we retreat. We're stuck.

the side onto the floe to shove the hull away. It feels strange to be off the ship after a month on board but there is no time to follow this line of thought. We manage to reverse and I leap back over the rails.

I climb up to the crow's-nest and listen to Greg's thoughts about the possibilities open to us. It appears that if we can turn the boat through 90° in the small area of open water available, there is a good chance of pushing our way between smaller floes to open water. From up here I can see that the empty expanse of the Ross Sea is tantalisingly close.

I climb down and explain to Don what needs to be done. He listens carefully, then Colin, in his usual unhurried way, suggests the best approach considering the limitations of the engine and the steering. Ken in his Akubra stands by the rail, leaning on the boat hook and looking as if he is casually waiting for the next heifer to come through the gates. Pete is obviously much more worried. The best thing to do in a situation like this is to put energy into getting out of it. There is just enough room for the boat to turn. The water forced back by the propeller pushes floes across the lead we followed into this small pool. The only possibility now is to find a way through.

Colin's engine repairs are thoroughly tested as we bulldoze small floes out of the way. Chris, Glenn, Margaret and I use a long beam to lever smaller pieces of ice out of the way. It is hard to tell how much success we are having, but we work enthusiastically. At the stern, Ken and Lyle push ice clear of the propeller with the flimsy boathook, calling for our assistance when large pieces get in the way. Meanwhile, Pete relays Greg's messages to Don at the wheel while Colin tends to the engine revs. Jonathan controls the gearstick between forward, neutral and reverse. For the first time, eleven people seems like the right number on board this tiny ship.

We manage to force our way 50 metres closer to the Ross Sea, but then we face a turn of 30° to follow a line of weakness through to a small patch of open water. Unfortunately the floe on our starboard side is too big to push aside, and that means we cannot make the turn. We back off and ram the ice ahead, but all we do is dint the hull and scrape off a good measure of red paint. Lyle, Chris and I jump overboard and try to push the bow of the boat across, but it is like trying to lift a very cold elephant by its tusks while standing on them. We struggle for another half-hour—until 1 am— before we all admit the obvious. We are stuck.

Friday, 29 January

Ice bumping against the hull throughout the night made sure most of us slept intermittently. At last Glenn and I discover an advantage of sleeping in the thwartships bunks. Because our heads are not next to the hull, the constant noise of the ice is not as disturbing. After twenty-two hours on my feet sleep comes easily to me.

Over a late breakfast we discuss the fix we have got ourselves into. A comment by Greenpeace yesterday implied that a US Coastguard ice-breaker might be in the region. Don and Colin are in favour of contacting the ship, and it does seem sensible to find out what vessels are in the area in case our situation takes a turn for the worse. There is little danger of the *Thistlethwayte* sinking at the moment because of the small size of most of the floes and the large amount of broken-up ice. A gale could change the situation, for though pack-ice does dampen big seas, the biggest floes around us would not have to hit the ship very hard to do some serious damage.

Since we are not yet in a life-threatening situation, Greg is particularly

The pack-ice dampens the movement of the ocean, so Don takes advantage of the almost motionless ship to repair the aerials attached to the mizzenmast.

concerned that we do not ask for help just for the convenience of an easy escape. The whole ethos of our trip is to demonstrate that a small expedition can execute an audacious plan without relying on the enormous resources of a government Antarctic body. If we ask for assistance at this stage we are admitting that we miscalculated, and to proceed afterwards would be hypocritical. I support Greg when he states that if we are rescued by the Americans he would prefer to abandon the climb and return to Sydney.

Against this background, Colin is concerned that ice continually bashing against the hull may damage the propeller or the rudder. We decide that the best course is to contact the Coastguard ship, tell them our situation and ask for weather and ice reports. This seems like a good bridging measure while we wait for conditions to improve.

After Don's organised but casual contact with amateur radio operators around the world, his talk with the Americans is like consulting Big Brother. He contacts the *Polar Star*, and to our amusement we learn that it is anchored at the ice-wharf at the United States's McMurdo base in the Ross Sea. The *Polar Star* refers us to McMurdo Relay, who in turn refer us to McMurdo Centre. We are amused again when Don attempts to spell 'Thistlethwayte' in radio code and leaves a couple of letters out. The radio operator at Mac. Centre curtly and efficiently gives us the information we require. It is strange indeed to make contact with authority again.

Though the Americans can be no help to us 430 nautical miles away, there is some security in knowing that others are aware of our plight. If we do need rescuing, we can send an emergency call to the *Greenpeace* which is approaching our latitude on its journey south. They are a long way east, but I am sure they would make the diversion if necessary. The *Greenpeace* is not ice strengthened, but there are two helicopters on board. Despite our prolonged consideration of these options, I feel confident that if the

southerly wind eases, the density of the pack will decrease and we shall be able to motor through the last 300 metres of pack into the northern limits of the Ross Sea.

Twenty-four hours after we became trapped in the pack, I climb up to the crow's-nest to stand watch. Only one person is needed for this duty until we are moving again. My job is to rouse the others if something untoward happens, not that there is much we can do except abandon ship and camp on the biggest of our neighbouring ice-floes.

About 150 metres ahead of the boat three penguins rest on a chunky piece of ice, and 200 metres beyond them is the open sea. I can hear the break of the waves against the edge of the pack. I could probably see Mt Minto but for the dark clouds on the horizon. Much nearer, water lapping against a big ice-floe sounds almost like a river.

The mass of cloud extends above us and the outer portions, highlighted in soft pink, hang down in folds which fan out like the indistinct digits of a hundred-fingered hand. The open sea to the south looks black beneath this mantle, its darkness emphasised by the whiteness of the ice. The unsullied white of the pack has lost its brilliance in the soft, beautiful light of the early morning, and yet the hidden power of the ice remains. The plates of ice move with the swell and softly scrape and thud against the boat. The ship is the only red piece in an enormous white mosaic. Some of the ice is almost transparent because it is waterlogged, while other pieces are the purest white imaginable. The water in between forms a network of black veins. The patterns of the ice change but so slowly as to be imperceptible, like the hands of a clock, or the sun or the moon rising across the sky. The all-night day means we have lost the special aura of moonlight, and I miss it more than I miss the darkness of night.

We decide it is wise to inform other ships in the region of our predicament. Don establishes that the nearest vessel is the *Greenpeace,* several hundred kilometres to the north-east.

A slight swell causes the hull to bump continuously against the ice. We anchor the boat to the largest ice-floe around us to minimise the damage.

Patches of black water seem to grow in front of me as I watch. The wind is coming from behind us now, from the north-east. At the same time, the pack is tightening behind us. If this wind continues we shall be able to escape. A pure white snow petrel flies past at high speed. I wonder where it has come from and where it is going.

Saturday, 30 January

I am woken by Glenn shouting down the stairs. 'Looks like we might be able to get out of here. Better get up and have something to eat before all hell breaks loose.'

'Just the ship breaking loose would be enough,' I say, but he is gone.

On deck and in the galley everyone is excited and busy, though it is hard to work out if anybody apart from Margaret is actually doing anything. I step out of the wheelhouse in time to hear Lyle swearing at the top of his voice. He runs past me thoroughly drenched and dripping with water.

'Been for a swim?'

'I was trying to shift the anchor when the shelf of ice I was standing on snapped,' he says, ripping off his clothes. Then he begins to swear again, calling himself all manner of things.

I go below and grab my cameras. When I come back on deck Lyle is dressed in a one-piece insulated suit belonging to Jonathan. I climb up to the crow's-nest where Greg stands impatiently.

He beams at me. 'Just look at that!' he demands even before I have pulled myself underneath the railing onto the small platform.

I turn and look ahead. Open water is maybe half a kilometre away now, but the pack-ice is much less dense. The black veins between the floes have expanded into the width of footpaths, paths filled with harmless slush.

Above: Jonathan decides that while we are stuck in the pack-ice we should test our handheld radios. Jonathan tunes in as Lyle wanders around the ice-floe reciting *Hamlet.*

Left: Colin enjoys the evening with the help of a quiet drink.

Gentle pressure from the bow should be all we need to make our way through.

'Fantastic,' I say. 'Now I know how Moses felt at the Red Sea.'

Colin starts the engine and we begin to move slowly forward. As we hoped, the ice is forced aside. Five minutes later the biggest floes are behind us. It is great to look back at our wake, a thin black line cut through the slush and smaller floes. When we have only 50 metres left to open water Chris and Glenn come floundering out of the Fish Cabin with their tape recorder and camera. The pack-ice finishes distinctly, which is very different from the way it began. The southern border looks as if it has been sliced cleanly and sharply, with no ragged edges. Our release from the ice has the perfection of a miracle: certainly we feel the same kind of joy. Glenn just manages to film the bow pushing through into open water while Chris clambers up the mast to record our jubilant shouts.

Jonathan waylays Colin as he walks back from the engine room.

'Colin, can I get a shot of you in your dreadnought suit?'

'Certainly,' says Colin. 'Shall I just pull my hood up?'

'Yeah, that'd be great.' Jonathan drops into his photographer's stoop: feet braced apart and head bent forward behind his camera.

Click-click-click-click — the sound of his motor-drive taking four shots in one second. He changes the aperture of his lens. Click-click-click-click. He turns the camera through 90°. Click-click-click-click.

'That's false pretences,' I comment. 'He said, "A shot".'

Click-click-click-click.

'Thanks.'

'That's okay.' Colin smiles with his eyes. The extra twinkle in their blueness reflects everyone's high spirits. He goes into the wheelhouse.

'Colin's so hard to photograph looking natural,' says Jonathan. 'When you get the chance you've got to make the most of it. And people only expect one snap, so the motor-drive takes them by surprise and you get them as they start to relax...'

'Or start to get bored.'

He nods at Pete and Ken standing by the rail at the bow, then he smiles at me. 'Look at the sailors talking about spars and nautical things.'

He wanders along the deck towards them and when I look up from my writing a minute later he is holding his light-meter in front of them explaining how it works. So much for nautical things.

Once more the ocean stretches blue and endless in all directions, and my eyes are left hungering for sculptures of ice. As I stare out to the distant line of the horizon I wonder if our passage through the pack was just a dream. Already my memories share the same unreality as images remembered from sleep. Even now, two hours since we broke free, the only proof that we spent time locked in the ice is the complete flatness of the water we motor through. And even this rare condition could be attributed to causes other than the dampening qualities of the pack.

During our month of sailing across the ocean I found variety in the colours of the sea. I felt the mood change as the swells grew bigger and then shrank again. My eye would latch onto an albatross and follow its glide over the wave tops, or my heart would dart and swoop with the petrels and prions, each bird a tiny focus of life in the vast expanse of water. Our two days in the ice were an interruption of this simplicity, so that now my senses are out of tune with the subtleties of the ocean.

I turn away from the rail and go below with the intention of relaxing for a few hours before our 2 am watch. The floor space is covered with Glenn's medical boxes. He has spread vials and packets over Lyle's bunk and his own, so Lyle is stretched out in Jonathan's bunk. Greg is asleep and Chris sits darning a red mitten with grey wool. I step between the piles of bandages and strange instruments and swing up into my bunk. Things quieten down when Lyle goes back up on deck for his turn at the wheel and Chris begins to read. Glenn repacks everything as supplies for the ship and supplies to go ashore, then heads up the ladder.

Minutes later Don's voice comes down the hatch. 'Land in sight...I think.'

I lie on my bunk wondering if this indefinite message justifies relinquishing the warmth of my sleeping bag. Chris decides that it is worth the trouble. At the same instant we both sit up and hurry into our clothes. Chris is first up the stairs.

Glenn and Jonathan wave towards the starboard bow. It seems impossible to believe that the cloud-like shapes on the horizon are our first view of Antarctica. Through the binoculars which are thrust at me I can see that the grey shapes are rock buttresses, and between them are patches of snow. This two-toned scene fills in an outline which is indisputably land.

Pete climbs out of the forecastle complaining, 'I was looking forward to a good sleep.' Despite his pronouncement, his grin radiates excitement.

Greg emerges bleary-eyed up the ladder and Margaret clambers out of the wheelhouse. The wind cuts through my few clothes and makes me feel naked. Bed is the place to be, I decide. When I turn towards the Fish Cabin I notice Lyle peering out of the wheelhouse in the direction of land. As helmsman he cannot come out on deck to share our excitement. I poke my head in through the door and say to him, 'The verdict is it's Tasmania.'

He laughs and glances from the dirty window down at the compass.

Back in my bunk, I snuggle into my sleeping bag. When I close my eyes I find that the two-dimensional image of the Antarctic coastline seen through binoculars has burnt itself into my mind.

The rocky Possession Islands echo in miniature the ruggedness of the mountain ranges of North Victoria Land.

Sunday, 31 January

I spent this morning doing all the small repair jobs and alterations to my clothing and equipment which I had planned to do during the voyage. It seems silly to have left these chores until we are sailing parallel to the Antarctic coastline. Now, as I write in the Pleasure Dome, I can see the Possession Islands slide across the frame of the window. The thick salt on the glass cannot filter out any of the majesty of the scene. Behind these rocky islands the Antarctic continent rises sheer for thousands of metres before disappearing into the clouds. Almost parallel to us is Cape McCormick, and 30 nautical miles south of that is Cape Hallet, our pre-ferred landing point. These capes form the teeth which enclose Moubray Bay. At last the names are more than words to me, and the romance and mystique I have attached to them grows.

It is very difficult to assess the ice conditions. Blue water on the horizon suggests open sea, but a nautical mile further on, another line of pack has crept over the horizon and poses an obstacle to us. We opt for caution and head out to the limits of these lines of ice even where it is possible to cut between them. There are no bergs amongst the pack now, and the floes are smaller than the ones which trapped us.

Mid-afternoon, on navigational duty, Pete and I decide we should follow a particularly wide lead in. Though we do not expect to be able to continue all the way to Cape Hallett, the lead will give us an idea of the density of the ice close to the landward limits of the pack. Then the lead opens up

and the way appears clear to the Cape. A perfect evening and magnificent finish to an amazing day. I sit on top of the Pleasure Dome well rugged up and stare out at the coast. Occasionally I drag my eyes down to my notebook as I attempt to capture my impressions. The sea is as flat as a pond and the skies are clear. The last of the clouds hang down along the flat top of Adare Ridge, 2000 metres above the sea. It is as if the earth were breathing and drawing the clouds inside the mountains, capturing our gaze and drawing it inside as well. Despite the magnetism of the land, our attention is taken by a school of whales several nautical miles ahead. Jets of water betray their presence when they rise to breathe. As if choreographed, the fountains shine golden in the sun.

'They're coming straight for us,' Greg calls out from the crow's-nest.

We continue our collision course. We slow the engines and then cut them altogether as we draw closer. The whales veer to the west and pass the ship 400 metres away.

'Fin whales,' says Pete.

We can hear them snort and blow, and then the splash of the water as they breach. Pete lowers his hydrophone into the water and Chris holds his boom-mike aloft. There is complete silence on board as we watch and listen. After the chugging of the engine and the continual slap of the water against our hull, these are moments of serenity on the calm sea. We hear Don announce his call-sign into the radio. I am surprised to realise it is 8 pm already. The day has gone so quickly because for once a great deal has been happening.

Pete curses as he crouches over his tape-recorder and presses his head-phones tight against his ears. 'I can hear Don, even underneath the water.'

The whales pass on a course for the mountains, surfacing every few hundred metres. Their spray looks like the co-ordinated puff of fireworks. Their backs break the water in a curve like a single toothed circular saw: thirty black and shiny blades slicing the water.

After dinner I climb to the crow's-nest again. The wind is bitterly cold, so that between photographs I am forced to hold my gloved hands against the side of my head to stop my ears from freezing. The snowy summits of the peaks to the west of us are tipped with a soft light which turns pink as I watch.

Greg climbs up and together we work out the best route through the ice for the next half mile. There appears to be ice around the toe of Cape Hallett, but we need to get much closer before we can tell how much of a problem or a danger it will be. I leave the task to Greg and head for the Fish Cabin to get some sleep. The excitement is exhausting.

Glenn's voice disturbs me. 'There's all this pack around lit up in orange and pink. And the sun's just setting on the horizon. Unless you really need to sleep it's worth getting up for.'

I sigh. I really need the rest. If we make a landing the hard work of unloading is likely to start as soon as we arrive. Only a minute later, or so it seems, Pete's voice intrudes upon my sleep. 'We're a couple of miles from Cape Hallett.'

My mind refuses to wake up. I put my wrist in front of my face and force myself to read the time—1.30 am. Only an hour's sleep, but it was better than nothing. I sit up and pull on another layer of clothing. Lyle shoots down the steps, sits on his bunk and immediately proceeds to cut out a disk from a piece of cardboard.

'What the hell are you doing?'

Left: **The soft colours of the night help disguise the danger of the pack-ice remaining between our vessel and the Admiralty Mountains.**

He pulls a ball of red wool from a plastic bag on his bunk before glancing up at me.

'Making a pompom for my scarf.'

The culmination of two years of planning and a month of agony at sea, and Lyle is making a pompom for the scarf he has been knitting since we left Sydney. I shake my head in disbelief. But then I think for a moment, and decide Lyle's behaviour is suitably bizarre. Our tiny ship steers cautiously between huge ice-floes while the mass and bulk of the unclimbed Admiralty Mountains demonstrate the only scale which is relevant here. Our excitement is a storm in a thimble in this frozen world. Sanity has different precepts now.

Left: Our first contact with Antarctica is an introduction to its peace and beauty. Clouds reflect in the still waters of Edisto Inlet.

ANTARCTICA

ANTARCTICA

'I very deliberately did not take one photo and did not write one word about the expedition. I just wanted to be right there at that minute, every minute, and nowhere else. And it was necessary, because on the surface it was such a simple operation just to go down to Antarctica in a little boat and go to climb a mountain, but that simplicity hid the complexity of the whole operation. For it to succeed there were a million different things to be dealt with at one time every day. No time for anything else.'

GREG MORTIMER

Monday, 1 February 1988

When I step out on the deck I am amazed to see how close we are to land. The ship has rounded Cape Hallett and we are in the shadow of Quarterdeck Ridge, a mass of rock rising 700 metres above the water. The sea is as smooth as a mirror and made black by the shadow. Land is only half a kilometre away.

Porpoising Adelie penguins returning to Cape Hallett are bloated with krill.

Previous page: Moonrise over Mt Trident

Greg is in the crow's-nest, and I decide to join him. I climb the ladder quickly because I am eager to turn my attention to the scene around us. Greg immediately thrusts his hands into my armpits to warm his fingers. On deck the temperature was perhaps −10°C, but the wind 13 metres above the deck makes my eyes and ears ache within minutes.

Greg nods ahead. 'You can see the abandoned buildings of Hallett Station.'
'Right.'
'And you see the pattern on the rocks?'
'Yes,' I answer, expecting him to launch into a geological explanation.
'That's penguins. Thousands and thousands of them.'

I cannot believe him, but as we draw closer I see that he is right. All that flat ground in front of us and almost 70 metres up the scree slope beyond is covered with Adelie penguins.

'I've never seen anything like it.'

Greg pulls his hands out of my armpits and laughs.

'The whole continent is like that. Unbelievable in different ways. All these strange animals around the coast, but inland no life at all. This place is like nowhere else on earth.'

I zip my jacket up around my neck and stare. The boat chugs slowly forward. Groups of penguins paddle leisurely towards the rookery until they notice the boat. Startled by the unfamiliar sight, they duck below the surface and shoot away like miniature torpedos. Occasionally one of them breaks the surface, then its momentum carries it through the air for a

Ken keeps watch from the bow as we motor towards Cape Hallett.

metre or so before it plunges back into the water and continues its erratic but graceful course.

'It looks good,' says Greg.

'What does?'

'The ice behind this peninsula of rock. See how it stretches right across the bay? It's been there all winter and is probably really solid.'

'So that's sea-ice, not ice on top of land.'

'Yep.'

I hope Greg's optimism is justified. Our concern now is whether we can find a place where we can anchor against the sea-ice. If not, we shall be forced to unload all our equipment and supplies into the Zodiacs and ferry them ashore. The biggest problem is the skidoo. This motorised toboggan weighs 200 kilograms even when stripped of its engine. It is too big to fit into a Zodiac, which means we would need to lash the two small inflatable boats together, and even then the machine would be insecure and difficult to unload. If we have to make that awkward transfer, at least the dead calm waters give us ideal conditions for the job.

As we motor around the flat tongue of rock where the penguins have made their rookery, I see why it is named Seabee Hook on the charts. A narrow isthmus connects the low island to the Cape Hallett peninsula and half encloses a tiny bay on its southern side. The rookery hangs off the hand of the peninsula like a swollen thumb.

Beside me Greg is excited, 'It looks great. Looks like we'll be able to anchor against the ice in Willett Cove.'

'This little bay?'

Adelie penguins dot the bare rocks of Cape Hallett. Behind them, the abandoned buildings of Hallett Station look out of place against this scene of mountains, sea and sky.

'Yeah.' Then he says, 'Up there is Football Saddle.' He points up the valley, which is the ice-filled extension of Moubray Bay. 'The New Zealanders landed a Hercules up there in 1967 when Hillary led that expedition to climb Mt Herschel.'

'If it's flat enough to land a plane on, it should be easy going for a skidoo.'

Greg shrugs, 'We'll find out in a couple of days.'

The ship is only 30 metres from the shore now. Up here in the crow's-nest I can see, beyond the dark rocks covered by hundreds of penguins, the still water of Willett Cove. The tiny bay is full of sea-ice, and a small iceberg seems to block the entrance. With no fuss, and as if he marked the boat against sea-ice every day, Don steers the boat towards the edge of it. We hit at an angle, and crunch into solid ice. Ken, Lyle and I drop the anchor overboard, then Lyle and I leap ashore. The anchor is heavy but the excitement of arriving and escaping the confines of the boat gives us the energy to run with it. Colin asks us to carry it as far as the rope will allow in case the ice cracks during the night.

'Fine, fine,' says Don casually. 'I'd happily stay here for a couple of weeks.'

When both the bow and stern lines are secured everyone jumps off the ship. Glenn sets up his movie camera to take some time lapse shots of our vessel with the outline of Cape Hallett behind. A group of us stand by the anchor and admire the boat. Penguins shoot up out of the water and land upright on their feet on the ice. They run towards our group, determined to reach their comrades sleeping on the ice 10 metres behind us. When only a few metres away they realise that something is not as it should be. They put their heads down and run between us as if we were not there. The penguins welcome the expedition to Antarctica by treating us like a bad dream.

We cannot believe our luck. Unloading will be so much easier with the ship anchored next to the sea-ice, and what is more, we can begin unloading tomorrow and spend the rest of tonight asleep. I glance at my watch. It is 3 am. What a full day it has been, and now we are too tired to spend much time ashore. Pete and I are last on deck. When I go down to the Fish Cabin I leave him looking at the rookery with binoculars.

Rather than going to sleep, I lie in my bunk and write my first impressions of the continent. I have never been on an expedition based so much on uncertainty—one of the reasons I am so incredulous now we have arrived. The strange nature of the place is another component. The city of penguins on Seabee Hook reminds me of my visit to Bodh Gaya, where Buddha was enlightened. When I visited the village, the Dalai Lama was giving an initiation to 200,000 Tibetans. His audience had travelled thousands of kilometres from the furthest corners of Tibet to visit this small holy village in India. The huge crowd surrounded the tent pavilion where the Dalai Lama sat and discoursed hour after hour upon a sacred Buddhist text. The message rang out across the fields through a network of loudspeakers. Cape Hallett is very different, but the city of penguins has the same density of life and the same other-worldliness. Here, instead of the tired and dusty plains of India, is range after range of majestic untouched mountains. The spirituality is here too, but it is raw and awaiting an interpretation.

I look up and notice that Jonathan is restless, so I lean across and whisper, 'Are you afraid to nod off in case you wake up in the morning and find we're still at sea?'

He smiles and shakes his head. 'I just can't sleep.'

Five hours later Greg wakes me. He says nothing, but beckons me to come on deck. A glance at my watch tells me it is a few minutes before nine and I curse silently. Another hour of sleep would have been great. Just the same, I throw on some clothes and climb up the stairs with a boot in each hand. Greg is at the rail wearing only long johns. The deck is warm from the bright sunshine so I place my boots on the deck and enjoy the feeling of my bare feet on the warm metal. There is not a cloud in the sky and we are flanked on three sides by mountains. The smallest of these is the flat-topped Quarterdeck Ridge, but because its base is only half a kilometre away it rises steeply above us. The dramatic peak of Mt Herschel is the nearest summit and a perfect sentinel for these mountains. Its steep, un-climbed eastern face and spearhead-shaped peak epitomise what the Admiralty Mountains have to offer: challenge, remoteness and an unworldly beauty.

The squawking of penguins drifts across the open water from the rookery. The boat is not moving at all. Our immobility after a month at sea would make me feel we are truly frozen in time were it not for the warmth of the sun reflecting from the snow.

Greg interrupts my contemplation of the scene. 'I don't know how many mornings like this we're going to get. This is one of those perfect days when Antarctica feels like the best place on earth.'

'Worth getting out of bed for.'

His grin and the gentle gaze of his blue eyes seems to say, 'We are here at last; the mountains are waiting and the rest is up to us'. It is another moment to be locked away with indelible memories of summits Greg and I have shared and ordeals we have survived. Each of those special moments has the sharpness of one of Jonathan's photographs, and the time between them has become blurred and jerky like a home movie.

Following page: **Midnight at Cape Hallett. Quarterdeck Ridge dwarfs the *Allan And Vi Thistlethwayte* and our equipment on the sea-ice. In the foreground, Adelie penguins sleep, huddled like small black stones.**

'It's so warm,' I say, turning my thoughts back to practical matters. 'I'm going to have a wash to celebrate'.

I go down into the galley where the floor is the same temperature as the Southern Ocean. My bare feet prompt me to light the stoves as quickly as I can. I put water and porridge on to heat, then hurry back out into the sun.

I strip off and sit beside the Pleasure Dome. For once the name seems appropriate because it is a pleasure to feel the warm metal against my back and the clean sunshine on my bare skin. One by one the others appear on deck. I remember the porridge, so I pull on my clothes and go below to stir it. Margaret is zipping up her jacket.

'You won't need all those clothes on outside. It's a magical day.'

She smiles and hugs me so tightly that I cannot breathe. As always, her enthusiasm is infectious.

'Go and see,' I urge her. 'I've got the porridge under control.'

Our excitement at arriving is betrayed by the huge breakfast we devour. The slight wind which picks up as soon as I begin my wash chills me instantly and increases my appetite. Everyone is full of energy. Lyle sums up his own feelings in a dispatch for the *Australian*, which he reads into the radio. He is overjoyed that the agonising sea voyage is finished, and that he can eat proper meals again. All of us have been worried that he may not have the strength to travel inland to Mt Minto, but Lyle himself has no doubts.

I am eager to stretch my legs on the continent but I know there is a lot of work to be done. One of the main tasks is unloading and stashing the extra year's worth of food which we have brought with us in case we are trapped here for the winter. Greg, Pete and I walk towards the penguin rookery in search of a route from this platform of ice to the rocky surface of the earth. Even though we have not yet abandoned the security of the ship, I already sense the vastness of Antarctica and its disconnection from the human world. The edge of the ice is broken up into a maze of miniature fjords, and every tiny peninsula we follow leads us to a moat about 5 metres wide. In an attempt to find a way across I leap over 2 metres of water. The ice I land upon snaps. Luckily my momentum carries me onto the floe but my shin slams into the new edge. I look around and see that I have landed on an island. My curses alert Pete and Greg, who laugh at my predicament. There is nowhere for me to jump to because everywhere within reach is undercut and may snap under my weight.

Greg edges out along a tongue of ice. 'I reckon here would be all right.'

I am sceptical.

'Put it this way,' he continues, 'You don't have any choice.'

I decide that to take a running jump would be unwise because the overhang I am now standing upon may break. Gingerly I step as close to the edge as I dare. This way at least I am jumping from solid ground. I visualise the mechanics of a grasshopper jumping, and try to put as much force as I can into my flight. I clear the opposite lip easily, but the ice is so thin the whole section snaps off with Greg and me on it. We leap to safety before it sinks under our weight, and agree that there is no practical route to the rookery from here.

On the way back we meet a Weddell seal sunning himself on the ice. He is nervous about our attention but not enough to move, even when we are only 3 metres away. His nostrils close tight with a snort each time he breathes. His huge dark eyes are the kind anyone could fall in love with.

Pete heads back to the ship while Greg and I make for the scree slope running down from Quarterdeck Ridge. The ice is cracked apart enough to

Our first day ashore passes quickly as we unload our supplies, separate the wintering-over rations, and assemble the skidoo (centre right).

force us further to the right than we wish. We take different routes across this jigsaw and reach the rocky slope several hundred metres apart. True land underfoot at last, the first for 1988. I climb across the ice slope to a stream of water running down from the lip of the hillside glacier. It tastes like what it is—the purest water in the world.

Back at the boat the unloading is already under way. The first job is to empty everything from the hold. With eleven people eager to work, the huge task goes smoothly. It seems wise to keep our supplies on the far side of the cracks in the ice, because the gaps may widen until the outer pieces are loose enough to drift off into Moubray Bay. When the wooden sled is unlashed from the aft deck we use it to ferry loads 40 metres in from the edge of the ice. This sledge, which was made specially for us in New Zealand and lovingly assembled on the Walsh Bay wharf by Lyle, slides smoothly across the ice. The big question is whether the skidoo can be made to go. My mechanical knowledge encompasses the principle of the lever and very little else, so the machine is a mystery to me. Chris and Lyle work at assembling the engine.

Margaret has anticipated the hunger brought on by the excitement of being here at last. We eat out on deck and use the interruption to our activity to admire our surroundings.

With everything out of the hold, the next job is to unload the forepeak. Some packs and boxes are wet, even though this compartment inside the bow is supposed to be waterproof. Colin's brow creases when he is told the news. 'Must have a look at that,' he mutters.

We sorted most of our vast amount of food in the old wooden warehouse at Walsh Bay, but some of the quantities seem inappropriate. Greg does some quick recalculations. We have two huge piles on the ice: food and equipment to stay at Cape Hallett; food and equipment to be taken with us on the sleds behind the skidoo. The first pile, our survival supplies if we are trapped for the winter, is comfortingly large, but the second pile seems huge as well. Will our motorised toboggan be able to pull it all? Probably not, so we quickly reshuffle the piles.

When the food is reorganised we turn our attention to the Zodiacs. Pete and Greg attach an outboard motor to one, while I inflate the other. When

both rafts are operational we begin to ferry the food across to Cape Hallett. We zoom around to the seaward side of Seabee Hook to get as close as possible to the few remaining buildings of the abandoned scientific station. The beach consists of large pebbles of volcanic rock, and everything is covered with penguin droppings. We drag the boats up beyond the reach of the tide then turn to face the eyes of scores of penguins. According to Pete's calculations, the rookery holds about 30,000 birds. Though strong, the smell is not as bad as Pete's reckoning led me to expect. Dozens of young birds cluster together as they wait for their parents to return from a day at sea hunting krill, the crustacea which form a vital part of the Antarctic food chain. Each adult which comes ashore is mobbed by hopeful youngsters demanding food. Pete discourages us from disturbing them more than necessary.

The buildings are penguin and seal proof, but easily unbarred by humans. Of the half dozen buildings left standing, we decide that the best place to leave our supplies is a fibreglass dome, shaped like a giant pumpkin, and already set up as an emergency shelter. The other buildings are the living quarters for the New Zealanders who in recent summers have been dismantling the station. We transfer all our supplies from the Zodiac to inside the 'pumpkin', and then we have a more thorough look around. I wonder how the 40,000 gallon fuel tank will be dismantled.

A painting on the side of one of the wooden sheds shows the station in its heyday. I am surprised by the extent of the former village, which even had an airport and aircraft hangars. A good job has been done of clearing away the debris—or so I think at first. Inside the hut which has been used as living quarters by the demolition crew, log entries reveal that many things, from tractors to building materials, ended up in the ocean. I suspect that in Antarctica's delicate environment, where most of the creatures depend on the sea for food, dumping in the ocean is more ecologically damaging than leaving everything in place on land.

In the kitchen area, besides cooking and eating implements, and the logbook, a few photographs decorate the walls. A scene from the New Zealand Alps is given the privilege of a frame, whereas Miss May and two Miss Novembers are merely pasted to the wall. The pinups seem singularly inappropriate for Antarctica because the models do not have a stitch of clothing between them. The hairstyles, modest poses and full, unathletic bodies of these coyly smiling beauties belong to the ideal of an era long finished when the station was abandoned in 1973. The meekness and inconsequentiality they suggest makes me almost embarrassed to write about them — a strange time capsule to discover in this timeless land.

We record our arrival in the log, then go outside among the penguins. Rather than driving the Zodiacs directly back to the ship we take a longer route around some of the icebergs in the bay. The afternoon sun shines through curtains of icicles hanging from the sides of bergs which have been hollowed out by the waves. The penguins who bask on these sheltered islands raise their heads in surprise when our noisy craft motor by. Thirty thousand penguins give a feeling of life and activity to Cape Hallett, but as I look at the mountains beyond the rim of sea-ice I can imagine the powerful silence up there, and the strangeness of a world without life.

Back at the anchorage, Chris and Lyle have finished assembling the skidoo. It does not work, so both of them are tight-lipped and glum. To improve their mood they help Jonathan and Glenn ferry another load of winter supplies across to the 'pumpkin'.

Don's radio sched. brings a reminder of time into our twenty-four hour day. He contacts the *Greenpeace* and we learn that they plan to visit Cape Hallett in about three weeks on their way north out of the Ross Sea. This is good news indeed because in the event of an emergency we might be able to radio them for help. Greg talks to Peter Malcolm, a British helicopter pilot, who had previously visited Antarctica with the Footsteps of Scott Expedition, and whom we had all met in Sydney.

I think back over our dealings with Greenpeace. My impression of a well-organised and professional organisation, which grew out of our work together for the Centrepoint Tower climb, was reinforced when I became familiar with their Antarctic programme. For a while we negotiated with Greenpeace in the hope that we might be able to hitch rides to and from Cape Hallett on board their vessel. Unfortunately, their ship was not scheduled to spend enough time in the Ross Sea for us to climb Mt Minto.

There is another satisfaction in having radio contact with the *Greenpeace* apart from renewing brief friendships and confirming ideals: there is some small measure of security in knowing that a ship with two helicopters on board and a crew committed to our own ideas of Antarctica as a wilderness, will be in this same region while we are climbing the mountain.

The climb of Mt Minto is the reason for our expedition, but through it we wish to demonstrate that small well-equipped expeditions can safely execute daring trips into the interior. We want to show that private parties can be more environmentally responsible than the large garbage-producing scientific stations, and thus have a more than equal right to visit the continent. A corollary is that we must maintain complete independence from government Antarctic operations. All of us have wondered what would happen in the event of an accident. Once we are away from the coast any kind of emergency would be a very serious matter, and the chances of a successful rescue slim, even if we manage to contact our ship.

After the sched., Greg and I adjust our ski bindings to fit our boots, but Margaret's call to dinner prevents us from going skiing. The feeling of excitement which has reigned all day mellows into a mood of satisfaction. We have achieved much and, so long as we can get the skidoo running, nothing should prevent us from leaving the day after tomorrow. If Chris and Lyle cannot find the problem with the skidoo, I am confident Colin will be able to work it out from first principles.

In these latitudes sunsets last for hours, but instead of admiring the beautiful light on the mountains around us, Lyle and I pore over the map and the aerial photographs Greg obtained from the US Geological Survey, and argue about which of the distant mountains is Mt Minto. Lyle maintains that the peak I thought was our goal is in fact Mt Adam. He convinces me, and suddenly the photos, the panorama in front of us and the map fit together in my mind. Each interpretation of the scene — the photographic, the visual and the diagrammatic — gives depth to the other two, and my confusion disappears.

At the head of the Ironside Glacier, a curving snow ridge sweeps up to Mt Minto's summit. The ridge looks like a safe and spectacular feature to climb, but we may well choose another route because our approach will be from behind. From here we must travel south across the sea-ice of Edisto Inlet then climb up over Football Saddle, the lowest part of the ridge between us and the Tucker Glacier. Our map shows the Tucker to be a broad glacier with a gentle slope which leads to within 40 kilometres of Mt Minto. From where Lyle and I stand on the decks of the ship, the mountain looks small and insignificant because the peaks in the foreground steal its grandeur. Already Antarctica is playing games with my senses. Minto is the highest point, not only amongst all the mountains we can see, but for several hundred kilometres in every direction. The soft light of night hides the crevasse fields which make the lower reaches of the Ironside impassible, and the clear air compresses the distance between us and our destination. I understand these tricks of perspective, and I know the Ironside is not a practical route, yet the sight in front of me seems to deny the facts. Everything is more extreme here, whether it is the cold, the foreshortening or the beauty.

Crevasse fields and icefalls bar access up the Ironside Glacier to Mt Minto (right of centre) which means we must approach the mountain from behind. The peaks to the right are much closer to the camera and appear taller than the highest peak in the range. The snow ridge rising diagonally right up to the summit is the ridge we eventually attempt to climb.

I stare at the scene for hours, both through the viewfinder of my camera and with the less critical eyes of wonder. All the energy of the sun is concentrated upon the summits of the Admiralty Mountains. The lower slopes and the foreground blend together, so that the soft shades of land and sky offset the pink and apricot peaks and their slowly changing shadows. Time seems to stop, and then go backwards. I shake my head and tell myself I am staring too hard. Then I realise the lengthening shadows are shrinking again. The sun is rising. I glance at my watch: midnight and time for bed.

The never-setting sun of summer blends sunset into sunrise and colours the mountain tops a delicate pink.

Tuesday, 2 February

After a good sleep, uninterrupted by cold hours standing watch, I awake to another glorious morning. While I am getting dressed the roar of an unfamiliar motor breaks the silence. I run up the stairs and see Lyle sitting on the skidoo, but already the engine has died. A cloud of grey smoke quickly dispersing shows that I did not imagine the sound. I return to the Fish Cabin to put on the rest of my clothes.

Downstairs around the galley table, Lyle, Chris and Colin discuss the skidoo over steaming bowls of porridge.

'What was wrong with it?' I ask.

'We had the fuel pump connected back to front, so the engine wasn't getting any fuel,' says Lyle with a touch of embarrassment.

'All systems go now, though?'

'A few adjustments to make.'

Margaret hands me a bowl filled to the brim with porridge and milk.

'Thanks,' I say. 'Don't have to worry about things jumping out of their dishes for a while, do we?'

Lincoln waxes our skis the evening before our departure from the coast.

'And the water goes down the plug-hole now,' she replies.

'Glad to be here?'

Her answer is a smile big enough to make me think that if I pulled her ears upwards the top half of her head would lift off.

'I don't even care that the water pipes were frozen.'

'How did you get them working?'

'Greg got at them with a blowtorch, and now I'm keeping hot tea towels jammed up against the pipes.'

'No rest for the wicked,' I say, though nobody could be less wicked than Margaret.

Outside on the ice I follow Jonathan and Greg's example and sort out my personal gear. My pack full of equipment was stowed in the forepeak during the voyage south, and I must check that I have everything I need for a month away. Despite my experience with cold climates, I had difficulty deciding exactly what I would need while I was still in Sydney. The sled provides a good flat area above the surface of the ice, so I spread my belongings along the top of it. Thermal underwear, a jacket of windproof Goretex and one of fibrepile, trousers of the same material, hats, gloves, mittens, socks, more socks, a woollen scarf and one of cotton, a lightweight jumper, a down-filled jacket, and a down-filled suit. These last two items seem unnecessary in the conditions of the last two days, but when we climb up away from the coast the temperature will drop dramatically. Antarctica's bad weather is legendary, so we have to be equipped for all possibilities. Already the height of summer has passed which means every day brings us closer to winter when the sun never shines. With my clothes in order I turn to my climbing gear.

Handling my ice-axe and mountaineering boots reminds me of our

ultimate purpose. Every day is special on an expedition like this, but the days spent climbing stand out above the rest. When I climb my attention is directed completely upon the act of climbing, and that sole focus makes me feel a part of the environment around me. Afterwards there is a sense of familiarity with the mountains I have been amongst, which cannot be forgotten. I put my ice-axe down with my other equipment and pack away the things I shall not need. The hardest decision is which books to take, and how much camera gear. I pick up my miniature tape-player then put it aside. Antarctica is the land of silence, and its few sounds will be music enough for me.

Greg lives very simply. He has few possessions and a very clear idea of his place and purpose. His quiet speaking manner hides his incredible determination. Because he conceived this trip and the way to achieve it, he is the undisputed leader amongst us. Our plan is daring because of the distances we must cover and the limited time available to us before the winter freeze. Greg's familiarity with Antarctica makes him believe our plan remains possible, and the rest of us can only trust his judgement. This is easy for me because we have shared desperate survival decisions on Annapurna and Everest, but I wonder at the source of everyone else's faith.

On one level, everyone's character has come out of the woodwork after a month at sea. Because there is so much to be done, everyone's method of action is now apparent. Jonathan has the ability to be busy no matter how much or how little there is to do. When he has finished everything else on his agenda, he picks up his cameras and photographs whatever is around him. Chris works hard, wasting no time on deciding what needs to be done. Perhaps his training as an engineer taught him this, or perhaps his natural efficiency drew him to engineering. As sound recordist, he faces a

Beyond the sleeping Adelie penguins, a grounded iceberg shelters the already quiet waters of Willett Cove.

difficult task. Both he and Glenn appreciate that the great difficulties to be faced in making this film will be the cold and the need for our cooperation. Small concessions are easy to make, but I doubt whether any of us will have the energy to repeat our actions for the camera. We continue to tease them about their argumentative fashion of working together. Glenn takes this baiting in the light-hearted vein it is intended but I think Chris is more touchy. He has shown himself to be competent in everything he tackles — from climbing Centrepoint Tower to adapting lightweight sound recording equipment for harsh Antarctic conditions — and yet I feel that he lacks confidence. Perhaps his exploits are attempts to prove something to himself, because he certainly does not need to prove himself to others.

Tomorrow we head into the mountains. In some ways, it will be sad to leave the ship. Margaret and Pete wish they were coming with us, and yet I know both of them will be happy once we have left. There is no shortage of practical biology for Peter, and Margaret, who can find joy in any situation, will love exploring Cape Hallett and this world of ice. Don will busy himself making radio contact with as many out-of-the-way places as possible, and will supervise Ken's and Colin's maintenance of the boat.

Colin has relaxed incredibly since we arrived. He has rediscovered the good humour that most of us had forgotten he possessed. In an old ship like the *Thistlethwayte*, where so much equipment has been improvised or repaired, Colin's job is enormous. For most of the voyage the responsibilities rested heavily on his shoulders. Now that we are at a safe anchorage and with a motionless ship, he has the time to finetune his improvisations to the engine. The hold is empty so he can regrease the new gearbox and check that everything is as it should be. This must be his idea of paradise — a wild and remote part of the earth, accessible only by boat, and the time and need to tinker with the vessel we all depend upon.

At two in the morning, Lyle's last act on our final day on board is to pull the photographs of his kids from the wall. He peels the sticky tape away from the back and places both snapshots carefully in his diary. I look at my photo of Barbara then reach out to do the same.

Wednesday, 3 February

The perfect weather has ended. Snow is falling gently when I go up on deck after a good night's sleep. The snowflakes which land on me melt quickly because my clothes are still the temperature of the Fish Cabin, a few degrees above freezing. The air and the metal of the boat are cold enough so that each flake sits where it lands.

Margaret dispenses with her usual good morning and greets me instead with, 'It's snowing!'

'I know,' I answer glumly.

It is typical for Margaret to think of the beauty of the scene rather than the inconvenience.

'Just like Mt Victoria out there now,' I say, rallying my good humour.

'And Greg didn't tell me to bring my skis.'

'No porridge for him, then.'

'He's already had it.'

The morning passes quickly while we pack our belongings and load the sleds. As well as the 4-metre wooden sledge, we are taking two fibreglass sleds called pulks. One is almost 3 metres long and the other only half that length. Our plan is to pull all three in a train behind the skidoo. There

is every reason to believe this should work, but a shortage of snow and lack of time meant we could not test the theory in Sydney. I am amazed by the amount of food and equipment we are taking. It looks like we must have too much of everything for six people for a month, but then I remember that we have to carry extra food as well as several large boxes full of film gear in case we are caught in a one- or two-week blizzard. I hope the terrain is not too rough for the skidoo.

Spirits are high in the galley at lunchtime. Colin tells a few jokes and repartee flies from all directions. It is 3 pm by the time we are ready to leave. The snow which was falling all morning has eased a little, and visibility has now increased to a few kilometres. The clouds hang threateningly close to the ground, ready to swallow us up.

Everyone gathers outside to watch when the procession is finally ready to depart. Lyle starts the engine, the rope tightens and the wooden sledge begins to move, the rope tightens on the pulks behind, and the mountaineering party is underway. A cry of jubilation from the spectators is interrupted by Glenn shouting 'Stop! Stop!' Hunched over the engine, Lyle cannot hear him, so Chris has to run up and almost shout in his ear. Chris and Glenn want him to repeat the departure so that they can film it again. They always appear to be ready after the action, but I know how hard it is for a film crew to capture enough shots of even a simple scene to be able to convey it to the viewer. Our departure from the ship is an important moment, and the bad light must make filming difficult, but Greg and I lose patience and ski off into the wilderness.

There are no mountains visible to draw us on, only the uninviting whiteness and the softly falling snow.

The skidoo train soon passes us, a comic line on the flatter ground, 200 metres to my left. Chris stands on the small platform at the back of the

Our skidoo and its train of three sledges drives into the mist, which hides from us the immensity of our undertaking.

wooden sled. Above the roar of the engine I can hear him shouting, 'Slow down,' but Lyle, sitting on the source of the noise, continues, oblivious. We will need to develop some method of communication with the driver before we reach crevasse country.

After an hour we reach our first obstacle — a field of sastrugi, or ice ridges, where drifted snow has been melted by the sun and compacted by the wind into hard ice ridges. The turning circle of the sleds is much too wide to follow the tight manoeuvring of the skidoo and so the sleds wedge themselves against the low ridges. Greg, Jonathan and I go ahead to find the best route. After 200 metres we are back on sea-ice which is flat and smooth for as far as I can see. Behind me, Lyle and Chris admit defeat and unhitch the two pulks. Chris pushes and pulls the big sledge from side to side as Lyle drives slowly forward, and in this way they find a way through the difficult ground. They unhitch the wooden sled and take the skidoo back for the two pulks. I turn and look at the small dot of Glenn, already at least a kilometre ahead.

'He's too far to the left,' says Greg. 'We want to head directly for the football.' He points a ski-stock at the rock face shaped like a football standing on end.

'I'll go ahead and try to redirect him.'

My skis glide smoothly over the snow which coats the sea-ice, and I appreciate once again the joy of using the perfect ski wax. It is easy to establish a good rhythm, and I am soon parallel to Glenn. I can see that he has spotted me and is taking a diagonal line to intersect my path. A few cracks split the sea-ice, but these are narrow with no hint of hidden crevasses. I suppose that the cracks occur with the tide or the swell of the ocean, but the pieces of the jigsaw are so huge the ice of the inlet feels completely stable.

'Amazing place!' Glenn calls out before I reach him.

Being towed behind the skidoo and the sledge on the smooth surface of Edisto Inlet's sea-ice, is a pleasant interlude during our first day of skiing.

'And this is just the beginning!'

'Mind-blowing, isn't it?'

We turn and watch the skidoo which is now powering across the flat. When it draws near we see that Jonathan is being towed on a rope in a frozen version of water skiing.

Lyle slows down and stops just beyond us. 'Want a tow?' Chris calls out from his position as shotgun on the back of the sled.

'For sure,' says Glenn.

'What about the the pulks?' I ask. 'You could pull them and this big one easily on this terrain.'

'We'll go back for them when we reach the next obstacle.'

'But there mightn't be one before we reach camp.'

'Well, we'll go back then. Want a lift?'

I take the line of nylon webbing which Chris tosses to me. Chris waves at Lyle, and the parade begins to move again. The line comes tight and I begin to slide forward as well. It is easy to maintain my balance, so I glance over my shoulder at Greg who is still skiing behind us.

'Doesn't he want a lift?' I call to Chris. Though he is only a few metres away I have to raise my voice above the noise of the skidoo.

'No. He's enjoying the ski.'

'Plenty of time for that,' says Jonathan.

I turn to face him and see that though he is being towed, he holds his camera to his eye to capture this scene. He is irrepressible.

I marvel at the effortless way we slide over the ice with our mountain of gear. Football Saddle may be a problem to cross, but there is a good chance that on the far side the huge Tucker Glacier will be as smooth as this.

I sit alone on the sea-ice at the head of Edisto Inlet. Occasionally I catch a syllable from the others at camp, even though they are a kilometre away. Here there are no trees, earth, or other obstructions to absorb the sounds, and there is no other noise to compete with the ones we make. The nearest natural sound, apart from the occasional rustle of my clothing in the wind, is the lap of the ocean against the edge of the ice 14 kilometres to the north.

We are camped where the sea-ice meets a long glacier running down from a 1000-metre ridge on the eastern side of Edisto Inlet, the frozen bay we travelled across today. Around me is a monochrome world, except to the south over Football Saddle; in that direction there is a touch of orange in the clouds. When Greg, Jonathan, Glenn and I began to pitch camp two hours ago, the sunset was beautiful. The ice-cliffs we camped beside for shelter glinted pink and orange, while towards the south the mist, which now envelopes us, drifted thinly around the low rocky peaks. We could see the glacial valleys opening onto Edisto Inlet, each one of them an invitation to adventure and discovery. The clouds to the north were dark with the reflection of the sea.

Now when I look up from my page, the clouds are dispersing. Black is forcing its way into the whiteness, and the landscape is taking shape once more.

The others will be cooking dinner by now, after a long wait for Lyle and Chris to return with the pulks containing our stoves. It is time for me to join them, not because I am needed, for there are many eager hands, but to celebrate our sense of freedom as the only humans in this majestic place. On my way back I step across a crack in the ice the width and shape of a motorcycle track, as if someone has ridden out of the side valley on my left and headed across the sea-ice to my right. The water in the crack has

frozen, split and refrozen a few times, creating a small ridge each time. The ridges are raised and weathered in the pattern of a tyre tread. The silence is interrupted by Lyle cursing loudly. 'I've fallen in the bloody water!'

I cannot suppress a quiet laugh. A few metres from camp the sea-ice is cracked open and our map tells us that the water under the ice is 400 fathoms deep. Though the fissure is only 2 metres wide, Lyle has managed to fall into it.

Back at camp our stoves roar noisily. Jonathan sits behind a windbreak of boxes, surrounded by packets of food, with pots of snow melting on the stoves in front of him. The others are carrying bags or equipment purposefully from one place to another. It is a human world again, one we shall pack up tomorrow and take with us. These few square metres of sea-ice will be as empty as they were before we arrived, and as they will be until the ice breaks out into the sea and becomes a landing pad for penguins and seals.

'He's fallen in again, I hear.'

Greg nods and grins, but refrains from the cruelty of outright laughter.

'What happened this time, Lyle?' I call into the pyramid tent where he is changing.

It is a joy to be away from the confines of the ship and to make camp on a surface which does not move. Beyond our camp, Felsite Island is frozen into the sea-ice of Edisto Inlet.

'I stepped onto some ice which I thought was solid and went straight through, but not right in like last time.'

'Save that for tomorrow, eh?'

He glances at me as he wrings out a sock but does not comment.

My feet are blistered from skiing energetically this afternoon, so I change from ski-boots into Sorels. These rubber boots have felt liners and are cosy and easy on the feet. I string up my Tibetan prayer flags between the sledge pole and the nearest pyramid tent. I bought these flags in Lhasa specifically for this journey. I did not know and still do not know what kind of forces rule Antarctica, but these symbols of Buddhist humility could not offend.

Three seals bask in the sunshine, having clambered out of tide cracks in the 2-metre-thick sea-ice. Behind the furthest seal, an oval-shaped rock-face has led the dip on the ridge to its left to be named Football Saddle. Crossing it is the first major obstacle on our way to Mt Minto.

Thursday, 4 February

The clouds vanish overnight and we awake to another perfect sunny day. While Jonathan prepares breakfast the rest of us dismantle camp. It is midday by the time we leave, which is three hours' improvement on yesterday. Maybe tomorrow we shall leave at a reasonable time.

Because of my blistered feet, I opt to ride on the back of the sled. Lyle drives again, and while the others are able to clamber over the fragments of ice piled up beside the water-lead Lyle fell into last night, we have to make a big detour back to the north with the skidoo and the sleds. Chris comes with us in case we need help. Everything goes smoothly across flat ice until we reach another crack. This time the metre-wide gap has a thin veneer of sea-ice which gives an illusion of safety, so I have to scout for a safe route before Lyle can continue.

We catch up to Greg, who is waiting for signals from Glenn and Jonathan. They have skied ahead to find the best way through the ice-cliff which marks the end of the sea-ice and the beginning of the Edisto Glacier. While

Our heavy sledge sinks into soft patches of snow, causing the skidoo to consume more fuel than calculated. *Left:* Lincoln and Greg push while Lyle drives. *Above:* Chris feeds the hungry motor.

Greg waits for a signal to indicate that there is a feasible way through this 5- to 10-metre barrier, Lyle and I photograph a pair of Weddell seals sunbaking on the ice, and Chris records their snorts as they breathe.

'I can see somebody waving,' says Greg. 'But I don't know whether he means we should come that way or try somewhere else. I guess we'll have to go and see.'

When we approach the ice-cliff barrier we hit patches of soft snow and the skidoo slows down as the sleds sink in. Lyle thinks the engine is straining too much with the extra effort so he decides we should go ahead towing the big sledge only. Greg helps to push and we manage to get the whole train to the base of the slope. There we are in luck because a curve in the line of the ice-cliff has allowed snow to accumulate and form a slope which runs up to within a few metres of the lip of the glacier. It takes the six of us two hours of hard work, chipping away at the ice with ice-axes and throwing down snow as fill to make a ramp for the skidoo to run up.

Lyle starts the skidoo at the bottom, sits there nervously for a few moments, then he guns the engine and zooms up the ramp. At the top he turns hard left across a gaping crevasse at its narrowest point. The bottom-less chasm would have swallowed him and the skidoo if he had hit it broadside or too far to the right, and this was the chief cause of his nervousness. It is a relatively simply matter to haul the three sleds up one at a time on the end of a 50-metre climbing rope. We eat lunch at the top and look at the route ahead. Football Saddle looks close, but we accept that we will not be able to cross it today.

While the others ski behind in our tracks, Lyle and I have a pleasant run over good snow. Though the surface is flat and firm, the slope increases to the point where the three sleds behind become too much of a strain for the skidoo. Once again we leave the two small pulks behind and continue on

to find a camp site. I am disheartened by the way our loads are slowing us down even though the gradient is slight; we will certainly have much steeper ground to cover later. Crossing Football Saddle will be a big event, because when we reach the Tucker Glacier it will be time to leave our first depot of food and fuel for the return journey. After that, with every day that passes we shall eat more food, use more fuel and leave more depots, so that by the time we turn off the Tucker and follow the steeper approaches to Mt Minto our loads will be much more manageable. Meanwhile I look up at the ridge running down to Football Saddle and wonder if any of the beautiful peaks which rise from its crest have ever been climbed. Certainly they would be much easier than Mt Minto, and yet they still seem aloof and untouchable. I turn around on the platform and look back down the glacier. The tiny dots of Greg, Chris, Glenn and Jonathan give scale to the wide valley and the 2000-metre peaks rising above it.

Eventually we choose a campsite beside the strip of moraine in the middle of the glacier still about 3 kilometres away from the saddle. My eye follows the line of rock debris to the black face of the Football Mountain. The rocks at our campsite would have fallen from that face years ago, and it will be many more years before the glacier carries them from here down

We camp next to the medial moraine of the Edisto Glacier. The moraine rocks provide a modicum of shelter for us and our stoves, as well as places to sit.

to the sea. Meanwhile, the piles of rocks provide shelter from the wind and absorb enough of the sun's heat to keep a small stream running even in these subzero temperatures. We return for the pulks before the sun drops behind the ridge and the cold makes setting up camp too unpleasant.

I cook dinner amongst the rocks. The water tastes beautiful, and saves time and fuel by eliminating the chore of melting snow, yet ice forms around the edges of the flow almost as we watch. Above the roar of the stoves we discuss the need to reduce our loads. Obviously the premise that the machine could pull as much as the sleds could hold was wrong. We try to convince Glenn and Chris to cache their 16-mm film gear here because the cameras, tripods and film stock make up so much of our load. They refuse to be persuaded. I shall go through my belongings tomorrow and discard spare clothes, and maybe a book or two. Because my ski-boots have given me bad blisters despite their separate felt liners, I shall leave them behind as well, and adjust my ski-bindings to fit my Sorels. The only reason I brought the ski-boots was for comfort and extra control, so because they have failed me on the first point I am prepared to forego the second.

After dinner the cold sends everyone into their tents, apart from Jonathan, who wanders around taking photos despite the wind. It is a few minutes before midnight Australian time which means the sun has already started to rise again.

Massive peaks of black rock separate the pink sky and grey clouds from their blended reflections in the snow around the camp. In the half-light the craggy mountains are no more than a silhouette between the heavens and the ice. It is beautiful, but the freezing wind forces me to accept that the only sensible place to be is inside my sleeping bag. I stand by the tent door, warming my hands in my pockets so that my fingers will be able to undo the door-zip, when the scene in front of me is transformed. The full moon rises out of the clouds above the Ross Sea, and instantly the scene takes on another dimension. The dark mass of the mountains is offset by the moon's glowing circle, and this play of light and dark echoes the balance between the broad, flat glacier and the expansive sky. Instead of crawling inside the tent I take my camera out to the middle of the glacier. There, away from the noise of the tents flapping in the wind, and the silent energy of my companions, I manage to forget the cold.

Friday, 5 February

The wind strengthened during the night so when we get up in the morning windblown snow rips at our faces. We have no time to spare, so we have to make the cache and pack up the camp as quickly as we can. The cache delays us because we have to go through all our loads and discard everything which could be classed as a luxury. The size of the pile we leave behind on the moraine suggests that we were overprepared with spares and extras. Even so, the sleds remain heavy.

Once again I man the big sledge, but today Greg will drive the skidoo. By the time we are ready to go, the wind has blown much of the surface snow away from the glacier which means we are faced with bare ice. The skidoo skids on the spot when we attempt to get the train of sleds moving. We pull the skidoo and the sleds through 90° and then skid our way across to the edge of the glacier where less snow has been blown away. Here we are able to make good progress for almost a kilometre before the slight hollow we have been following opens out onto another sheet of hard green ice.

Greg waves me forward. 'I'm going to try traversing,' he says when I

Jonathan stirs soup (above) which takes a long time to cook because the air is so cold. Through the steam Glenn's face shows the effort of a hard day's work.

reach him. 'Maybe we can zigzag up to the head of the valley at least. We have to hope the snow hasn't been blown off the side of the valley as well, or we'll never get this thing over the pass.'

The gradient is gentle, but even when we head diagonally across the slope we lose control. The wooden sledge starts to slide sideways and I can do nothing to stop it. Greg does not realise what is happening and within seconds the uneven pull has tipped the sledge over. Instead of waiting for the others to walk across to help us turn it upright again, we unhitch the skidoo and head back for the pulks. I jump off as we slow down, but my feet shoot out from underneath me so that I land on my back on the ice and slide slowly towards the pulks. Greg laughs, then points up at a vague ramp of snow which cuts diagonally up across the side of the valley.

'I'm going to see if I can get the skidoo up there,' he shouts against the wind.

'Okay.'

I pick myself up and watch him drive across to the bottom of the ramp. Rather you than me, I think, because if you lose traction or hit a patch of ice halfway up you might slide all the way back down again. But Greg steadily chugs to the top of the ramp and out of sight. A few minutes later he reappears, and drives back down to me.

'How is it?'

'Great. We should be able to get all the way to the saddle. Let's try it with the pulks.'

I clip the tow rope to the rear of the skidoo then hop on the back. The ramp is much broader than it appears from below. To our joy the skidoo pulls the load well, despite the gradient, although I have to jump off and push to compensate for the loss of traction when we hit patches of hard ice. There are a few worrying moments when we start to slide but Greg manages to steer across onto snow. The angle eases but there is more ice, so I have to run behind until we reach firm snow again. Greg takes off now, perhaps thinking that with speed our momentum will carry us over any other patch of green ice, or perhaps just trying to make up for lost time. When we reach the gentle slope leading up to the pass we bounce over a few small snow ridges. The first of them almost throws me off the skidoo, so I grip more tightly to the netting which holds the jerrycans in place, and position my feet more securely. These prove necessary precautions because a minute later there is a mighty wallop as we break through a crevasse. Luckily our momentum carries us across. I jerk my head around to watch the pulks. The long one smashes into the edge of the gaping hole behind us but the smaller one, which could have easily disappeared inside, bounces clear to the right. Greg stops, and I cautiously go back and peer down the hole. Walls of blue ice lead down into blackness.

'A big one?'

'Yeah,' I say, sitting on the skidoo again. 'A bottomless pit.'

'Hmm.' He starts off but does not slow down. Ahead of us everything is white. Looking over Greg's shoulder, it is impossible for me to see where the windblown snow ends and the surface we are driving over begins. A greyness appears ahead, and I realise that this is the air above the pass. Next I see some rocks showing through their covering of snow.

'This is it! The saddle.' I shout against the wind.

Greg does not turn but he nods his head.

We pull up next to the rocks.

'What if I leave you here with the pulks, and go and get the others?'

'Okay.'

He hesitates.

'It's okay,' I repeat. 'If the skidoo breaks down, or if this snowstorm becomes a proper blizzard there's a tent in one of the pulks. There's a stove and about three weeks' food. I'll be all right.'

'Well, I'll leave you this down suit.' He throws me the suit which we have kept bundled up on the back of the skidoo as emergency clothing for the driver. 'I'm sure I'll get back down to the others. The only problem is that I might not be able to make it back up today.'

'Think positive.'

'Yeah.'

I unload the jerrycans from the back of the skidoo and unhitch the pulks. Immediately Greg turns the machine around and heads away into the whiteness. The ice crystals bite my face when I turn to look at the view. There is nothing to be seen but swirling snow. I stack our supplies next to the rocks so that if the snowfall becomes serious and everything is buried at least we will know where to dig. The rocks themselves are kept clear of snow by the wind, although the gaps between the small granite boulders are full of ice. After a quick bite to eat, huddled behind the jerrycans, I decide to walk along the ridge.

The wind continues to blow strongly, but enough of the cloud layer has lifted to reveal the Tucker Glacier. The pervasive whiteness makes it impossible for me to get a realistic sense of perspective and distance. From where I stand, the foreground obscures the slope we must descend to reach the Tucker. Ahead of me is a small rocky peak which I know will be a good vantage point if the clouds do not drop again.

It is strange to be alone again after five weeks' confinement with the others. The further I get away from the saddle, and the pile of food and equipment, the more carefully I step. The last thing I want to do is slip and twist an ankle or break a leg. The others would find me up here eventually,

Clouds hovering over Football Saddle make us feel more vulnerable.

but even so I feel very isolated. I remember Greg's story of the loneliest moments of his life, which he told as we stood on the decks of the *Thistlethwayte* on the day we reached Antarctica: 'I was dropped off by helicopter on the escarpment over there,' he said, pointing at the steep slopes of the Adare Peninsula as we motored by, 8 nautical miles out to sea. 'You can see how steep it is—real cliffs. The helicopter would just hover with one skid almost touching the ground while I got out. I had a pack with two weeks' food, just in case a storm blew in and they couldn't come back for me. For two hours I'd do the geology I had to do, and then the chopper would come back and take me somewhere else to do the same thing. But talk about isolation...I've never felt so alone.'

'But it would be easy enough to handle for two hours.'

'It was the longest two hours I have ever spent. Each time.'

It is the intensity of the feeling which matters, not the duration.

The ridge steepens and the broken black rock I have been climbing since the pass gives way to granite again. Here the rock has been weathered by the wind into tiny pinnacles, reminiscent of the ice 'mushrooms' amongst the pack-ice and on the glacier. The wind must blow constantly. Certainly it shows no signs of abating now.

I climb a little higher and look to the south. The dark waters of Edisto Inlet appear hostile beneath the storm clouds. Already I am beginning to forget my friends on the boat because I am so deeply absorbed by the almost living presence of this continent. Australia and my life there is a world away. I glance down at our supplies on the saddle and spot the skis I shoved endways into the snow as markers. At the moment visibility to the north-east is good, but there is no sign of the skidoo.

I turn and continue to scramble carefully up the rocks until the clouds lifting from the Tucker prompt me to stop. The black shapes of rock buttresses on the far side of the valley reveal that the highest mountains are not entirely snow covered. The landscape looks bleak and distinctly uninviting, and yet this huge glacier and its mountains are only the beginning of the journey. Our goal lies more than 100 kilometres beyond this place, and our summit is twice the height of any of the huge dark shapes showing through the clouds. Despite a month at sea to acclimatise me to the extraordinary, I can hardly believe our destination is the scene in front of me. The only way to cope with the enormity of our task is to take each day as it comes, and deal with the problems as they occur. For the moment that means paying attention to each step I take.

After reaching the summit of the small peak I scramble down its south ridge for 300 metres until I can look across at the saddle. Directly below where we have dumped the gear, the slope quickly steepens into an ice-cliff, and to the left of this lies a series of crevasses. We must find a way down much further to the left. It is difficult to judge distances over the snow in the bad light of this storm, but there appears to be a route down a broad snow slope curving back to the right beneath the ice-cliffs. No sooner have I decided this than I see the skidoo motoring steadily towards the pass towing the wooden sled behind. I scramble back up to the summit and wave my arms wildly, but the two figures show no sign of seeing me when they stop at the pass. Within minutes they have clipped the empty pulks to the skidoo and are heading back the way they came.

An hour later the six of us and all our supplies are reunited at the pass. When Lyle takes off his windproof to replace it with his down jacket he is astonished to see it lined with white.

'Frozen condensation,' he mutters. 'I've never seen that before.'

It is too cold to celebrate reaching the top of the first big obstacle between us and Mt Minto. Instead we hurriedly eat some lunch behind the shelter of the big sled, repack our loads and start down the slope—only to find that the windborne snow has collected into deep drifts a short way below the pass. The sleds sink in like anchors and refuse to move. Greg and I decide the skidoo would have a better chance if the others took control of the pulks until we get down the hill. The sledge runs a little better without the two pulks until one side of it bogs in a soft patch and the whole thing tips over. The six of us spend half an hour digging it out, and then the skidoo refuses to start. Chris and Lyle fiddle with the spark plugs and the fuel line, and eventually the machine roars back to life.

We come to a steep slope. I lean on the simple brake-board with all my weight until enough snow jams underneath to slow us down.

The slope levels out and Greg stops the machine. I jump on the brake.

'Let's have a look ahead,' he says. 'It seems to drop off here.'

We walk down the slope which is as steep as the one above but without the cover of deep snow.

'I won't be able to hold the brake on this,' I say. 'I wonder what would happen if we just let it go?'

'With the luck we've had today, it would probably end up in a crevasse. Doesn't look like there's any down there, but the light is too bad to tell.'

We trudge back up to the skidoo.

'It's 10.30,' says Greg. 'Let's stop here and worry about it in the morning. The trouble with round-the-clock daylight is you forget to sleep.'

Midnight and we are still sitting out in the snow having dinner. It is a cosy scene with the stoves set up between the sled and the skidoo. A pyramid

Following page: **Beyond our camp, the Victory Mountains rise 2000 metres above the vast glacier. We cannot help but feel small and insignificant.**

tent forms the third side of the square and the open side is a panorama of the vast Tucker and Whitehall Glaciers. The peaks of the 2500-metre mountains flanking the glaciers are hidden in the layer of grey cloud which stretches over us and dissolves into white mist at what appears to be the head of the valley. I know from the map that the Tucker Glacier continues for at least another 80 kilometres around the bend.

As we eat, we discuss the amount of fuel the skidoo is consuming. Continual relaying of loads over the last three days means that we no longer have enough petrol to complete the return journey. Our figures for fuel usage were obviously based on a skidoo working in much easier conditions. We decide that Chris and Jonathan should return to the ship tomorrow with the skidoo, to fetch more fuel. With no load they should be able to get back to Cape Hallett in a few hours.

Saturday, 6 February

Yesterday's clouds obscured all but the vaguest hint of the magnificence which surrounds our camp. We eat breakfast in the sun and look out over the wide glacier and the dozens of peaks and side valleys which line it. Today there is not a cloud in the sky.

'What if Pete has convinced them to go out into the bay to find some whales?' Glenn asks.

'They won't have done that yet,' says Chris, who always has an answer for Glenn. 'You know how long it takes them to make a decision.'

'If they've got any sense, they'll refill the water tanks before they go anywhere,' says Greg, heaping some more sugar into his porridge. 'That'll take at least a day, and I reckon yesterday would've been too bleak for them to bother.'

'It's right on 7 am,' says Jonathan. 'I'll try and raise Don.' He huddles over the small grey box like a witch over a cauldron. 'Mountain to ship. Mountain to ship. Come in please.'

'Ship to shore party. Ship to shore party,' Don's voice crackles through the speaker. 'Can pick up your signal but cannot copy you.'

Jonathan fiddles with the controls but still Don cannot understand him.

'Cannot copy you. Is every one well?'

'Roger. Roger. Roger.'

'Understand all well. What is your current position? Over.'

'Just beyond Football Saddle. Just beyond Football Saddle.'

'What is your current position? Over.'

Jonathan fiddles frantically with the knobs while repeating the sentence. Finally Don understands him.

'Copy you much better now. We had a visit from the US Coastguard vessel *Polar Star* yesterday. They left us some chocolate ice-cream. Won't be able to save you any, though. Over.'

'Two people returning to the ship for fuel. Do you copy?' Jonathan fears that his signal will fade again so he has no time for smalltalk.

There is a pause.

'Copy that. Two people returning to the ship for fuel. Is that correct?'

'Roger. Roger. Roger. Please prepare the 44-gallon drums.'

'Copy that. We will prepare the 44s.'

'See you later today.'

'Okay. See you then. Ship signing out.'

'What about knocking off a quick dispatch for the *Australian*, Lyle?'

He grimaces. 'I suppose so.' He picks up Jonathan's radio logbook and

rests it on top of a barrel. Half a minute later he is scribbling furiously.

I watch the busy antics of Jonathan who is triple checking everything before heading off, just as I would do. Greg sits on a black barrel and watches quietly. At 10.30 Chris and Jonathan leave. We watch the skidoo motor up the slope, Jonathan in the driver's seat, the damaged pulk dragging empty behind, and Chris on skis trying to keep up. They crest the ridge and disappear. Silence settles around us. It will be so good to be camped in one place for two days, especially in a spot as beautiful as this. The air is warm enough for us to sit around with bare hands and feet. The temperature is probably only one or two degrees above freezing, but in the absence of wind the sun feels warm. We spend the next few hours relaxing and tinkering with various tasks. The three days since we left the ship have been full from the moment we leave our sleeping bags till we crawl back into them in the evening. After yesterday's blizzard today's sunshine is particularly sweet.

Lyle cooks lunch of scrambled eggs. His first experience with egg powder is a great success. He is really enjoying being here, applying himself to everything and finding pleasure in the simple living forced upon us by the cold and our limited resources. A few days ago he said, 'I gave up regular climbing about ten years ago, and then, like Rip Van Winkle, I wake up to a new world of MSR stoves, Gore-tex and you guys who've explored practically every mountain range on earth between you.'

Eventually we stir ourselves to sort out a load of jerrycans and food to pack the small pulk. Our idea is to make a depot on the Tucker so that the skidoo will have a smaller payload next time we move camp. Glenn stays behind so he can put away damp clothes and sleeping bags if the weather changes for the worse. He is pleased to have the opportunity to film both our departure and the panorama around the camp.

The steep slope below presents no problems, because it is easy to control the pulk as it slides gently in front of us. When the angle eases we don our skis but soon find we cannot get enough traction to pull our load. Walking proves to be hard work because we sink in up to our ankles or calves with every step. On the infrequent patches of ice, the pulk slides easily and seems to be only a quarter of the weight. The snow stretches out flat before us. Apart from regular scrutiny for crevasses we do not need to watch where we place our feet. I look across the glacier to the Victory Mountains. The peaks are between 2000 and 3000 metres high and I can only presume that most of them are unclimbed. Scientific parties may have been dropped on the slopes or even the tops of some of the mountains by helicopter but I am sure that the sharp ridges and huge rock faces which catch my mountaineer's eye have not been touched by more than admiration.

For me this apprenticeship of glacier and cold is essential to exploring Antarctica because these features form the essence of the continent. The approach to a mountain is always a vital part of the climb. It is a time to allow body and mind to adjust to conditions which will only become more extreme as we slowly gain altitude and draw further away from the coast.

After about 3 kilometres of plodding we decide to cache our load. The sight of our tracks disappearing back towards the dot which is our camp is a reminder of how irrelevant our presence is to a place which on every other day exists without life. No animals live up here, and the only plants are rare patches of lichen on the rocks. Here on the glacier, where we eat our lunch before heading back to camp, there is nothing except snow and ice. It is daunting to think that from this place to Mt Minto and back again we will see no other living things.

'Mountain party to ship. Mountain party to ship. Come in please.'

'Yes. Hello, mountain party. How are things at your camp?'

'Hello Don. All's well here. Took a load out onto the Tucker Glacier today, and now we're having dinner. We could hear you talking to Jonathan but we did not copy him.'

'Are you familiar with their situation? Over.'

'No, Don.'

'They estimate they are 3 kilometres from the ship. We have a sched. with them at 10 pm and again at 11 pm. Copy that? Over.'

'Yes, but what is their situation? We have not been able to contact them.'

'They left the skidoo at the ice-edge and are manhauling their pulk. They now have 3 kilometres to go.'

'Why are they manhauling? Over.'

'Because the sea-ice has broken out from Edisto Inlet.' Don suddenly realises that we had no way of knowing this dramatic change because he repeats the statement. 'The ice has broken out from Edisto Inlet. We had a busy morning because we had to move out of our anchorage.'

'Where is the ship relative to its previous position?'

'Do not copy you, Greg. Please repeat.'

'Where is the ship relative to its previous position?'

'Sorry Greg, I don't copy you. We have three people listening hard and none of them can understand you. Suggest you try again at 10 pm. Try again at 10 pm. Ship signing out.'

'Roger, Don. Mountain party out.'

Greg puts the microphone down but says nothing.

'Bloody hell,' I mutter.

Lyle shakes his head. 'The forces are immense. All that ice.' He thinks for a moment. 'I wonder where it broke out from.'

'He said Edisto Inlet so that probably means the whole bay.' Greg says matter-of-factly. He adds no comment, and this tells me that his mind is running wild with implications and possibilities.

'That means where we dug the ice ramp,' says Glenn.

'Be great if the ship could come and pick us up from there.'

Lyle glances at him. 'Sure would.'

It is strange to talk of the return when there is still so much ahead of us. Our few days away from the ship seem like weeks to me, and next month is an eternity away.

'The breakout might have been much closer to the ship,' says Greg. 'Remember that the crew have no idea where the sea-ice ends and the glacier begins. We'll have to wait and talk to Jonathan at ten.' He pauses. 'I guess it looked all right for them to go out on it, but then it got worse than they expected. It's a bit alarming.'

'I wonder what they're up to now.'

'Never a day goes by...' says Lyle, and he does not need to finish the sentence. We are having to battle for every step of progress. Greg looks intense and worried.

The 10 pm sched. tells us only that Chris and Jonathan are safe and have just been picked up from the ice by Pete and Ken in the Zodiacs.

Lyle and I rig up the radio so that Greg can operate it from his tent, then the four of us crawl into our cosy sleeping bags. I write my diary until my alarm rings. 'It's five to eleven, Greg.'

'Okay.'

Inside our tent, Lyle and I listen to him call up the ship.

During the attempt to collect more fuel for the skidoo, Chris contacts the ship in the hope that a Zodiac can be sent to pick them up from the disintegrating sea-ice of Edisto Inlet. But for the emergency radio a disaster may well have occurred.

'Copy you loud and clear, Greg. The next voice you hear will be Jonathan's.'

'Hello, Greg. Do you copy?'

'Hello, Jonathan. How are you?'

'Pretty exhausted, but okay apart from that.'

'So what's the story?'

'The skidoo is on sea-ice about 7 or 8 kilometres from the ship. We had to come by foot from there but we manhauled the empty jerrycans in the pulk. It will take us at least two hours to get ourselves organised here. It's too dangerous to go back over the sea-ice because the floes are starting to break up. So we'll have to go back along the edge of the shore, or maybe the Zodiacs can get us closer. We had a lot of trouble with the skidoo. It's misfiring, and we bent one of the bogies, but we won't try and repair it until we get back to camp.'

'It sounds pretty tenuous, so don't rush it.'

'Okay. Actually, Chris has been pretty good at holding me back, so that we can sort out the best option.'

'Sounds like you make a good team. Why don't you have a good sleep and we'll sched. again at 8 am?'

'Make it seven.'

'Okay. Out from here.'

Alone in his tent, Greg turns off the radio but says nothing.

Lyle writes his diary, then pauses with the end of his pen in his mouth.

'From what Jonathan said, the skidoo is still on sea-ice. The problem is if the rest of the bay breaks out...' Again, Lyle does not have to finish his sentence.

'I can't believe it,' I say. 'All that ice just gone.'

'Yeah. All that ice we travelled over for a day.'

'Two days.'

'We camped on the bloody thing,' he says, then a moment later adds, 'I fell *through* the bloody thing.'

I laugh, and Lyle joins me, relieved by the humour which releases our tension. There is nothing we can do from this side of the saddle. We are so small and insignificant, but I feel secure in this tent and warm in my sleeping bag. Outside the wind is the only noise, flapping Greg's tent a couple of metres away and rushing over the ice beyond. There are no rocks near us for it to swirl around, and the nearest trees are on a different continent.

'You know,' begins Lyle, lifting his head from his diary again. 'This trip is outrageous. Try to look at it from a distance: a small ship a long way from home; getting stuck in pack-ice but pushing on; getting here then the ice we sledged over disappearing out to sea. Cape Hallett felt incredibly remote, yet look at us now. Out here with food and fuel and a small machine, gradually pushing ourselves even further away from everything that's familiar to us. It's going to be really hard to convey the stretched nature of it all when we get back.'

'It's hard enough to comprehend it now.'

Sunday, 7 February

My alarm wakes me at 6.50 am. I call out to Greg so he can turn on the radio. Reception is good and Jonathan says they will leave the ship in about an hour.

'The theory on board puts the blame for the breakout on the American icebreaker which visited the other day,' Jonathan tells us. 'It parked by ramming itself two ship's lengths into the sea-ice, and when it left it broke the seal of the ice across the lip of the inlet. It's an amazing scene down here, so much clear water now. We'll save time by going at least part of the way in the Zodiacs. I expect we'll arrive late this afternoon or this evening. See you then. Signing out.'

Greg turns off the radio and we all go back to sleep until 10 am. Even then it is only the crunch of Greg's footsteps in the hard snow outside which wakes me. Minutes later there is the comforting roar of the stove. Inside the tent it is hot and stuffy, so I untie the door we closed last night to stop snow blowing in. Outside it is a perfect sunny day. I wriggle out of my sleeping bag and into my long underwear, then drag myself out to enjoy the sun.

While Greg makes breakfast I do some yoga on my sleeping mat on the snow. It is my first thorough session since leaving Australia, and I relish the relaxation of body and mind which comes from the practice. A good sleep, windless and sunny skies, great yoga, all followed by a delicious breakfast of porridge and omelettes. Every day should start like this.

At about 1 pm the four of us set off to make another supply dump. This time we take a lighter load because we hope to push out onto the main part of the glacier past the first crevasses.

Greg and I set off while Lyle and Glenn make last minute adjustments to their packs and skis. It is much easier going today, not only because the pulk is loaded more lightly but because the surface is firmer. When Glenn and Lyle catch up to us we put on our skis and all four of us attach ourselves to the pulk. Soon we work out a rhythm and make good speed. At yesterday's depot we add one more jerrycan and a carton of biscuits to our load. The snow ahead is firm, so we soon pass the toe of the ridge which we had set as our destination. We turn left and head out towards the middle of the glacier. The snow is perfect for our hard green wax so our skis glide smoothly over the level surface of the glacier. We pass a few depressions which are probably old crevasses drifted full of snow or new ones opening up. Because I am in front on the longest rope, it is up to me to choose our route between these potential dangers. Soon we reach open crevasses whose threat is far more obvious. My attention is focused on

Back at Football Saddle we are unaware of Chris and Jonathan's dangerous plight. Greg prepares dinner.

finding the best line between the cracks and the depressions, and I enjoy the discipline of the task.

When we are past the crevasse field we decide to cache our load. It is a beautiful spot, and we celebrate our progress by having a good lunch of biscuits, nuts, dried fruit and chocolate.

Greg hauls the empty pulk back to our first depot. Lyle and Glenn remain there with him for a snack. I do not want to be chilled by the cooling of my sweat so I take the pulk and keep moving. Already my muscles are starting to feel in shape only a few days after escaping from our month-long detention on the boat.

'Reading you well, Greg.' Don's voice crackles over the radio. 'I'll tell you the situation. This morning Ken, Margaret and Pete took Chris and Jonathan back up Edisto Inlet in the inflatable boats, but when they got to where they had left the skidoo there was only open water. They think the skidoo either fell through the ice or drifted out to sea on a floe.'

The rest of the sched. is idle chatter compared to this bombshell. The four of us are stunned by the news.

'You've got to laugh,' I say, but no-one does. I do not feel much like it either. In fact, nobody has anything to say at all. We have reached terrain where the snow machine can be of the most use and, at that moment, it is lost. It seems that the gods are playing with us, making sure that we take nothing for granted. Perhaps they are making sure that Mt Minto remains unclimbed.

I return to cooking dinner while Lyle puts his energies into repairing the big sled. Glenn plays with his film gear, trying to improvise a sound recording system without the microphone Chris has taken with him. Greg disappears inside his tent. Soon soup is ready but we drink it in virtual silence.

I call everyone again when dinner is cooked. Greg announces that with twists and bends and avoiding crevasse fields we have 125 kilometres between us and Mt Minto. 'Eight days at 15 kilometres a day pulling all this stuff behind us.' He waves his hand at the camp.

Hard work.

'At least it will simplify things.'

Somehow I had known we would not return to the ship with the skidoo, feeling it was just a matter of time before the machine would die. That premonition is irrelevant now. I get back to the work of melting snow so I can fill our water-bottles and have plenty of fluid for Chris and Jonathan when they return in the early hours of the morning. Perhaps they will camp at the depot of food and gear we left on the moraine on the Edisto Glacier.

While I tend the stoves I think that there will be some joy in skiing up the glaciers towards Mt Minto. The loss of the skidoo means we will revert to the kind of travel I understand, progress by the toil of our muscles. The purity of physical effort is a nice idea, but I remember that with the skidoo we made only 30 kilometres in three days. From here onwards—without the skidoo—our daily average must be half as much again if we are to make it to the mountain and back before the sea begins to freeze over in early March. Don gave the first of March as a deadline and we must work to that. When reduced to such figures our chances seem slim.

I turn the stoves off, pull my hood tight around my face, shove my hands in my pockets and walk a few metres beyond the tents. The Tucker Glacier is covered in shadow. The furthest of our depots of food and useless skidoo fuel is less than halfway to the bend in the glacier. That bend marks

the start of a 60-kilometre stretch of glacier which we must follow before we can hope to see Mt Minto. And then, before we can try to climb it, we must traverse another 40 kilometres of steeper glaciers and passes. Greg maintains that it is still possible for us to do all this and return to the ship by the beginning of March. As I stare into the distance, I cannot help remembering that many Antarctic explorers have died trying to do the possible. The place is so beautiful that I feel lured onwards despite the hostile climate and the vast scale of everything. For us, Mt Minto might be a siren on a rock. Absence of life is the natural condition here, but I will not draw the obvious conclusion about our presence—my premonition this time is that we shall survive.

Jonathan and Chris plod into camp shortly after midnight. When I stick my head out of the tent I see Glenn filming their arrival. Each of them is pulling a small pulk which they swapped at the ship for the damaged larger one. They look dispirited, apologetic and exhausted, but glad to have reached the end of their long hike.

Jonathan is still as voluble as ever, and he gives us a summary of their misadventure: they were driving across the sea-ice about 5 kilometres from Willett Cove when Chris saw the ship out in the middle of the Bay. Moments later he realised that the gaps between the floes were not only wider than two days earlier, but were widening by the minute. The sea-ice was breaking out of Edisto Inlet—and they were in the middle of it. Chris urged Jonathan to turn around but first they had to switch off the engine and try to straighten a bent driving wheel. They gave up the task as hopeless after a few minutes, only to find that they could not restart the motor. Chris checked the spark plugs and eventually got the machine going again. Meanwhile the gap between them and the nearest landwards floe had increased to a metre in width. They were stranded.

As the sea-ice broke up, Chris and Jonathan were forced to jump the water leads in a desperate and tiring attempt to reach safety.

Chris gunned the engine and pointed the skidoo at a place where the edge of the floe was uplifted, forming a natural ramp. The skidoo shot over the gap and landed on the far side. The next hour was a desperate search for a route back to solid ice. Finally they parked the skidoo 2 kilometres from the water's edge, on what appeared to be solid sea-ice, then spent the next five hours jumping from floe to floe in an attempt to reach the ship. Twice Jonathan landed in the water, but his pack and the empty pulk he was hauling stopped him sinking past his waist. Regular radio contact with the ship encouraged them to continue, and finally Ken and Pete drove the Zodiacs between the floating mosaic of ice pieces and managed to pick them up.

Back on board they devoured one of Margaret's meals, organised everything we needed back at Football Saddle, swapped the damaged pulk for two smaller ones, and slept for a few hours. To their horror, when they returned by Zodiac in the morning, open water stretched another kilometre past the place where they had left the skidoo. Its disappearance was indisputable. They left the jerrycans of fuel with Ken, Pete and Margaret in the inflatables, then began the long grind of hauling the two empty pulks over the pass to our camp.

Minutes before Jonathan took this photo, this expanse of water showed only as a split in the ice a few centimetres wide. He and Chris were left in no doubt about what was happening — the ice they were standing on was breaking up and floating out to sea.

Even when told first-hand, the story is scarcely believable. The four of us do not have much to say. The skidoo was such an integral part of our trip that we feel lost without it. The reality of the situation takes longer to hit us because we were not witnesses to the dramatic changes on the other side of the pass.

'We'll talk about it in the morning,' says Greg.

'Are you angry with us?' Chris asks.

I look at him and see that he is serious. Of course this is not a matter'for anger. We are lucky that Chris and Jonathan did not disappear with the skis, the camera and the microphone which were left with the skidoo. The whole misadventure is proof of how insignificant and fragile we are amongst the forces which govern Antarctica, so feelings of guilt are not appropriate.

'Angry is too polite a word,' I reply melodramatically, trying to make a joke of it, then pull my head back into the tent.

From the silence in the third tent, I deduce that for once Jonathan is tired enough to go straight to sleep. I lie down in my sleeping bag and listen to the low mumble of Chris's voice as he talks to Glenn.

My next thoughts are that it is morning already.

MOUNTAINS OF INSTEAD

MOUNTAINS OF INSTEAD

'Clear, unscaleable ahead
Rise the Mountains of Instead,
From whose cold, cascading streams
None may drink except in dreams.'

W. H. AUDEN

Monday, 8 February 1988

Our third morning at Football Saddle is sunny and still. Under such peaceful skies and with the sunshine raising the temperature above freezing, it is easy to forget how hostile this environment can be. But the skidoo tracks around the camp remind us.

More details from Chris and Jonathan about their epic on the sea-ice make me realise how little I understand the forces which operate in Antarctica. At least from here onward we shall travel along huge glaciers, formations familiar to me after years of climbing in the Himalaya.

'Don is worried about being the last boat in the Ross Sea before the winter freeze,' says Jonathan over breakfast. 'In fact, he desperately does not want to be in that position. The Italians at Terra Nóva Bay, and the Americans and New Zealanders at McMurdo will all be leaving next week. And Greenpeace is planning to come by Cape Hallett on the twenty-first. That's the date we have to work to.'

'We agreed on 1 March,' says Greg. 'Do you think he'll leave without us?'

Jonathan shrugs. 'They don't want to spend the winter here either.'

We digest this information with the biscuits Lyle spreads with honey and jam. Jonathan's news compounds the pressure of time put on us by our late arrival in Antarctica and the loss of the skidoo. Our only chance of success lies in reducing our load by half so that we have some hope of hauling our own supplies. After leaving a large dump of gear on the far side of Football Saddle, halving our loads again seems almost impossible.

'Well, first, we've got to find out if everyone wants to go,' says Greg. 'Does everyone want to manhaul?'

Jonathan answers immediately. 'Chris and I talked about it yesterday. It was pretty depressing manhauling all the way back here, following the snow-machine tracks and thinking how badly we screwed up. We decided between ourselves the only possible course of action is to cut our loads right down and go for it.'

'That's basically how *we* feel,' says Chris. 'But how about everyone else?'

'I'm quite happy about manhauling,' says Lyle. 'What I'm not really happy about is our being left in the Ross Sea after the twenty-second. That's a dicey situation. It's cutting things pretty fine in terms of getting out this year.'

The Tucker dwarfs any other glacier we have trudged along. The tracks left by our skis and sleds seem to disappear towards infinity.

Previous page: Photographing the halo around the sun has made the landscape look dark — an illusion in this land where for three months the sun shines every hour of the day.

'We won't be able to climb the mountain and get back to the ship in that time,' says Greg. 'Not up to the mountain and back again, starting at 10 each morning, and hauling big loads to start with.'

'We've got to try to start earlier...'

'Fifty kilograms a person is a big load, and we'll be leaving from here with at least that much. It's a hell of lot to carry.'

There is a moment of silence.

'Well, it's either that or stay here,' says Jonathan. 'Basically what we're deciding is whether or not we're going anywhere.'

There is another silence before Lyle speaks. 'I think we all agree that we should go on. From any point of view it's the thing to do. We're sitting here with heaps of food and we've got two weeks, at least, so we might as well go for it.'

'I don't feel like heading back to the ship now,' says Greg.

'No,' agrees Lyle quickly.

'I don't think anyone does,' adds Glenn. 'So let's just pack up and go.'

'Okay,' says Greg. 'Let's say we give it a couple of days and then we'll reassess our chances?'

Glenn nods. 'If we get blown out by a blizzard, well, that's that. If we get good weather, then we get there.'

'We have to bear in mind that we could go for a week and then get blown out,' I say, wanting to make sure we all understand the commitment we are making. 'There's still 120 kilometres between us and Mt Minto — then we have to get back.'

Greg takes up the point. 'It gets more tenuous by the day because we haven't got any rapid way of retreating, especially now we're a pair of skis short as well. It's just about more serious than not having the skidoo. Walking in soft snow, which one of us is going to have to do every day, is bloody slow.'

Above a small peak near Football Saddle, the rising moon shines through clouds which have drifted up from Edisto Inlet.

'Yeah, that's what I'm most annoyed about,' says Chris.
'So let's get out of here.'

After the loss of the skidoo, we can only continue in our attempt to climb Mt Minto by halving our load and manhauling our sledge behind us.

Once again we go through the routine of cutting down our loads. This time we have to be ruthless. Glenn and Chris put their 16-mm cameras in the pile of gear to be stashed, and Glenn leaves about seventy per cent of his extensive medical kit. I leave behind my second camera body and abandon some dirty clothes. Apart from that there is very little I can leave behind. Not to take my two books would be to invite one of the week-long blizzards which Greg casually mentioned as characteristic of this region. Lyle reduces the weight of the sled by removing the brake board and the now redundant platform and handles. We decide we can survive a blizzard with one pyramid tent if necessary, so we add the second pyramid to the pile.

When Greg, Lyle and I are ready, we set off with the big sledge. We have some difficulty holding the load on the steepest part of the slope below the camp, so near the bottom we let it go. It is a joy to see all that weight scoot down the hill and continue for another half kilometre along the flat. When we catch up to it we pull it for a short distance before we stop to put on our skis. The surface of the glacier is firm, so we make reasonable time. It is continual hard work, but after two days and three nights at Football Saddle it is good to be pushing ahead.

Jonathan volunteered to be the first to go without skis. By lunchtime he is almost a kilometre behind but he is in good spirits when he catches up.

Theoretically, skis spread one's weight and reduce the likelihood of breaking through the crust of snow over hidden crevasses. Somehow, though, I manage to position my skis so they run the length of a crevasse. One second I am contentedly puffing along in the sunshine with the Tucker Glacier stretching endlessly in front of me, and an instant later I drop completely out of sight of the others, lying sideways and jammed between two walls of ice. The gap widens beneath me and disappears into a frightening bluish darkness so there is nothing for me to push against to extricate myself. I try not to wriggle in case I slip loose and fall the full length of the rope running between me and the big sled. With the sled as an anchor and Greg and Glenn to haul me out, I know I am not in danger. Nevertheless, I am reluctant to fall any further into this cold hole. It is like being dropped into a bottomless deepfreeze without warning. Despite the restriction of my ski stock being jammed beside my leg, I manage to raise an arm enough for Glenn to grab it and drag me out. Glenn looks startled at this introduction to the hazards of glacier travel but Greg stands back quietly laughing. Revitalised by the cold and the rush of adrenalin I brush the snow from my clothes and shiver. A few metres behind us, Jonathan looks around him warily. Without skis he is much more vulnerable.

A mountain called Trigon Bluff on the map marks the point where the Tucker Glacier takes a right-angled turn and heads almost due north for 60 kilometres, and this peak seems like a good point to aim for. It is 20 kilometres from our Football Saddle camp, but we need to make that sort of distance each day if we are to have any hope of succeeding.

Hours later, when we stop to pitch camp at 7 pm, Trigon Bluff scarcely seems any closer, but at least Football Saddle appears further away. The air is so clean and sharp here, it is impossible to judge distances. There is nothing in the foreground or even in the distance to give scale. Only the flat horizon to the east tells us that the mouth of the Tucker is a long way down the valley.

'How are you feeling about things now?' I hear Lyle ask Greg when we are pegging out the last of the tent guys.

'A bit better after today, but I think we still have to get rid of some more weight, just to make this manhauling more comfortable. We only covered 11 or 12 kilometres.'

Lyle agrees. 'It would have been good to reach the corner today, but still, it's been a productive day considering the late start.'

Making camp is a little quicker now that we have less gear, but unfortunately we also have less energy for the task. Though the weather appears stable, we must be prepared for a blizzard to hit the camp during the night. The three tents are pitched close together so that all their guy lines are interconnected. Jonathan heaps blocks of snow onto the nylon material at the bottom of the pyramid tent's outer wall. We clip the pulks to the tent anchors, and every object which might blow away is taken inside.

With the camp organised we join Greg who huddles over the stoves in the lee of the big sled. There is hardly a breath of wind, but in these temperatures the stoves need all the protection we can give them. Cooking is a slow process, so we have plenty of time to talk. Soon the sun dips behind the Victory Mountains and leaves the Tucker in shadow. I know it will not get dark, and that the sun will appear again in an hour or two, yet the increased cold is no easier to bear. I am glad of my down suit. Here, almost at sea level, I would quickly overheat if I wore it while manhauling, but it is a cosy luxury during the evenings.

Jonathan rubs his hands together to warm his fingers after taking photographs of the camp. 'Blizzards aren't as cold as this, generally,' he says.

'What? Are they quite warm?' asks Chris.

At first I cannot believe my ears. 'Are you serious? Quite warm!' I burst out laughing.

'Not warm,' Chris quickly qualifies. 'I mean above freezing.'

'Not far below anyway,' answers Jonathan.

Top: Amongst the things we leave at Football Saddle is some of our emergency food. Greg makes the hard decision of how much to leave behind.

Above: Chris skis along the Tucker Glacier dragging a pulk behind him. Beyond the horizon, to the far right, the Tucker meets the sea. The slopes to the left rise up to Football Saddle (not shown).

Following page: The magnificent scenery of the Tucker Glacier is some compensation for the hard work of manhauling our sledges.

It has come to the ridiculous point where we regard freezing temperatures as quite warm, and I suppose that when we return this way the Tucker will seem almost like the tropics. The cold we will face 4000 metres higher on the slopes of Mt Minto is unthinkable. I can only hope that since we will be gaining altitude slowly we shall scarcely notice the change in temperature.

Tuesday, 9 February

An overcast sky greets us in the morning. Antarctica feels a lot less friendly on a day like this. The cold encourages us to dismantle our camp quickly and get moving up the glacier. Today I volunteer to walk, in the hope that wearing my mountaineering boots will take some pressure off the blisters on my heels. The others attach skins to their skis for a better grip on the snow as they haul.

We rope ourselves together in a long chain in anticipation of the inevitable crevasse field of fractured ice, which must occur where the glacier rounds Trigon Bluff and heads north-west. The smooth crust of surface snow obscures the dangers. Only Greg remains unroped, believing that if he stays at the back and follows our tracks, any crevasse which is likely to break open will have done so by the time he reaches it. Because I sink into the snow with every step, I have to hurry to keep up with the big sledge. Occasionally my foot pushes through into a small crevasse and I have to call for the others to stop while I pull it out. Once, when they do not hear me, the rope from my waist to the sledge comes tight and drags me over onto my face. Before long Lyle, who is route-finding at the front of the big sledge, starts to break through as well, despite his skis. From that point onwards he, Chris and Glenn proceed with more caution, so I find it easier to match their pace.

Lunch is a quick affair because we are cold, not only from the weather but also from falling into crevasses. When we round the corner of Trigon Bluff the danger of crevasses lessens considerably, and so half an hour later we untie from our ropes. There is great satisfaction in having a new panorama open up to us, even though the sky remains overcast and the surrounding peaks stay hidden in clouds. The glacier seems to run ahead of us interminably before it disappears into whiteness. The effect is eerie because, paradoxically, the reduced visibility increases the feeling of space around us. We no longer suffer the illusion, caused by the exceptionally clear air, of being in a narrow valley surrounded by small mountains. Now we can see that the valley is very wide, which tells us that the mountains whose summits are hidden must be huge. Of course, our map gives the heights of almost every peak, but the map is only paper with numbers on it, whereas the cloud layer converging with the white horizon is real.

Once unroped, we are all able to move at our own speed, which means we have much more control over our body temperature: we can stop when we need to put on or take off clothing, without inconveniencing everyone who is tied to the rope. Such temperature control is important in Antarctica, not only because of the obvious dangers of frostbite and hypothermia, but because sweat from over heating can quickly freeze and reduce the insulating properties of clothing. In the Himalaya, the shortage of oxygen at high altitude makes an easy climb difficult and a hard climb almost impossible, but it is always reassuring to know that a day or two's descent will bring thicker air and warmer temperatures. In Antarctica, there is no possible relief. The height of summer has passed, so that every day the sun dips a little lower to the horizon and the twilight lasts a little longer. The only retreat is back along the line of our ski tracks.

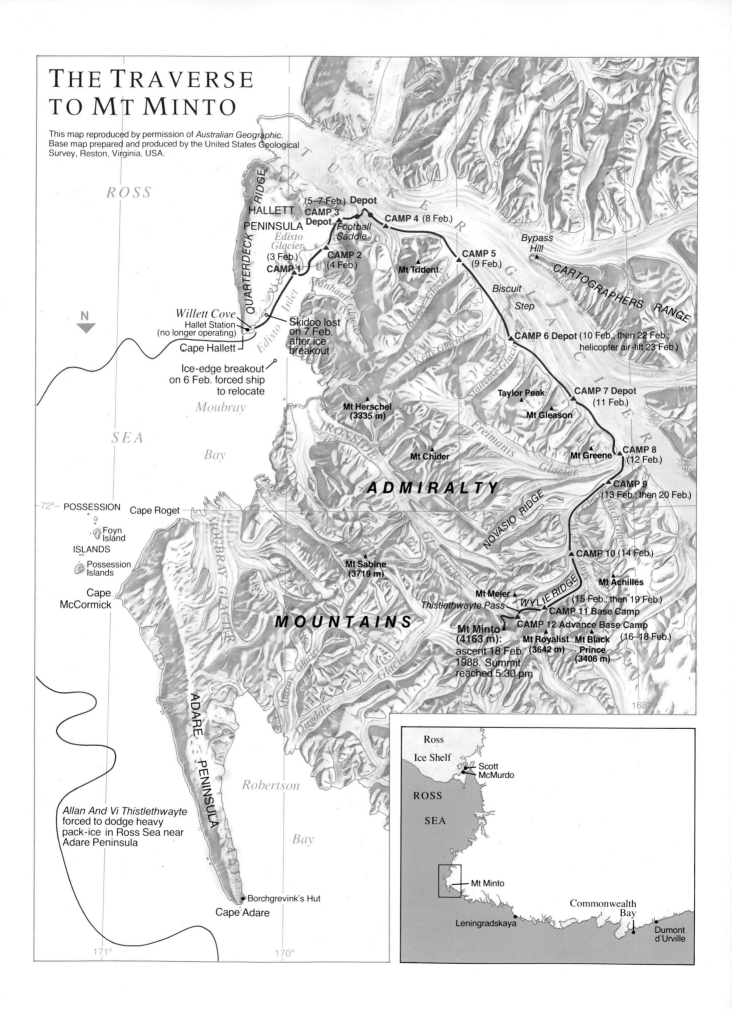

THE TRAVERSE TO MT MINTO

This map reproduced by permission of *Australian Geographic*.
Base map prepared and produced by the United States Geological
Survey, Reston, Virginia, USA.

ROSS

TUCKER

HALLETT PENINSULA

QUARTERDECK RIDGE

Edisto Glacier

(5–7 Feb.) **Depot**
CAMP 3 Depot
Football Saddle
CAMP 4 (8 Feb.)

CAMP 2 (4 Feb.)

(3 Feb.)
CAMP 1

Mt Trident ▲

CAMP 5 (9 Feb.) ▲

Bypass Hill

CARTOGRAPHERS RANGE

Biscuit Step

N

Willett Cove
Hallett Station (no longer operating)
Cape Hallett

Skidoo lost on 7 Feb. after ice breakout

Ice-edge breakout on 6 Feb. forced ship to relocate

Edisto Inlet

Ironhaul Glacier

Kelly Glacier

Torrens Glacier

GLACIER

CAMP 6 Depot (10 Feb.; then 22 Feb.; helicopter air-lift 23 Feb.)

Moubray

SEA

Bay

Mt Herschel ▲ (3335 m)

Staircase Glacier

Taylor Peak ▲

Mt Gleason ▲

CAMP 7 Depot (11 Feb.)

Mt Chider ▲

Freimanis Glacier

Mt Greene ▲

CAMP 8 (12 Feb.) ▲

Glacier

ADMIRALTY

72°— POSSESSION

Cape Roget

ISLANDS

Foyn Island

Possession Islands

Cape McCormick

MOUBRAY GLACIER

Mt Sabine ▲ (3719 m)

MOUNTAINS

NOVASIO RIDGE

Fitch Glacier

CAMP 9 (13 Feb.; then 20 Feb.) ▲

CAMP 10 (14 Feb.) ▲

Mt Achilles ▲

Mt Meier ▲
Thistlethwayte Pass

WYLIE RIDGE

(15 Feb.; then 19 Feb.)
CAMP 11 Base Camp ▲

CAMP 12 Advance Base Camp ▲
(16–18 Feb.)

Mt Minto (4163 m):
ascent 18 Feb. 1988. Summit reached 5.30 pm

Mt Royalist ▲ (3642 m)

Mt Black Prince ▲ (3406 m)

ADARE PENINSULA

Caulfeild Glacier

Murray Glacier

Dugdale Glacier

Robertson

Bay

Allan And Vi Thistlethwayte
forced to dodge heavy pack-ice in Ross Sea near Adare Peninsula

Borchgrevink's Hut ●
Cape Adare

171°

170°

Inset map

Ross Ice Shelf

Scott ◄ McMurdo

ROSS SEA

▪ Mt Minto

Commonwealth Bay

Leningradskaya ●

Dumont d'Urville ●

I welcome the freedom of being unroped. After all, freedom is what this place is about. With Jonathan a few hundred metres behind and the others the same distance ahead, I can stop and hear nothing except the sound of my breathing. My mortality makes me feel like an aberration in this place.

After cooking dinner, Greg stands up to stretch his legs while I prepare hot drinks. 'This is crazy,' he calls out from 20 metres away. 'Look at where you are.'

He gestures at the five of us huddled between the sled and our three tents, earnestly talking about something irrelevant. Beyond the clumsy domesticity of our tiny cluster of sleds and tents stretches a world of limitless beauty.

At the end of the day I sit with my sleeping bag pulled up around my shoulders and write my diary. It has been our best day's progress by far. We hauled our sleds 17 kilometres to this camp on the eastern edge of the Tucker Glacier. We are surrounded by mountains now, though the peaks to the north are too distant to be seen clearly. They rise beyond an horizon of ice, a daunting indication of how far we have to go. After a good day's march everyone is in high spirits. I feel committed to the project now, which is a matter of believing we can do it. Mt Minto is out of sight beyond the furthest mountains, but we have food for three weeks and lots of determination. If the weather is kind to us we may succeed.

I can hear Lyle's voice in the pyramid tent. 'It's amazing just to think where we are. It's a valley 20 kilometres wide and we are only the third party to travel up it. Ever.'

'Really?'

'Yes, two geological parties were before us. Others have come in by helicopter to do survey work. The maps are made from aerial photographs.'

I think back to walking along the glacier surrounded by unclimbed peaks. These are not just bumps on ridges whose major summits have been climbed, but range after range of mountains where no-one has been. This morning on the opposite side of the Tucker we stared across at the northern-most slopes of the Victory Mountains. Two-thousand-metre granite faces rose up steeply from this huge glacier which is only 100 metres above sea level.

If I unzipped the tent door I would see a mountain which brought comparisons with the French Alps from Greg and Jonathan who have climbed there. Buttresses of granite 1400 metres high ask for the footsteps and handholds of climbers, but we do not have the time to oblige. Next to this peak is a massif of sharp ridges which reminds me of New Zealand. 'Similar sort of rock,' said Greg. Steeper here, though, I think, because all the loose stuff is frozen into place. Comparisons must be put aside because the overall effect is like nothing I have ever seen before.

Wednesday, 10 February

What a day! I lie exhausted inside my sleeping bag and scribble in my diary. In terms of pure effort, today was one of the hardest days I have had in the mountains for a long time. After yesterday's grey skies, this morning's sun was strong enough to thaw the glacier's frozen crust. Ten centimetres of soft snow on top of the ice slowed down the sleds dramatically. Jonathan, Glenn and I had a particularly hard time because we were pulling the big sledge. Jonathan nursed a sore arm and is suffering from a sore back caused by the desperate forced march after the loss of the skidoo. These

ailments have prevented him from pulling his weight, and have kept Glen and me from commenting about it. The sledge was overloaded anyway, but the soft snow slowed us to a snail's pace at the slightest tilt of the slope from level to uphill. We all knew that in these conditions the day was going to be painful, but I saw some point in getting it over with as soon as possible. Jonathan seemed unaware of his easy riding and made no comment when asked to speed up, except to suggest I take over the lead. We increased our pace, but even so the others with their single pulks continued to draw away into the distance. It was frustrating to work so hard for so little gain.

The hard work of sledging and the mental strain caused by the harsh conditions and our awareness of the time restriction can be seen on the faces of Chris (left), Lincoln (centre) and Lyle (right).

And now I am exhausted. As soon as the tents were up I crawled inside the pyramid and got into my sleeping bag because I felt that my body did not have the strength to keep warm outside. This meant leaving the rest of the domestic chores to everyone else, but I feel I have pulled more than my share today. I mumbled something along those lines to Greg who seemed to understand. Survival in this environment means looking after oneself first. Only then does one have the resources to help the team.

When I arrived at camp I was angry with myself for draining so much of my energy on the straightforward task of sledge hauling. Such bursts of determination I usually reserve for a push to the summit or to get myself out of a dangerous situation. If I continue driving myself at today's pace I will run out of steam before we reach the mountain.

Lyle brings me a hot drink—a real luxury. Now that I am warm and somewhat recovered, I feel guilty at being in here out of the cold. I wriggle out of my sleeping bag, put on my down suit and boots, then go outside. The others crouch around the sleds and the stoves, and chat about the day's progress. We are 19 kilometres from last night's camp, and have managed to skirt a ridge on the glacier known as Biscuit Step. Everyone feels optimistic. We have built up so much momentum already that we do not even talk about turning back.

I look around at the setting for our camp. We are a kilometre or two from the point where the Staircase Glacier enters the Tucker. This flat-bottomed valley seems to be a made-to-measure glacial highway leading to Mt Chider, whose peak shines temptingly in the sunlight at the head of the valley. Our camp is shaded by the Cartographers' Range on the western side of the Tucker, but half of the steep north wall above the Staircase is still bathed in the yellow light of evening. A thin streak of cloud echoes the line between sun and shadow and helps give some scale to the 2000-metre face. The face itself is corrugated by a series of parallel rock ridges and ice gullies which run from the glacier directly to the top of the ridge without a change in angle. If these mountains were accessible to climbers this wall alone would have a dozen different climbs upon it, every one of them a classic. Mt Chider and all these other peaks will have to wait for another expedition.

After dinner I head back to the tent where Greg is already unpacking his sleeping bag. I crawl in through the small door and broach the subject which has been on my mind since we reached camp.

'I'm worried about Jonathan.'

Greg looks at me with surprise. 'Why?'

'He just didn't seem to have his heart in it today. Glenn and I were grunting our guts out while he seemed to be off with the fairies.'

'You've got to remember the epic Chris and he had with the skidoo,' Greg says calmly. 'I reckon he's been running on adrenalin since then, trying to make up for the loss even though the situation was out of their control.'

'We can't afford to have him burn himself out at this stage,' I say. 'God knows he's experienced enough in the mountains to be able to pace himself.'

'Well, maybe today your pace was a lot faster than his. Too fast for your own good.'

'Maybe. Perhaps the sled was just too heavy. I can't afford to keep on putting out the amount of energy I used today.'

'Take one of the pulks tomorrow.'

'That won't solve the problem.'

'But it might stop you worrying about it. Jonathan will be okay.'

I suspect that Greg is right. The real problem is the heavy sled and not Jonathan.

Greg drags the stove box inside so we do not have to get out of bed to melt snow in the morning, then we settle into our sleeping bags and look at the maps.

I am in favour of leaving a big cache here and convincing Chris and Glenn to leave more film equipment behind. We can also cache a good supply of food and fuel. If we do that we should be able to reach the Man O'War Glacier in one and a half or two days. Then we could push on up the Man O'War for another two days, before making an attempt on the mountain from there. That would mean going lightweight—just the two dome tents and no sleds—on a five-day burst. Then it would be back down along the Man O'War to where we are now. If all goes according to plan we could be back here, with the mountain climbed, ten days from now—but things rarely go according to plan in the mountains. With lighter loads, we should be able to get back to the ship from here in four days, making a total of fourteen days from today. That will be two or three days after all the other ships have left the Ross Sea for the winter. Don and the others will just have to chew their nails.

Greg has totally disappeared inside his sleeping bag. Our tight schedule gives us very little time to ourselves so I take advantage of this quiet period at the end of the day to catch up on my diary. A few minutes ago I heard my first Antarctic avalanche, a sound much more common in every other mountain range I have visited. Here, the intense cold freezes everything

into place despite the pull of gravity. The result is a silence so complete that even the normal mountain sounds are rare. The only sound now is the scrawl of my pen in my notebook. Everyone else went to bed an hour ago. Outside the sky is grey with clouds, decidedly wintry looking. Hopefully tomorrow the sun will spare us and the snow will be firm enough to haul loads along more easily. Packing up camp without the sun will be unpleasantly cold, but that is the price we have to pay for good sledging conditions. Already I have learnt that nothing is given away in Antarctica.

Our camp is shaded, but half of the steep wall above the Staircase Glacier is still bathed in the yellow light of evening. A thin streak of shadow from a cloud helps give some scale to the 2000-metre-high rock face.

Thursday, 11 February

The day starts dramatically with an argument about Chris and Glenn caching their exposed film stock with our pile of food and stove fuel. The 16-mm film weighs quite a few kilograms and the Super Eight cassettes now add up to a sizeable weight as well. They are very reluctant to leave any of it because to get the shots has taken so much effort. Greg and I maintain that if they are to get any footage of the mountain being climbed they will have to leave this film behind, because we need to take every possible measure to reach the mountain with enough strength left to climb it. Meanwhile Jonathan stays out of the way in case we suggest he leaves his exposed film here as well, even though his is much lighter. Finally we compromise and let them pack the most important film. Sledging sequences and camping scenes can be reshot if it comes to the worst, but the loss of the skidoo cannot. The snow around is perfectly flat for at least a kilometre in every direction, so there is nothing our cairn of snow can be confused with. We have to hope there is not a blizzard blowing when we come back this way. Jonathan sticks a section of radio aerial in the top of the cairn and attaches his spare underpants to it as a flag.

Our manhauling begins with 2 kilometres of easy flat ground across the mouth of the Staircase Glacier, then we slog up a slight rise. Chris leads the way on the big sled with Greg and Lyle on shorter ropes. The slope makes me glad I am pulling one of the pulks even though I am walking and not skiing. The angle is not great but the slope continues for a kilometre or more. After three days of manhauling we have gained only 200 metres in height, but today we must gain another 200 metres if we are to maintain the average daily distance essential for our success.

The hill we climb has blocked our view up the Tucker since yesterday lunchtime. Travelling at a slow pace in such a vast environment means our surroundings change imperceptibly. It is exciting to crest the ridge and observe the changes in the scene in front of us. In the distance is a white horizon where the Tucker disappears out of sight. Appropriately, the glacier runs off our map so we have no way of knowing how long it is nor where it finishes. The Man O'War Glacier is easy to identify after referring to the map because of the steep cliffs on its northern side which force the Tucker Glacier to make a short detour to the west. These cliffs are very steep, and shaded beneath the midday sun. Ahead of us is our first downhill run since leaving Football Saddle. The slope is gradual but the others are able to get up a rhythm on their skis and make good speed. I take some photographs, then trudge along their tracks. I soon catch up to Glenn and Jonathan who have stopped to film and photograph. It is a perfect day, and Antarctica feels benign. Jonathan has his arm in a sling but is in good spirits, and he seems much more aware of the environment than he did yesterday. I, too, pay more attention to my pace. If I arrive exhausted at camp this evening I will have no-one to blame but myself. Glenn and then Jonathan head off, leaving me to trudge after them. I catch up to everyone an hour later at our lunch stop.

On the lower reaches of the Tucker Glacier, the sun drops behind the Victory Mountains, but instead of darkness the earth shadows and crimson sunsets such as this one seen from our camp near the Cache 'n' Carry Glacier are a photographer's paradise.

'You just missed the clock,' says Glenn.

I stare at him blankly. 'What do you mean?'

'Lyle reckoned he heard a clock, but when I took his pulse we worked out it was his pulse he was hearing.'

'I must be dead myself,' I say. 'I couldn't hear a thing back there.'

Our camp this evening is a hollow in the glacier probably made by a crevasse which collapsed months or years ago. We are at the bottom of a steep, broken glacier which has no name on the map. We jokingly label it 'Glenn's Cache 'n' Carry' in remembrance of our heated discussion this morning. The spot is the first sheltered campsite we have found on the glacier.

I decide to cook tonight to make up for not helping the previous evening. Constant attention is required to melt blocks of snow while stirring whatever is cooking on the other stoves. I cook up huge pots of dhal and rice and a smaller amount of curried potatoes and peas. Dried potato spoils the appearance a little, but the flavour is good and all our stomachs are filled.

Afterwards, while water is heating to top up our waterbottles and make a last hot drink for the night, I walk away from the lee of the tent where I have set up our makeshift kitchen to stretch my legs. It is almost midnight. Chris, Glenn and Lyle are standing around the dome tents with their hands in their pockets, admiring the sunset colours in the clouds over the Victory Mountains and the Cartographers' Range.

'Beautiful, isn't it?' says Chris.

'Sure is,' agrees Lyle, and Glenn and I echo him.

'Funny thing,' says Chris. 'We all agree about it, but all four of us are looking in different directions.'

Friday, 12 February

The sky is overcast this morning, which is good, because it means the snow will remain firm and the big sled will run well on the surface. Glenn, Greg and I are to pull the big sled today. Despite the food we have eaten, the fuel we have used, and the cache we off-loaded yesterday morning it does not seem any lighter. Glenn goes out in front on the long rope and sets off like a leopard seal after a penguin. Greg and I glance at each other but say nothing. The slope ahead will slow him down to a realistic pace. His urge to get there as soon as possible is admirable, but he needs to save some energy for the end of the day or he will end up feeling as I did two days ago.

I am impressed by the way Lyle and Glenn are coping with their first expedition. Both are ready to listen to advice and are not shy about asking questions. Chris, on the other hand, is much more self-reliant. Since he has climbed mountains in New Zealand, the problems and dangers of snow and glaciers are not so new to him, and having worked for years as an instructor for Outward Bound, he is accustomed to being the one with all the answers. There is no arrogance in this attitude — he simply had to meet the demands of the people he instructed. Perhaps this habit of having to seem all-knowing is why he tends to take advice as criticism, or perhaps he just objects to the joking way I express things. Jonathan is perfectly well, and obviously happy to be here. He is at ease now, even though always busy with camp chores or photography. Greg is his usual imperturbable self, taking quiet delight in our adventure whenever he can forget about the back-breaking work of manhauling.

Our vital cache of food, fuel and exposed film stock is a lonely sight on the vast Tucker Glacier.

Lunchtime on the Tucker Glacier, almost at the point where we leave it. The sun has been co-operative by breaking through the cloud to keep us warm while we rest. There are plenty of clouds in the sky, but hopefully they will remain where they are until we are ready to move on.

Three or four kilometres beyond this spot we shall turn left up the Man O'War Glacier. A strange name for an Antarctic glacier, I think, because nothing could be further from the stupidities of human conflict than this place. Then I remember that these are the Admiralty and Victory Mountains where the peaks and passes bear the names of ships, naval commanders or famous battles.

Chris catches up to us as I slice the cheese. He is last today because he is walking, and this seems more of a disadvantage because the conditions are good for skiing. Even so, it is still hard work for Greg, Glenn and me with the big sledge. No doubt it is hard for everyone, and each thinks his own lot is the worst. Chris says nothing in reply to our greetings as he drags his pulk in a circle around the food barrel.

'Bit of a slog, isn't it?' I offer.

'Yeah, more so today than yesterday because it's warmer and the snow is softer.'

As he speaks I think the opposite: the snow was softer yesterday because the sun was shining most of the day. I keep my opinion to myself and turn to Greg who is perched on top of the sledge, knees up against his chest.

'You look like a vulture there.'

'I feel as hungry as a vulture right now,' he replies.

'And your neck is getting longer every day.'

'Too right.'

I use the climbing term for boldness in the face of danger: the further you stick your neck out, the more likely it will get chopped off.

Glenn (left) and Chris check a movie camera strapped onto the big sledge for some close-up footage of manhauling. Tasks such as this keep the film crew busy even during those rare moments when the rest of us relax.

The climb up away from the Tucker begins in the afternoon. We decide to trim the corner off the right-angle turn by taking a short cut over a low ridge. The last part of the climb is too steep for us to manage, so we call Lyle down from the crest to help. At the top we see that there are crevasses in front of us, so we unclip and ski across to where we can look ahead. Back in harness again, Glenn, who is in front, asks advice about route-finding through a crevasse field.

'Just take what looks like the best route,' says Greg. 'Just tell yourself that no other mountaineering party has ever been stupid enough to drag such a big anti-crevasse anchor behind them as this one.'

Unfortunately the crevasses are too open and unstable for us to take a direct route. Instead we have to drop down into the shallow valley below the crevasse field. The cloud level drops as well, and it immediately begins to snow. When we get to the bottom of the valley we decide to camp. It is only 6.30 but we are tired, and once we climb out of the valley the visibility may not be good enough for us to pick another safe campsite. It looks as though we shall have to be more careful about crevasses from here onwards.

'I'm impressed with these radios,' I say to Jonathan as he disconnects the radio from the aerial after our evening sched. with Don. To save power we do no more than give our position and confirm that we are well.

'Yeah, they are good,' he replies. 'But if we lose radio communication we're suddenly in a serious position. I mean, *we* know we're still okay...'

He leaves the rest unsaid. After a week of silence, or even a few days, Don and the others on the boat may decide that we have met some dreadful fate. Once they have reached that conclusion there is nothing to keep them in Antarctica. The history books are full of stories of climbers

Just a few days after leaving the coast it becomes too cold to cook outside, so we move the kitchen into the polar pyramid tent. With the kerosene stoves alight, the tent warms up quickly and becomes a drying room for everyone's inner boots and gloves. Lincoln tends the stoves while Greg changes his socks.

who have struggled down from their mountain days later than expected, only to find that their base camp has gone because their companions had bridged the gap between fearing the worst and accepting it as reality. I remind myself to ask Greg what arrangement we have made with the ship if radio contact fails.

'This is frozen,' says Lyle, rummaging in the supplies outside and opening tins.

'What is?' asks Jonathan who is in the pyramid tent beside me melting snow for soup. 'The tuna?'

'That was, too, but I mean this fetta cheese.'

'It's not all that cold at the moment. It must have frozen last night. There hasn't been much chance for things to thaw out.'

I write in my diary while Jonathan cooks. As Greg said today, 'Life is always hard down here. You sweat pulling the sled, and as soon as you stop you freeze. Even at night in your sleeping bag your toes are toasty warm and your nose is freezing. You can never really relax. Crevasses appear in unexpected places and storms blow up in a few hours and last a week.'

The cold is always with us. Even when the sun is hot on your face, the sweat is freezing on your back.

Saturday, 13 February

I awake to the sound of the stove. I groan as I stretch my body out straight. It is light, of course, the strange red light of the inside of the pyramid tent, but there is no way of guessing the time. I sit up and look with bleary eyes at Jonathan.

'What's the time?'

'Six-thirty.'

Too early to get out of my sleeping bag, I decide. Instead, I swing my body around until my head and feet have changed places, then I open the door. The sky is overcast but the cloud layer has lifted to several hundred metres above the glacier. It is not snowing at the moment, but I cannot see any more than that without finding my glasses.

'Overcast,' I pronounce, and snuggle back in my sleeping bag.

It seems like a minute later, though it is actually 7 am, when Jonathan wakes me, this time with the instruction, 'Take this.'

I take the steaming bowl from his hand. The fluid looks like Milo, with brown lumps of undissolved chocolate circling the bowl in search of the spoon which stirred them. I taste it.

'Shit!'

Tact, never my strong point, is totally absent first thing in the morning. The bitter taste of coffee overrides everything else, and I am not a coffee drinker.

'Too strong,' I explain apologetically, 'But it might be okay for the others.'

I reach outside and grab one of the snow blocks I cut last night and piled up next to the door. The coldness of the snow in my hand helps to wake me. When I drop the lump into a steaming billy it dissolves instantly. I lean out again and reach for another. Beyond the sound of the stove in the tent I hear an unfamiliar noise. I glance in at the stoves but their sound and the appearance of their flames is normal.

The second block of snow slides into the billy but it is more stubborn about dissolving. 'There's a plane out there,' I say.

Jonathan purses his lips as he concentrates for a moment, then nods.

I put my head outside to listen to the distinctive sound of a prop-driven aeroplane getting closer.

'There's a plane above us,' I announce loudly to the others. They will have to wake up in a moment because Jonathan is pouring their drinks.

'Must be a party working in the area,' says Greg's sleepy voice. 'Or somewhere nearby.'

'Nearby' has a different meaning in Antarctica, especially for the scientific teams who do most of their travelling by aeroplane and helicopter. Because we are pulling sleds we feel every inch of the ground we gain. For days we have been working our way up the enormous Tucker with painful slowness, even though our map shows the glacier to be virtually level. Now we are faced with the Man O'War, whose gradient is steep enough to bring the contour lines much closer together on the map. We are worried about how we shall cope with the steeper terrain that the plane flies over with ease.

I suppose we shall never know the plane's destination. Anywhere else in the world we would not even waste time wondering. Here in Antarctica, though, any form of life is so out of place that evidence of other humans is intrusive and disturbing.

Manhauling puts a big strain on our bodies. We suffer from sore backs, tired muscles and blistered feet. Greg does some repair work on his heel at lunchtime.

By the time we have packed up camp and loaded the sleds the sun has dissolved the clouds. We ski slowly along the bright snow under a blue sky. The day's toil is as bad as we feared. Greg thought that Lyle and I should join him with the big sled because this is likely to be the strongest combination. The three of us grunt in unison while our huge load ploughs into the snow behind us. Jonathan walks, and it proves to be a bad day for walking as well. Soft snow has drifted deeply into the gullies we are forced to traverse to avoid a big crevasse field. As Greg and Lyle and I start the slow plod up what we hope will be the steepest hill, Chris and Glenn film us. Jonathan cannot be seen. No doubt he is floundering in the soft snow of the gullies.

The only hope of getting the big sled up the hill is to zigzag. The corners are especially difficult because we have to drag the sled through 90° or more, and the snow jams underneath the runners. Progress is painfully slow because we gain only a few metres' height with each long zig or zag. The slope, like all such climbs, seems never ending. Finally, the gradient eases just enough for us to be able to keep a straight course.

The sudden noise of an avalanche provides some relief from the routine. Lumps of ice tumble down the steep wall flanking the northern side of the Man O'War and come to rest at least 2 kilometres away from us. With a scale as large as this, 2 kilometres seems close. The spectacle provides a good excuse to interrupt our torture. We sit down and eat lunch while we wait for Jonathan.

'The going looks almost flat from now on,' says Glenn.

'Looks it,' I say, 'but it's not.'

'How do you know?'

'It only looks level because the mountains either side rise up so much higher, and this valley is so much narrower than the Tucker.' Valleys have played this trick on me before. 'The steepest part's behind us, but it sure isn't flat ahead.'

'I hope you're wrong.'

'So do I, since we're stuck with this bloody big bastard.' I kick the sledge.

'Last hill for it, though,' says Greg, 'I think we'll leave it behind tomorrow. If we make a big cache of food and fuel we should be able to fit everything we need into the three pulks.'

Jonathan trudges up to us, but rather than cursing the soft snow he calls out, 'Got a great shot of the avalanche. What about you, Glenn?'

Glenn reveals what he had neglected to admit to the rest of us. 'They always told me at film school, "Reload as soon as you finish shooting a roll." I knew it wouldn't be long till lunch, so...well, I didn't.'

'Silly bugger. Might have been the only one we'll see. These mountains are frozen solid.'

'Okay,' says Glenn.

'That one only fell because the rock wall is really steep with a huge weight of snow above it.'

Glenn cuts him short, 'Okay, I said. The camera's loaded now.'

Jonathan sits down with a smile. Anyone else would be annoyed at being so far behind but he accepts such delays as the price of good photography. The many seasons he has spent in mountain ranges all over the world have given him the confidence to be happy alone in such isolated places, as well as the knowledge to judge when he should keep his cameras in his pack and stick with us.

Chris wears a scarf across his face to protect it from sunlight reflected off the snow. We discover that the most comfortable method of manhauling is to wear our harnesses back-to-front, so that the tie-on point faces the sled.

Following page: Chris, hauling his sledge slowly along the Tucker Glacier, is dwarfed by the ridges of the Cartographers' Range.

The webbing of my harness bites into my hips with every slow slide of my skis, and my back aches from the weight of the sledge we drag so slowly. It is heartbreaking to raise my head and see the white slope in front of us. It is not a matter of pushing on until we reach the crest — there is no crest. This slope goes on for at least another 10 kilometres. Beyond that, the glacier swings to the north out of sight. I synchronise the slide of my skis with Glenn in front and Greg beside me. The effect is hypnotic, deadening.

Our progress is so slow that to an observer it might seem that our joints are slowly locking up with cold. The surface of the glacier is hard because the loose snow has been blown away — reducing the friction on the sledge — but the angle remains constantly uphill. The pain is made easier to bear by the fantastic scene around us. The valley of the Man O'War is only 2 or 3 kilometres wide, but I can set my eyes on a feature ahead and watch the intervening distance diminish and disappear. On the Tucker the view seemed to take a whole day to change noticeably because the scale of everything was so large. Here, the mountains remain big but the valley is relatively narrow, and that is a much more comfortable perspective. We plod slowly towards a beautiful pyramid peak. Unlike its neighbours, it rises only a few hundred metres above the glacier and would take only a few hours to climb...How frustrating it is to have no time to spare.

We hurry towards our mountain, like six ants in a frozen desert chasing an arbitrary goal. In the tracks of Sisyphus, we haul the weight of our ambition in our sleds. We are vulnerable, determined, and insignificant to everything except each other.

We stop shortly before 7 pm because we can take no more. Low cloud drifting up the valley wipes out our retreat, so our attention focuses upon the route ahead. At the same instant the three of us excitedly realise that the peak appearing around the ridge to the left is Mt Minto. For the first time since leaving the ship we can see our objective. We find the energy to keep moving until the ridge to our left no longer obscures our view of the peak. Its mass rises behind the mountains in the middle foreground, a distinctive pyramid of rock with snow trapped between the arms of its ridges. From this angle Mt Minto is an inspiring sight and a noble objective. I feel strangely relieved because we no longer have to trust the map.

Greg skis another hundred metres towards what appears to be a small dip in the glacier in the hope of finding a more protected campsite. Lyle and I are content to sit on the sled and stare at the mountain.

'There's a huge crevasse over there, a real monster,' Greg says when he returns. 'We'll have to stay here. It's pretty exposed but probably a bit more sheltered than if we continue over that rise.'

Chris and Glenn, who were filming our arrival, ski across to us and we begin to set up camp. Jonathan has been swallowed by the clouds behind us.

Our beards are heavy with the frozen moisture from our breath. My long hair is dusted white as well. Frozen breath is not a commodity I had heard of before this trip. We look as if today's efforts have aged us 100 years. We are now 1200 metres above sea level, and presumably that is the main reason for the drop in temperature. Today we gained more altitude than in five days of hauling along the Tucker—some compensation for travelling only 7 kilometres.

We are rewarded for our efforts by the beautiful orange light which bathes everything around us when the sun approaches its low point. I rush around with my camera, all the time making sure there are no hidden crevasses where I walk. In other mountain ranges the superb colours of sunset last only a few minutes. Here the progression towards dusk is almost imperceptible. The only changes are the already long shadows lengthening a little more and the orange losing some of its pink tinge. I do not need to hurry. With this beauty frozen into slow motion I am once again over-powered by a feeling of timelessness.

Everyone is in bed, satisfied after a good meal cooked in the pyramid by Chris and Glenn. Greg is asleep beside me, while Jonathan and Lyle share the second dome.

Writing my diary is awkward because my right-hand woollen glove has holes in the thumb and two of the fingers. I am trying to avoid contact with the plastic barrel of the pen because it is cold even through my inner glove. Tonight is certainly the coldest we have experienced. I decide to give up the struggle, because I am eager to sleep and let my muscles relax in the warmth of my sleeping bag.

Just before Greg nodded off he said, 'At last it's cold enough for these Mountain Designs bags to be useful.' Indeed it is. After Everest I wondered whether I would ever again be cold enough to need a sleeping bag as warm as this one. Tonight answers the question. Mt Minto is still 40 kilometres away and 3000 metres above us. It sounds daunting, but already we have travelled 123 kilometres from the ship, and for almost 100 of those we have hauled everything ourselves. Spirits are high now we can see our objective again, though all of us are tense in anticipation of what it holds for us. We are a long way out on a very fragile limb. I cannot help thinking that we have experienced only Antarctica's kinder moods, and these are more than harsh enough. I dread being shown the malevolence of the continent.

Sunday, 14 February

Another late departure this morning, when we can least afford it. First we make a cache of food, fuel, and the wooden sled, then Chris and Glenn interview us about our progress so far and our thoughts about what lies ahead. Greg is obviously itching to get going throughout the discussion, and I share his impatience. Poor Chris and Glenn work so hard and yet we barely tolerate their small intrusions into our routine. They must do every-thing the rest of us do, and film it all as well.

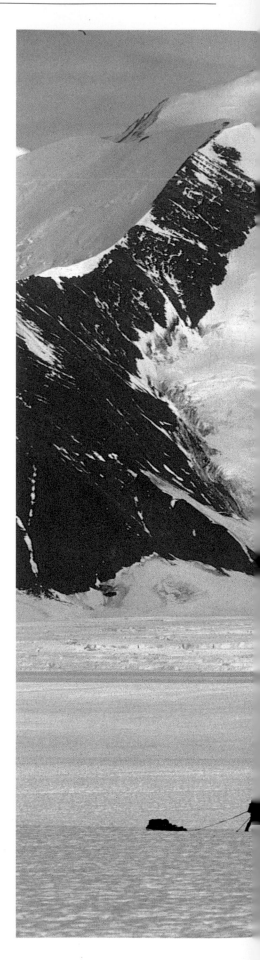

It is midday before we set off. Once again I volunteer to go without skis. My years of experience in high mountains have taught me to walk efficiently in snow. It will be hard work but I know I can cover a good distance, and have strength to push on tomorrow. I start ahead of the others, hauling the bag we formerly had strapped to the sled. The idea is that this will drag as easily as a pulk, but instead it acts more like a snow anchor. One hundred metres from camp I stop, transfer everything into my pack and take the haul bag back to camp. Meanwhile I am overtaken by Greg and Lyle hauling one pulk, and Jonathan with another. When I start walking again I find that the weight on my back makes me sink even further into the snow.

'Leave something for us,' shouts Chris, who has obviously spotted my difficulties from where he and Glenn are repacking the film gear into their pulk.

I accept the offer gratefully, dump a bag in the snow for them to pick up on the way past, and begin to plod along the scour mark left by the others' pulks. It seems ludicrous for the person walking to carry a heavy pack because the extra weight makes every footstep sink deeper into the soft snow. However, the routine for the day is established and we cannot afford to waste more time rearranging loads or swapping skis. I shall have to make the best of it.

'Funny weather,' I say, apropos of nothing, as I peel another clove of garlic for our dinner.

'Yeah,' says Greg, huddled over the full pot of rice, stirring it carefully.

'This afternoon I thought it was going to blow up in a big way,' I say, remembering how the wind burnt our faces as we trudged into it. 'But now it looks like it's going to be all right again.'

'It does that a lot up here,' says Greg. 'Building up then disappearing, and then one day, without warning, whammo! A blizzard hits you!'

If Antarctica feels the need to remind us of its powers, now would be an appropriate time for a blizzard to come. Whenever we have felt the masters of our chosen universe and assumed we knew what lay ahead, Antarctica has dealt us a blow. Weeks ago, when we were almost celebrating our triumph over the pack-ice before we were through it, we became stuck for thirty-six hours. At Football Saddle we assumed we would have a good run up the Tucker with the skidoo, then the skidoo was taken away from us. Our confidence grew again when we were able to maintain a good daily average while manhauling, then the steep slope of the beginning of the Man O'War stopped us from covering more than 7 kilometres, less than half the distance we must achieve each day. Once again our goal seemed to recede from us. With 25 kilometres remaining to the mountain and 100 kilometres of manhauling behind us, we must not take the good weather for granted. The last thing we need up here is a two-week blizzard.

Everyone else goes to bed immediately after eating dinner, but I kneel in the dim light of the doorway and laboriously darn my glove. I can repair only one finger before my fingers are too cold to direct the needle.

I pull on my boot liners and crawl out of the tent to clean my teeth and stretch my legs before curling up in my sleeping bag. Outside is one of the most peaceful and beautiful scenes I have ever witnessed. The temperature must be below −20°C with the result that almost everything is frozen into stillness. The only proof that what I see is not a painting in soft colours is that *this* scene is perfect. Nothing could improve the sharp lines of the

Mt Kyle at midnight.

mountain ridges and the smooth curves of their snow slopes. The air here is purer than anywhere else in the world, and the cold makes sure nothing shimmers or distorts the scene in any way. The other side of the glacier, 2 kilometres away, seems no more than an arm's length beyond the prayer flags flapping gently in the breeze.

This evening I tied the line of Tibetan Buddhist flags between a tent guy and the tip of a ski poked into the snow. I do not know which Tibetan prayers are blowing out on the breeze, and I am not sure if I stitched them onto the cord in the correct order. Much more important to me is that, as the first visitors to this place, we acknowledge the holiness of our surroundings.

Monday, 15 February

In contrast to the sleepy slowness of our talk, the steam from the porridge and tea rushes through the beam of sunlight shining in the open door of the tent. There is a breeze outside but the stoves and sun make it muggy inside. Greg gives the porridge a stir and then lies down again.

'You know when I was in the storm with the Germans?'

I nod, remembering his tale of a two-week storm in the mountains a short way south of here, when he was working as a geologist.

'There were two bosses—real heavies—who were in these tents', he nods at the pyramid we lounge in so comfortably this morning, 'and the rest of us were in Salewa tunnel tents. The wind would flatten them, so you'd be lying there with the roof pushed down to 20 centimetres above your face. It was the worst storm I have ever been in. God, it was boring after a few days. Anyway, the wind dropped enough for the rest of the expedition to fly in one of the choppers from the *Polar Queen*. We just

stood around staring at it, like we'd been on another planet for the rest of our lives. And the pilot—it was one of those times when it was really inappropriate to say anything—was so obviously amazed at how we looked that he shook his head and let out this involuntary teutonic "Wo!"

'It was like that with us yesterday. I was rushing around doing everything, trying to get away early. And everyone was just standing around.' He pauses. 'Well, not everyone, but almost. And I was so pissed off. This place does things to you. It really is a different world.'

'Yeah.' I nod and fumble for a spoon inside the food bag. 'I know I was angry in the morning, mainly at myself. I stomped along cursing myself and everyone else, even though I realised there was no basis for it. There's a yogic pose which dissipates anger. I told myself I'd do that when I got to camp, but after an hour I was into the rhythm of the walking, and it was good to feel my body working well. I didn't care that you guys were so far ahead.'

I stir the porridge and ponder the meaning of such anger.

'The irritability comes from working so hard and having no time to ourselves,' I say after a moment. 'And then there's Chris and Glenn's bickerings. They know each other well, and they don't seem to take offence at what they call each other. I suppose it's no more than their method of working together, but it does set the tone. Also there's Glenn's way of abusing his camera loudly when it plays up, which it does a lot in this cold. I suppose it amounts to nothing.'

'But we should watch it.'

I nod, and say, 'We are under such pressure to reach the mountain and get back, that it's little wonder we all feel the strain now and then.'

'So long as irritability doesn't interfere with our judgement. This is too unforgiving a place for that sort of mistake.'

We get on with the business of breakfast. It is a good day outside and

Mt Minto, at 4163 metres the highest peak in North Victoria Land, rises behind the peaks of the upper Man O'War Glacier.

that inspires us to hurry. Greg heads off first but Lyle and I soon catch up to him. Because he is walking, he breaks through the crust of firm surface snow with almost every step. We take over the lead for the next hour or so. The glacier rises gently but continuously in front of us, which makes breaking the trail hard work. Even though our loads are still heavy, we feel free now we have left the sledge behind. It would be back-breaking work hauling the wooden monster through this soft snow. After a chocolate stop Chris and Glenn go ahead, and Lyle and I are able to follow their tracks with little effort.

As I ski along I consider the aggression which flares up occasionally. Those brief exchanges of words are intended seriously only in the moment of speaking. Everyone except the participants laughs at the clashes because we all realise their true purpose is to relieve tension. They occur when the energy we have summoned to motivate us either dissipates or takes off in the wrong direction, which can happen when the harshness of the climate or the enormity of our task gets the better of us.

When I feel in harmony with my body, I work rhythmically; there is no mental tension, only the natural strain of my muscles. Whenever I feel out of kilter with myself and the task at hand, everything seems too much of an effort, and I use my anger to drive me on. Sometimes the anger is directed silently at the others. Afterwards, this clearly appears ridiculous, because each of us is responsible for our own presence here. We blame each other for our problems because we get tired of constantly blaming ourselves.

The shortage of time to reach our goal and make the return journey before the onset of winter forces us to push ourselves to our limits everyday. Greg stops to catch his breath.

We crest a steep slope between crevasses and are faced with an incredible panorama of the highest mountains of the range. Steep granite buttresses rise for 2000 metres from this valley, while even larger peaks loom up behind.

'There's few places in the world where you can see a mountain panorama better than this,' Greg says, euphorically. 'Maybe not anywhere. And we're the first to see it.'

'You reckon?' asks Chris, probably wondering whether he can get Greg to repeat this into a microphone.

'The Kiwis who climbed Mt Adam didn't come up here,' says Greg. 'And the only other land parties just continued up the Tucker.'

That such beauty can exist unseen for eons makes me feel yet again that humanity is only incidental to this earth, and that the existence of things has nothing to do with our perception of them.

'Wow.'

Lyle's usual succinct, appropriate commentary is reduced to one syllable of wonder.

'So that's Mt Minto behind?'

'Must be. It's bigger than all the others.'

Late in the afternoon, with only a few kilometres remaining to the head of the Man O'War, we pause for a drink. We are nearing the top of the slope which has taken more than an hour of effort so far.

'People would kill for this snow on the Australian ski-fields,' I say.

'They'd kill for it anywhere,' answers Greg who is walking behind the pulk which Lyle and I are hauling.

'Yet we just complain because it buries our skis and gives us cold feet.'

'That's less of a problem if we keep moving.'

I take the hint and I swing the pack onto my back again. A few minutes later, as the soft powder brushes past our ankles with the smooth slide of

our skis, Lyle says, 'The only problem with all these glaciers, rock buttresses and ice-cliffs is that there's nowhere to put a T-bar.'

'We may live to see those days,' I say.

'Yeah,' he puffs. 'There's already talk of building a hotel near the Australian base at Davis.' He is quiet for a moment then begins to fantasise. 'We could come up here in our seventies, ride the chairlift up to the restaurant, and sit there drinking hot chocolate while the young men chat up the snow bunnies, and people from all over the world ski by in their multi-coloured suits. The guy who mans the chairlift would come in at the change of shift and say with scorn, ''You're too old for this, grandpa.'' And I would look at him just long enough to hold his attention, then I'd say, ''Shut up, sonny. I was here before you were *born*''.'

I laugh because this ludicrous scene is capped by a cliché which makes it real. Our social habits can reduce the most magnificent places to venues for such ego-boosting pastimes as flirting and one-upmanship. Memories of the indulgent games from the human world stand out in my mind, because more than anywhere else I have been—or can imagine—Antarctica is impersonal.

We are in the heart of the mountains now, camped only 4 kilometres away from Mt Minto, with the diversion we must make around the intervening peaks adding another 2 kilometres. After a climb of 700 metres today, we are at 2400 metres, and the cold has increased accordingly. The snowfield at the head of the Man O'War Glacier is relatively enclosed, which makes it much more sheltered here than anywhere else we have been since leaving Sydney Harbour. The powder snow was hard work to travel through, but the nearness of our goal gave us the energy to cover 20 kilometres. Here we shall make our base camp and push on with only two days' food and our two lightweight dome tents.

Dozens of side glaciers flow into the Tucker, each with its own realm of unclimbed peaks.

While I scribble in my diary, Lyle snores gently beside me. The half-light of midnight is creeping noticeably closer to darkness every night. The return of darkness is a comforting reminder of that other world where everything fits into place, or rather, of that world whose miraculous nature we learnt to overlook in the process of growing up. Our confrontation with Antarctica's different rules has reopened my eyes to reality—but it is a long way to come for the lesson. Too late to start on that one, I think, and decide to put my pen away. The next few days are going to be hard but exciting, which means I need my sleep. Lyle's snoring is unlikely to disturb me. When the hood of my sleeping bag is pulled tightly around my face even the silence extending for thousands of kilometres beyond our camp will be muffled.

We make our base camp at the head of the Man O'War Glacier and hope that the clouds obscuring the magnificent granite peaks around us are not the first signs of bad weather.

THE RIGHT
HORSE

THE RIGHT HORSE

'Expeditions to the Antarctic are all about taking risks. Sometimes you back the right horse and sometimes you don't.'

JONATHAN CHESTER

Tuesday, 16 February 1988

Spirits are low when we awake. Snow falls steadily from a heavy sky. Greg is withdrawn, though whether he is tight-lipped with worry or anger I cannot tell. He says very little while we have breakfast and get ready to go. Despite the poor conditions and the 3000-metre pass we must scale to reach Mt Minto, there is no discussion about not pushing on. We have built up so much momentum it would take more than a small storm like this to stop us. Of course, I cannot help thinking that this snowfall might be the beginning of a real blizzard.

Greg and Jonathan set off on skis hauling the small pulk. Lyle trudges along in their tracks. He has left his skis with Glenn's and mine, as anchors for the pyramid tent we have left behind. Our packs are more than heavy with emergency clothing, sleeping bags, climbing gear, stoves and food. I leave very little behind, so I do not have to wonder if I have everything I want. When I am about to shoulder my pack Chris and Glenn ask me to explain our strategy for the film. I face the wind so that they can protect the camera and microphone from the windblown snow. It is bitterly cold as I answer their questions and I wonder if the harshness of the environment will come through on film.

'Okay,' says Glenn. 'Thanks.'

I turn my back to the wind and swing my pack onto my shoulders. I warm up quickly as I trudge along in Lyle's footsteps. Chris and Glenn overtake me when I pause to remove some clothes from underneath my windproofs. The others have stopped a short way up the slope leading up to the pass. When I catch up to everyone, Greg and Lyle are just about to continue.

'The pulk's digging into the snow like a bulldozer,' says Jonathan. 'So we're going to leave it here. That pile is for you to take, if you want to sleep in a tent tonight, that is.'

I curse before dropping my pack onto the snow. Then I stuff the tent, a fuel bottle and a bag of food into my already full pack and strap the ice-saw onto the side.

'Give us a hand getting my pack on, will you?' asks Chris. Such manoeuvres are always more difficult when wearing skis. I lift his pack and hold it in place while he eases his arms through the straps.

'Is yours as heavy as this?'

'No,' I reply.

'Why not?'

'Because I'm wearing my mountaineering boots.'

Despite the bad weather we leave our base camp and plunge into the whiteness.

Previous page: Looking west towards Mt Royalist at sunset from the slopes of Mt Minto.

130

Chris grunts when I let go and leave him with the full weight. 'I wonder if the ski back down here will be worth the effort of the extra weight.'

'Not for me, it's not.'

He puts his hands through the wrist loops of his stocks and starts to ski up the hill. The skins on his skis grip well, and he steadily gains on the other four who are walking and sinking in up to their ankles. Maybe I should have brought my skis after all. I shall keep this thought to myself because I advised Lyle and Glenn not to bring theirs. . .

I leave Jonathan to anchor the pulk in such a way that it will be secure in a strong wind but easy for us to find even if it snows heavily. I soon catch up to Glenn and Lyle who walk slowly behind Greg. I feel a little guilty because I have not broken the trail at all today.

'Let me plug the footsteps for a while, Greg,' I call out.

He stops for a moment while I plod past him. He says nothing and does not even look at me.

Breaking trail is hard work because the slope is much steeper than anything we have encountered since leaving the ship and the snow is always up to my ankles. It could be worse, I tell myself, it could be up to my knees. The effort is offset by the satisfaction of gaining height quickly.

I look up and see Chris sitting on his pack in the snow when the slope temporarily eases off.

'Hard work,' I gasp as I throw my pack off and flop on top of it.

'Yeah,' he agrees. 'There's a huge crevasse just behind me. It was the perfect excuse to wait for the rest of you.'

'So we can all fall in together?'

He shrugs. 'Maybe we should rope up. There's more ahead.'

'Looks okay if we skirt it widely enough.'

He nods.

Carrying heavy packs through fresh snow is tiring work. Lyle rests for a few minutes beside the path we have trudged in the snow.

'What's your excuse now?'

He smiles. 'I'm lazy.'

Greg, Lyle and Glenn plod up to us and collapse on top of their packs. Nobody says anything.

Chris looks at Greg. 'You unhappy?' he asks.

Greg shrugs then stands up and unstraps his skis from his pack.

'Chocolate?' Lyle offers everyone.

I wonder if Greg is annoyed by our overall slowness. I remember on other mountains I have been unable to keep up with him, and yet today he trudges along slowly. Perhaps he feels the weight of our inexperience: Jonathan is competent and independent, but often frustratingly slow; Glenn and Lyle are crossing their first high mountain pass; and Chris has done only a little more. Once we are over the pass, we will have to climb up to get back out again. If anyone is injured or frostbitten, or if a blizzard traps us beyond the limits of our two-day food supply we will be in great danger. All of us know this, but nobody is more aware of it than Greg. Perhaps he is preoccupied with the commitment we are making, but I doubt it, because he thrives on living to his limits. I tell myself to stop thinking about his mood, because it is his problem. He has given every indication of wanting to be left to himself. I think how strange it is that in this huge and lifeless land we cannot escape from each other.

Greg and Chris head off on skis with Lyle and Glenn following on foot close behind. Jonathan puts away his camera and clips his boots into his skis. I trudge off after the others. We zigzag between a few large open crevasses. There is no sign of the ice beneath us being undercut, so I feel reasonably secure. Higher up, Greg has taken a route across a steep slope of hard snow above a crevasse, so everyone is moving slowly. If this was my first time on hard steep snow I would move cautiously too. Though we

Jonathan opts to carry his skis rather than cache them, in the hope that they will make the descent of Thistlethwayte Pass quicker and safer.

carry ice-axes, it is unlikely that any of us could stop our fall before disappearing into the crevasse. Maybe we should have roped up, but everyone is past it now except for Jonathan and me.

The sun breaks through the clouds and immediately I am hot. When I take off my fibrepile jacket the wind begins to blow more strongly, swirling snow and particles of ice along its path. I zip up my windproof and keep moving. We are high enough now to be engulfed by the clouds. When mist is blown around us, its frozen moisture cools me instantly, but as soon as the sun appears again the heat reflected from the snow makes me sweat. I remain dressed as I am, accepting that this is the best compromise, but I walk slowly so that I do not sweat too much. After about half an hour I catch up to Lyle and Glenn, who take turns in breaking trail. Up ahead, Chris and Greg move much more efficiently on skis. They are barely visible near the crest of the pass.

As we climb higher we become more exposed to the wind and I no longer have to worry about overheating. I take over the lead from Glenn and put my energies into punching a line of footsteps through the crusty snow. The wind seems to be strengthening and I begin to grow cold. At first I walk faster in order to warm up, but I realise that I will only tire myself out. There is no alternative but to stop, get my fibrepile jacket out of my pack, grit my teeth and whip off my windproof jacket. Though I wear thermal underwear and a woollen jumper the freezing wind makes me feel naked. I pull on my fibre pile jacket, and jerk my windproof back on, then grab my pack and start walking even before I lift it back onto my shoulders. The only advantage of carrying a pack as fully loaded as this one is that it towers over me and protects my head from the wind.

The angle eases, but the featureless snow gives no clues to the nearness of the crest. For fifteen minutes or more I think that the top is only 50 metres away. We should name this place Thistlethwayte Pass, I tell myself, because, like the boat journey to Antarctica, this trudge seems never-ending. I laugh at the idea until a better reason for the name occurs to me. These are the Admiralty Mountains where there is a tradition of naming peaks and glaciers after ships or naval battles, and there is also a tradition worldwide of naming geographical features after expedition patrons. Thistlethwayte Pass it shall be, if the others agree to it.

Chris and Greg have long since disappeared. I gave up following their ski tracks an hour ago and I begin to worry about losing touch with them altogether. There is enough snow swirling in the air near the crest to blur the outlines of Mt Meier to our right. If the visibility gets any worse we could be in a serious situation. Jonathan is a long way back, and Glenn is starting to drop behind. At last I realise that the snow beneath my feet has levelled off. The crest of the pass is a huge flat area about 300 metres wide and stretching perhaps a kilometre between Mt Meier and the smaller peak to our left. I decide that the best course of action is to hurry ahead and try to see where Chris and Greg have dropped off the broad slope of the pass. My deep footprints should be visible for an hour or more even if they begin to fill up with snow, whereas the ski tracks might easily disappear within minutes.

'What about lunch?' Glenn's scream makes me turn and look into the wind. He is 150 metres behind me on the crest of the pass, hunched over his axe to rest. It is not the crazy question it seems, because in this cold our bodies burn a lot of energy, and to keep warm we need to eat. However, it would be stupid to stop here in the most exposed place we have been yet. I do not attempt a reply to Glenn because I know the wind will whip away my words. Instead I hurry down the slope. Soon the snow becomes knee-

This hole where Lyle stepped into a hidden crevasse is dramatic proof of the worth of skis in crevasse country.

deep, so to lessen the effort I take giant strides. This becomes easier as the angle increases. There is no danger of crevasses, and with an endless and featureless snow slope stretching before me I do not need to watch where I put my feet. I stare across at a rocky ridge, sweeping up like the spine of a gigantic brontosaurus. As I watch the ridge disappears and reappears through its veil of light cloud and windblown snow, but the summit is never clear. This must be Mt Minto, I tell myself, because there is no other mountain big enough.

I spot Chris and Greg a few hundred metres away, down to the left. I run down the slope as best I can, swinging my legs out to the sides to wade through the deep snow.

'How's it going?' Greg calls out when I get close to him.

'Fine, especially now I'm out of the wind.'

'It's still blowing even down here. How's everyone else?'

'That's Lyle coming now.' We look up at a figure following my line of footsteps. 'Glenn's not far behind him, but I haven't seen Jonathan for a while.'

Greg nods, and turns to watch Chris ski down the hill. We see him attempt a turn in the soft snow, but he falls over.

'Let's go and join him,' says Greg. 'Hopefully it's sheltered down there.'

The slopes of Thistlethwayte Pass rise behind our two small tents and lessen the feeling of being alone in the middle of nowhere. We are camped at 2800 metres at the head of the Ironside Glacier, the same spot where we huddled in the snow and ate our lunch. We decided that if the strong winds developed into a blizzard we would have a better chance of crossing the pass again from here than from the base of Mt Minto.

Seventy kilometres to the east of us this glacier calves icebergs into Moubray Bay, only 5 kilometres from the *Allan And Vi Thistlethwayte*. The upper slopes of the Ironside Glacier lose height very gradually, so even without clouds filling the valley, the steep lower reaches would not be visible. If the weather is clear tomorrow we should be able to see Edisto Inlet and Cape Hallett from the slopes of Mt Minto, which rise another 3 kilometres across the valley. This is a big 'if', since everything depends upon the weather. We will need more than the determination that we have built up during our endless days of manhauling, so we pray privately to whatever gods we believe can make tomorrow into a perfect day.

All of us are in good spirits now that we have reached our destination. Greg, Jonathan and I agree that Minto's south ridge is the obvious route. Chris has climbed enough simple mountains to have faith in his ability to overcome the obstacles. I sense that Glenn, as a novice to mountaineering, feels the task will be beyond him. Lyle, though equally inexperienced in the mountains, has eighteen years of rockclimbing behind him. He has learnt the discipline of disregarding everything except the movement of his body over the rock, so the adjustment to climbing a big mountain is really a matter of scale. Greg, Jonathan and I can make the important decisions about weather, avalanche danger and route finding, and leave the others to concentrate on the physical demands of climbing the mountain. As long as the terrain is not too steep and the conditions are favourable, there is a good chance that we will all reach the summit.

I glance up at the peak of Mt Minto while we work around the campsite guying down the tents. The mass which looms large above us seems benign one minute and hostile the next. I suppose these impressions simply reflect my happiness to be here and the subconscious memory of the fear which humbles me during every climb.

Wednesday, 17 February

Today is to be our summit day. We have come so far, at the cost of so much effort, to reach this place, and feel that we have already paid the price for the summit. I cannot believe we will not be given a chance to climb Mt Minto. But when I think that such an attitude presupposes a dispenser of justice, I also remember the impersonal nature of Antarctica. The whims of this continent connect with our fancies only by chance.

We wake to skies swept clear of clouds by a ferocious wind. Our small tents shake wildly, although they are securely pitched and sheltered behind a wall of snow blocks. Up high, the snow is whipped from the summit of Mt Minto and sent into mad spirals by the gale. Lower down, the outlines of the ridges are blurred by the windblown snow. Glenn passes in our tea and porridge, and though the signs are not good, we have to get up. Putting on the numerous layers of clothing takes time, especially for me because I give extra attention to my feet.

Outside, the scene is awesome. The Admiralty Mountains are proving that Antarctic beauty can be ferocious. The lines of snow which sweep over the broad basin at the head of the Ironside Glacier look like wind-driven sand. Huge white whirlwinds hang in the hollows of Mt Minto's steep south-east face, and the snow still blows from the summit 1400 metres above us. Now is not the time to try, but try we must because we will never forgive ourselves if conditions improve and we have wasted our only chance.

We sit in the lee of the downhill tent and watch the mountain. At the first sign of improvement we decide to go. Everything is packed and ready, so within minutes we are away. After a few hundred metres I remember that I forgot to zip up the inner door of the tent. With this wind blowing,

From left: Greg, Lyle, Glenn and Chris huddle together to eat a late lunch once we have crossed Thistlethwayte Pass. Chris attempts the nearly impossible task of warming his foot by rubbing it.

snow will sweep underneath the fly and gradually cover everything inside. I curse, throwing my pack down, and jog as best I can back through the soft snow to the camp. As soon as I turn my back on the mountain the wind begins to howl. This is madness, I tell myself, when I crawl inside for a few minutes' shelter, but the others are pushing on and my place is with them. I zip up both tent doors this time and stumble back to my pack. Already it is completely covered with snow and, when I look up, I can barely see the last of my friends disappearing into the whiteness. We cannot climb in this, but the storm might pass as quickly as it has descended. Unlikely though. I put my head down and trudge along the line of footsteps.

Whenever I raise my head my face is stung by the windblown snow and ice, so I quickly learn to watch my feet. Plodding through snow is such a boring activity, yet I seem to spend large segments of my life doing it. Usually it is a means to an end, but I know we shall not achieve that goal today.

When I reach the slopes of the mountain I glance up, and two figures separate from the huddle ahead and start walking towards me. My five companions are vague dark figures in the storm, but I recognise Greg's gait. The decision to retreat is obvious but I keep walking towards them because I will get cold if I stop.

'Your turn to plug steps,' he says when only a few metres away. 'Back to camp.'

'Yours were full of snow even though I was only twenty minutes behind you, so I get to break trail twice.'

'Lucky you.'

'Yeah.'

'Crazy to go on,' he says as an afterthought, thinking that I might want a late part in making the decision.

'Yeah.'

I turn around and head back to the tents. Fogged goggles make it hard for me to see my footsteps, especially since the snow being blown along the surface of the glacier has almost filled in the trail already. The energy I had stored for the climb has evaporated in defeat. The plod back to the tents seems twice as far.

We crawl inside the tents and instantly the cold feels much less fierce. We eat some nuts and a few biscuits and discuss what to do. Everyone is prepared to delay our return journey for one day, even though we have only enough food for tomorrow. There is not much to talk about because our options are clear-cut. One day's delay is unlikely to make the difference between escaping and spending the winter here, but it just might. The effort of reaching this place has provided enough momentum to make us accept the risk. The six of us snuggle into our sleeping bags and catch up on a few of the hours of rest denied to us in our rush to beat the winter.

When I wake up, Greg is asleep and Lyle is writing furiously in his diary. I reach for the few sheets of paper which I brought, as my final weight cutting measure at the last camp, instead of my diary.

I think of failure and what it would mean to each of us. Jonathan gave up his place on Australia's Bicentennial Mt Everest Expedition to come on this trip because our goal had more appeal. Unlike such large expeditions, we do not have the resources to besiege a mountain into submission. Now the elusive virginity of Mt Minto—which is much of its attraction—is likely to triumph again because we have neither the time nor the supplies to wait for good conditions. We are paying the price of being a small team. The odds have always been against us, but that makes the prospect of

Despite the deteriorating weather, we push on towards Mt Minto. When we reach the lower slopes of the mountain, the blizzard worsens and we agree that to continue would be suicidal. There is no option but to return to our two small tents.

success even sweeter and, I realise now, failure easier to accept. Jonathan must be asking himself whether the unique experience of our journey thus far is worth more than a chance to climb the highest mountain in the world.

Like me, Lyle has the time this afternoon to think of things other than the mechanics of getting ourselves to the mountain. Unfortunately he seems to have focused on the possibility of being trapped here for the winter; when we are 150 kilometres from the coast with a storm blowing it is not a good time to consider the odds. He is worried, and wants an instant transfer home to his wife and children.

Glenn and Chris regard the expedition primarily as a film-making exercise and so they can take some solace in knowing that they still have enough material for an impressive documentary. Just being here in this camp is an outrageous situation, and if they can manage to capture the tenuous nature of our position they will have a good film. Chris had just begun to direct more of his energies towards the ascent of Mt Minto. Today I could feel his frustration when we finally accepted the inevitable and headed back to the tents. He is accustomed to being more in control of events. Greg has spent too much time in the mountains to waste anger on the weather, even though the summit means more to him than to any of us. As for me, I think of other things.

I think of Tim Macartney-Snape, my companion on every expedition except this one. Last year the international expedition he joined failed to climb K2 in Pakistan. There, too, the weather kept them from the mountain. Perhaps the time has come to think of other rewards than the fulfillment of goals. Who else understands a summit achieved, anyway?

I think of friends and family, sunny days at Palm Beach and lunchtimes at Manly to celebrate the past. I think of Sydney—all those anonymous faces crowding the shopping centres and offices; all those number plates making a constantly changing cypher which the eye cannot help but try to decode during the wait for green from red.

I think of Barbara, and though she is just as far away as everything and everyone else, she feels much closer. For the first time in weeks I have time to think about more than the means of climbing Mt Minto. Indeed, I must think beyond the goal we have set ourselves, because it appears that we shall not achieve it. We have to gather our energies for the long return journey without the boost which comes with success. Part of that process is to detach my mind from Mt Minto. This afternoon there is the time and room in my head to consider more than how soon I have to get out of my sleeping bag, how cold are my toes, or how vast is this frozen land.

I think of the fruitcake Barbara made us which we cut a few days ago and finished eating last night. A good omen: the best fuel to take us to the summit. I think of the other charms I have brought with me—a jumper knitted with love, which kept me warm on Everest and on the journey south to Antarctica; a balaclava made by my mother fifteen years ago (she never expected that the penguin she knitted into the design would ever confront 30,000 originals); my coral and Tibetan turquoise beads which have remained around my neck since we left Australia; the Tibetan prayer flags which flutter behind on my sled or my pack every day. As well as these objects I invest the events around us with significance. I think of this bad weather as a deliberate lesson given to us before the perfect day of tomorrow when we shall make the climb; a lesson in patience and acceptance of our essential impotence; a chance for us to recover some strength after two weeks of effort which have felt like a year.

Once I would have scoffed at this attitude and called it superstitious. In a

Lyle writes his diary while wearing gloves which he has patched with chinchilla material taken from Lincoln's spare hat.

way I suppose it is, yet because I grant these objects and events no special powers, they are not talismans for immortality. Instead, they remind me that the world beyond myself is still a part of me, and so they become tokens to protect me from loneliness and despair.

Greg wakes up, sits up, and rubs his eyes. 'Good sleep,' he mumbles. 'Time for some food.' And then he comes to life, woken by his sense of humour. 'What shall I wear?'

I laugh at this reminder of the mores of the world we left behind.

'This hat? The blue jacket?'

Lyle sits up, but his laughter is half-hearted.

Greg reaches for the bag of nuts and dried fruit. 'The way I look at it, we might as well pig out, because we haven't got enough fuel to cook more than dinner and breakfast. No point stringing it out.'

'We're strung out enough as it is,' says Lyle, reaching for the bag.

'We're okay.'

'Depends where you look at it from,' says Lyle. 'If you look at it from an armchair in Sydney...'

'That's just what I've been writing about,' I say, taking a handful of nuts.

'If you look at it from an armchair in Earlwood...' teases Greg, 'Camille would think we are really strung out. Just as well she doesn't know, or she'd be very worried.'

Lyle groans and lies down again.

I extract my fingers from my sleeping bag and prepare to write. 'It's great having an empty head,' I say, referring to the mental space to consider things.

'I hate having an empty mind,' says Lyle. 'All I do is worry.'

'No,' pronounces Greg. 'An empty mind is good.'

The ridge of Mt Minto which we wish to climb forms the righthand edge of the shaded face on the left. The base of the mountain is still 3 kilometres beyond our two small tents and the low wall of snow blocks we have built as extra shelter.

'Why? All I can think about is what to do next.'

'Well, what else do you ever want to think of? And I don't mean continually going over plans for tomorrow or next week.'

As if to illustrate his point, Greg wriggles out of his sleeping bag. 'Yes. Definitely my blue trousers.'

He pulls them on, slips his feet into the liners of his mountaineering boots and crawls out of the tent. I hear him telling Chris, Glenn and Jonathan to make room for him to cook dinner. The tent unzips and Greg crawls inside and begins to chat. I hear his delight when he discovers an untouched bottle of fuel. From the tone of Jonathan's voice I can tell he is depressed. Chris and Glenn say almost nothing, such is the power of their frustration.

There has been no time when our commitment to this venture has been as strong. The weather has forced us to stop and consider where we are, and the implications of being so isolated. We cannot change channels or snap out of the dream; the otherworldliness outside is *real*. Beyond the meagre shelter of our tents, it is 150 kilometres back to the ship, and a storm is blowing over the 3000-metre pass above our tiny camp.

Thursday, 18 February

Jonathan wakes first and has breakfast ready by 6.30.

'Here's your tea, you guys.'

Glenn's voice comes from the same end of the tent as my head so I roll over and fumble for the zip. Clouds of frost fall on me from the inside walls. I curse, then unzip the door to take the steaming bowls of tea.

'How's it look?' Greg asks. He is not referring to the tea.

'Ahh...' I try to decipher the meaning of the thin clouds around the outline of the mountain. 'Foreboding...could go either way,' I decide eventually. 'Looks cold though.'

We drink our tea, and I pass the bowls back for porridge. Greg unzips the second door which is near his head.

'Hmm,' he says. 'I see what you mean.'

Glenn passes in our porridge. Busy noises come from the other tent. We will have to try it, I tell myself, on the chance that conditions get better rather than worse.

'Oh, well,' says Greg without his usual enthusiasm.

'So what do we do?' asks Lyle, who has been lying in his bag silently awaiting the verdict.

'We go and climb it,' says Greg.

With no further discussion we dress and prepare for the climb. I decide to wear my down suit over thermal underwear and a light woollen sweater. I shall take my fibrepile jacket but leave my trousers behind. If I keep moving I should be warm enough—and with 1400 metres to climb and descend we will not have much time to sit around. Jonathan, Chris and Glenn are almost set to leave when I crawl out of the tent. Our backpacks are ready from the day before and so all we have to do is shake the windblown snow from them. I shove my fibrepile jacket inside my pack and look for my right-hand woollen glove.

'Not much snow has fallen,' says Greg. 'You can see our footsteps clearly.'

I glance up to where Jonathan has already begun to walk.

'Sounded like it was snowing all night, though. I guess it was just blowing around.'

It is 7.15 when Lyle heads off after Jonathan. Chris and Glenn are ready to leave, but are checking with each other again that they have everything they need for the filming. I crawl back inside the tent and ransack it in the search for my glove.

'See you along the way,' says Greg.

'All right.'

I look inside my sleeping bag, then under my sleeping mats. Nothing. I must have dropped the glove yesterday in my weary plod back across the glacier. I swear at myself and my stupidity. The person with the most reason to fear frostbite is now the least well equipped to protect his hands. Ever since being severely frostbitten ten years ago I have been more susceptible to the cold. I shall just have to be careful and warm my hand in my armpit as often as I can.

I zip up the tent door and its vestibule, and look across at the others—a line of figures dwindling in size as they approach the mountain. Already the conditions are improving; the thin cloud has dispersed. The summit is clear and the highest rocks are free of snow.

Our weeks of struggle have brought us to this. Without discussion we get up and go. All possibilities, all ifs and buts, were thrashed out during the long haul up the glaciers. Yesterday we were preoccupied with the weather, the mountain, our reasons for being here, and then all those things were put into a different perspective by our retreat. But today there is none of that. Our purpose is as clear as the mountain in front of us. More than that: it is the same.

I shoulder my pack and set off after my friends. Jonathan's footsteps are close together and by stepping into them my progress is as slow as everyone else's. That is okay because there is no hurry yet. It will be a long day and I know I shall catch up soon enough.

I realise that this purpose and determination is mine alone, and yet I have extended it to include us all. Our small band has become close-knit through our struggles together: through such shared experiences as the precise matching of muscle for muscle when a team of three hauls the big sled uphill, or through the same numb-fingered pain as we struggle with the tent-poles at the end of the day while all thoughts are directed to our sleeping bags where hands and feet will slowly warm again. Perhaps this morning my friends are full of doubt and I am the only one filled with clear-sighted determination. I think not, because I know this sort of day is made for Greg, at least. All the energy he has put into making the expedition work will be focused to burning point today. Tomorrow, of course, we must head back to the boat regardless of what happens in the next few hours. But I will not think of tomorrow.

I gain slowly on the others and stop fifty yards behind Greg and Glenn to take some photos and adjust my clothing before plunging into the shade of the face. Away from the sun's rays it will be many degrees colder. Even now it is $-5°$ or $-10°C$, so it would be wise to keep moving. I look up at the mountain. The summit lies back out of sight, so the mountain's fore-shortened bottom quarter appears to be a huge peak itself.

I decide to photograph the mountains stretching down the Ironside Glacier. Yesterday it was all obscured by cloud. The view will improve higher up, but these snaps are almost a precautionary ritual to hold back the cloud—scenes deferred for a better camera angle get obscured by mist and storm. I allow my superstitions to influence me again. Be aware of everything today, I tell myself. See what is influencing you and ignore what is not real. This state of heightened awareness is the deepest satisfaction of every climb.

I shoulder my pack again and follow the others, restraining my energy

and excitement. Greg is in the lead. He has chosen a horizontal line across the face to bring us to the ridge at a point several hundred metres above its junction with the glacier. The advantage of this line is that we do not lose height by skirting the bottom of the face to reach the base of the ridge.

I catch up quickly because of the condition of the snow. Foot holes made in the soft snow alternate with the thin lines of boot edges on hard snow. Everyone treads carefully on the hard stuff. I glance down. A slip might finish at the bottom of the face — probably harmless enough because the slope is gentle and the distance only 100 metres. Just the same, it is an experience to be avoided. I step across carefully. Ahead of me the others move again from the deep and secure boot-prints in the soft snow onto the hard surface. They balance across to soft snow again.

Perfect conditions for cramponing, I think, so I swing my pack off my shoulders and unbuckle the crampons from the side. The metal frames are still firmly tied together with their straps to keep the points from ripping holes in everything they rub against. The lounge-room floor at Sydney where I fitted them to my boots seems a long way from here, even further than 4000 kilometres and two months away.

My fingers fumble with the buckles. I am thankful that I am struggling with them here on easy ground instead of balancing in footsteps chopped out of the ice. I clip the crampons onto my boots and welcome the security of their sharp metal points digging into the snow. Their promise of the climbing to be done fills me with joy, and I think of how long it has been since I faced the tensions of an expedition summit day.

I have no time for more than fleeting thoughts of the past, so I shoulder my pack again and follow the line of footsteps. Because they are not

From the lowest slopes of Mt Minto the summit lies back out of sight, so a bump on the ridge actually looks like the highest point. We traverse across to the righthand ridge then follow it upwards.

wearing crampons, my companions need to take extra care not to slip. I catch up with them quickly, just as we gain the rocky ridge. Everyone stops to share a block of chocolate and delight in the view. The sky is completely empty of clouds, and so we are sure of at least a few more hours of clear weather. The others sit down, take photos or stare out across the panorama which until now was hidden by this ridge.

Jonathan hands me a couple of squares of chocolate but I feel an urgent need to continue.

'I'm going to keep moving so I don't get cold,' I say.

The ridge above is broad, with an easy angle, and promises straight-forward climbing. The rock proves to be broken up and dusted with snow, not set in ice as I expected. My crampons are a hindrance here so I stop to remove the metal frames from my boots. Greg and Lyle catch up to me as I strap them back onto my pack. Below, Jonathan is putting away his cameras and Glenn and Chris are fiddling with the film gear. I hope everyone shares my need to hurry.

I swing my pack onto my shoulders again. It is a good weight, containing nothing superfluous. The ridge steepens slightly and the change in angle lets me use my hands on the larger pieces of rock. Time goes quickly as my mind deals with the simple equations of handhold, foothold, handhold.

Greg has set himself a slow pace, perhaps to match the others, or because he knows how long a climb it will be. I feel full of energy and know I have much in reserve. I begin to draw ahead. It is a joy to be absorbed by climbing again, even over such simple terrain as this. The wind still blows cold and strong from our left, starting somewhere in the unknown frozen wastes of the inland. When I need to look to the left I do so with my head down to prevent the hood of my down suit being ripped back off my head by the wind. The condensation from my breath slowly freezes on my sunglasses. Every few minutes I scrape away the thin film of ice with a gloved finger. I can never really clean it, so I have to be content with imperfect vision. The small clear sections of glass make me feel I am wearing blinkers. My eyes ache with the cold, and every minute or so I close them for a few seconds to warm my eyeballs.

I yelp with triumph when I reach the point where the ridge bends back to the left and the crest is lit by the sun. An increase in the wind offsets any heat that may have been in the sun's rays. A level part of the ridge, steep-flanked like the crest of an enormous cathedral roof, leads me to a sheltered spot where I wait for the others.

In the distance, the dark water of Edisto Inlet forms an isolated patch of blue between the Ironside Glacier, the steep mountain walls which flank it and the peninsula of Cape Hallett behind. I take photographs of the others climbing along the ridge towards me, but it is so cold I have to warm my fingers between each shot. I wonder how Glenn will manage with his movie camera because he needs to keep his finger on at least one button while he films. With loose snow swirling off the ridge above us, he should get some dramatic footage if his camera does not seize up. A more likely problem is that the film could tear in the extreme cold. I take a shot of Greg a few metres away, then warm my fingers in my armpits. I am glad that I have limited myself to still photography.

'Bloody cold,' Greg says, shrugging the pack off his shoulders and sitting on it.

'You could say.'

Lyle balances along the crest towards us. 'Halfway?' he asks.

'A third. Maybe less,' Greg replies. 'But I think we should have lunch here because we may not find another sheltered spot higher up.'

Lyle and I pull the lunch out of our packs. We are protected from the worst of the wind, but with temperatures as cold as this the slightest breeze makes a big difference. Chris flops down beside me. I size him up as a human hot-water bottle. My left foot, especially susceptible to cold since the bad frostbite a decade ago, is dangerously numb.

'Do you think I could stick my foot inside your jacket?' I ask.

'Sure.'

I struggle with my gaiters and with the laces underneath. The cold has made the plastic outer boot hard and inflexible, so it is a struggle to remove my foot. Chris unzips his down jacket and I shove my foot inside underneath his armpit. Now I can turn my attention to the lunch.

The cheese is impossible to cut with my Swiss army knife so I put the block on a rock and chop it with my ice-axe. The block splinters into shards when I chip at its edge, and when I give it a hearty blow to the middle, again only small pieces shatter off. The clumsy business of picking these pieces up with cold fingers is made more awkward by having one foot inside Chris's jacket. Lyle chops at the salami with his ice-axe while Greg breaks up the chocolate with a rock. The nuts and dried fruit are gobbled quickly because they are easiest to eat. We do not talk much as we eat except to curse the cold, which manages to frustrate even the simplest actions. Our movements are slow, clumsy and frequently interrupted as we thrust our gloved hands inside pockets or down jackets to warm up.

'Probably be quicker to crampon from here,' says Greg, 'and we should get on with it.'

'I'll film everyone getting ready,' says Glenn.

'Then maybe you should get ready first.'

It is another ten minutes before we are set to go. Lunch has been a long interruption to the climb, but eating food is a vital part of keeping warm.

The broken rocks of Mt Minto's south ridge provides straightforward climbing. The 3000 metre high mountains in the background form a barrier between the Ironside Glacier (seen here) and the Tucker.

The wind seems to have strengthened during the hour we were stopped. Greg briefs Lyle and Glenn in the use of crampons because they have used them only in practice sessions. They could not have chosen a more remote place to learn. I would be frightened silly if I were in their position, because our lives depend on the correct use of our ice-tools.

We crampon past Glenn's camera and begin to climb the icy slope. The angle is not very steep but the surface is hard and it would be difficult to arrest a fall. The sharp points of the crampons have to be set firmly in the ice before each step. The wind blows constantly, but it eases a little before the strongest gusts, and this variability makes the climbing precarious. I breathe heavily from the exertion, and my balaclava forces the moisture from my breath up beneath my glasses where it coats the underside of the lenses with rime within minutes. To save myself the constant chore of trying to clean my glasses I stretch the opening of my balaclava down around my chin to free my nostrils and mouth. Now, with the skin of my face bare to the elements, I need to keep my head turned away from the wind to protect myself from frostbite. I climb up in steep zigzags, keeping my back to the wind when I climb up and left. This means I am climbing backwards half the time, which is awkward, but at least the system allows me to see.

Lyle is climbing strongly, demonstrating the determination which made him such a formidable rockclimber. When I glance down I notice that Jonathan and Glenn are dropping behind. Glenn will be okay with Jonathan nearby to assist if he has trouble. I wonder how each of them are managing with their different photographic obsessions. This is definitely not the weather for practising these crafts — nor for being on this mountain at all. I get the feeling that we are here very much on sufferance.

Every step we take calls for the utmost concentration as we cross the hard ice below the summit.

As I look down, the indefinable presence of Antarctica overwhelms me like nostalgic memories of a lover met but once in a land foreign to both of us. Though not yet the stuff of memories, Antarctica is the same: known and yet unknown, familiar while remaining unattainable. And dialogue with this land is even more elusive. It is all we can do to survive, and somehow the reduction to this most basic level of existence bonds us to the world.

Greg interrupts the thoughts which punctuate my careful placement of one foot after the other.

'Looks like we'll be able to climb up beside the ice-cliff without even having to cut across onto the rock.'

I bend forward over my ice-axe to rest. 'Yep.'

'How's it going?' Greg shouts into the wind even though Lyle is only a few metres away.

'Good,' he shouts back.

I can tell that he is smiling even though his down-jacket hood obscures most of his face. For some reason he is not wearing glasses or goggles. I presume he has given up the battle to keep them clear of ice.

Chris is another few metres below watching Glenn and Jonathan move up slowly. It is too cold to stay still, so I climb away from Greg.

Behind Greg, the Ironside Glacier curves down towards Cape Hallett. The blue waters of Edisto Inlet can be seen between the end of the Ironside and the white crest of Quarterdeck Ridge.

Fifty metres higher, the rocky ridge becomes steeper, and narrows the crest of ice we are following. I do not like the thought of climbing close to the lip of the ice, because such edges have a tendency to break off. Greg fell 50 metres in Peru when the summit of the mountain he was climbing collapsed under his weight. The rope stopped his fall but he cracked his collarbone. Here we have the recipe for another such disaster. The right-hand slope, which drops steeply to the lip of the ice-cliff, is smooth and slippery enough to make a fall impossible to stop. The only safe way to climb this section would be to take the rope out of my pack so we could safeguard each other if the ice does break. I look for an alternative and notice that there appears to be a straightforward route through the rocks to the left. Without conferring with Greg I move across to investigate. A short gully leads through steep ground, then it is easy going over loose rock to a tongue of snow. The heat of the sun has been absorbed by the rocks around the tongue, and so the snow is much softer than the ice we have been climbing since lunchtime. I stop and take my camera out of my pack to snap Greg traversing towards me. Together we climb the snow tongue up to a small saddle on the ridge. From here we can see the remaining 250 metres of the mountain. We slap each other on the back because we know that the summit is within our grasp. Above us the terrain is steeper but seems to pose no real obstacles.

'We'll only just make it,' says Greg. 'The wind is strengthening all the time.'

'Let's try cutting diagonally across the face. It's in the shade but it should be out of the bloody wind.'

'Looks steeper,' he says, obviously thinking about the inexperience of Chris, Lyle and Glenn.

'Better than getting blown off your feet,' I say. 'I'll go on and make sure it's all right.'

'Okay.'

My excitement gives me the energy to climb quickly, but I move too fast and have to stop for breath after a few minutes. I remember that we are 4000 metres above sea level now, and our bodies are affected by the reduced oxygen. The effect here is nothing like the debilitation experienced on Himalayan mountains twice this size, but climbing is still much harder work than at sea level. I stop and look back to where Greg waits for the others. He is looking down so I cannot signal that the route ahead looks good. There is no point shouting because the wind will swallow my words. I pull my sunglasses from my face and, despite my short-sightedness, I can see better without the ice-coated lenses. Two figures—probably Lyle and Chris—are now with Greg.

The cold prods me into action again. Every minute or so a strong gust of wind swirls across the face and threatens to blow me off balance. When I hear the roar of an approaching gust I shove my ice-axe into the slope and stand firm. Now that I have traversed out onto the south-east face of the mountain, the slope drops in one uninterrupted sweep to the glacier 1200 metres below. The climbing is straightforward, but the relatively sheltered aspect has worsened the snow conditions. Snow patches adhere to the slope, and I know that standing on them may be enough to cause a small avalanche. Nevertheless, I am tempted to climb across the patches because the soft snow gives way around my foot and makes a level footstep. After hours of climbing the hard sloping ice my ankles beg for the opportunity to stand square.

I choose a more or less straight route diagonally across the slope, aiming for a break in a major rock buttress which runs down from the summit ridge. A short steep gully leading up to the notch is the only obstacle. In the gully there is no option but to climb the steep, unstable snow. I spread my feet as far apart as I can and stretch up with my ice-axe. I hope that if one of my footsteps collapses the other foot or my ice-axe will hold. If not, there is a good chance that I would be able to use my ice-axe to stop myself on the next patch of soft snow, but it is not a theory I wish to test. Luckily, I do not have to. When I reach the security of the notch in the rock, I look back along the line of my footsteps. Three figures are following me; presumably it is Glenn and Jonathan who are still out of sight.

Above me, another gully leads up to a steep band of rock below the summit ridge. From here it appears that the rock is climbable, but in these temperatures and without a rope, it is not a sensible option. The ice is obviously not very deep here, so the easiest course is to choose a gully packed with enough snow to lead all the way to the top. By chance, 100 metres to my right, a broad snow-filled gully runs down from what appears to be the highest point. I take a diagonal line across the slope until I reach it. The wind strengthens with every step upwards, and gives an extra fierceness to the cold. Perhaps at this height the wind has been as strong all day.

Distances are always deceptive at the top of mountains, because of foreshortening, and the anxiety to reach the summit. But for once, the summit rocks are closer than I thought. As I approach the crest the wind whistles wildly, unmuffled by my balaclava and the down hood.

Below the last rampart, a few metres from the crest, wind from a different direction in days past has gouged a ledge large enough for me to sit upon. The wind howling above makes me decide that this is a good place to stop. I turn around and ease my pack onto the ledge, so that when I swing my feet up I can rest sheltered and secure. The snow drops away steeply beneath my cramped haven. My secure position allows me to relax a little and remember where I am. I can see my five companions in a line along the shaded face beneath me, and a long way below them lies the bright white snow of the glacier.

I decide to wait for them to reach me, but then I notice that the small dot in front, presumably Greg, has stopped above the steepest part of the gully. Someone must be directly beneath him and out of sight because I can see only four figures now.

Greg is not moving. Perhaps he is waiting for me to signal that this route is indeed the best. I shrug my shoulders out of my packstraps, making sure that the pack stays firmly on the ledge. Then I remove my mittens, unzip the top of my pack, and carefully pull out my goggles to protect myself from the wind above, which must be at least as strong as it sounds. Away from this place in a different world, the noise of windblown trees often makes the wind sound more furious than it is. Here, the noise comes only from the air rushing over rocks and against itself.

I shove my sunglasses into the top of my pack, slip my arms back into the packstraps, then pull my goggles over my eyes and try to adjust my improvised face mask. Proof of the effort of the climb is a lump of frozen breath below my bottom lip. My beard has frozen into it, and when I try to pull the mask up over my mouth I wince with the pain despite the numbness of the skin around my whiskers. I have no option but to let the ice do the insulating. When I try to fasten the hood of my down suit I find that the velcro tabs are coated in ice as well. I rub both sides vigorously with my mittened thumb then hold the two parts together for a few seconds until they freeze.

When I look down through my ice-free goggles Greg is yellower and clearer, but still in the same position. I summon my concentration and move carefully off the ledge. The rock I have sheltered beneath has good holds along its top edge. I pull myself up easily but the overhanging boulder on the crest provides only enough space to crawl to the side. My pack makes this manoeuvre impossible, so I have to squirm along on my stomach. I try to move gently to avoid ripping my down suit on the sharp rocks. I have a vision of its cozy warmth disappearing in a windswept puff of feathers. When I edge my head around the corner I am stunned by the force of the wind. I turn away and glance down to where Greg is still perched at the top of the gully.

Take it easy, I tell myself, or you'll be literally blown away.

I clasp the shaft of my ice-axe then stretch out and swing the pick into the snow of the flat summit ridge. With my axe as a firm handhold I inch myself out onto the crest. The wind buffets me as I crouch there. I look around quickly, not feeling the coldness of the wind, only its force. To my right the ridge rises steeply to the lip of the face I have just climbed. The high point is only 5 metres above me, but such a steep slope will not be possible to climb in these ferocious winds. When I swivel on my haunches to look behind me, I am amazed by what I see.

We were wrong, is my first thought. The main summit is 200 metres along the ridge, and 30 metres above me. Despite the map, we had thought that the summit was here where I crested the ridge. Certainly it appeared that way from every viewpoint below, but it was yet another Antarctic illusion.

I hesitate for a moment, wondering whether the wind will blow me off the mountain. By keeping low with my ice-axe ever ready to hack into the slope as an anchor, I work my way 10 metres to the left. To my surprise, the wind eases dramatically. I look back and see that I crested the ridge at its narrowest point where some sort of vortex is created by the closeness of the southern and northern faces.

I feel secure now, and safe enough to turn my attention to this remote spot which we decided to make our goal. The view is stupendous. To the north I can see over smaller mountains to huge icebergs floating in Robertson Bay. To the east of the bay the rocky peninsula of Cape Adare juts out like a giant finger. To the south-east is the view I have been admiring all day: the long serpentine curves of the Ironside Glacier leading to the waters of

Edisto Inlet. Seventy kilometres away from where I stand on top of this part of the world is Cape Hallett, our starting point. The rest of the panorama is taken up by mountain ranges stretching into the distance. I pull my watch out of my pocket. It is 3.25 pm; eight hours to ascend the 1400 vertical metres from the camp to here. A good day's work.

I look more closely at my immediate surroundings. The summit ridge itself is a huge ramp sloping gently down to the north, widening as it rises towards the summit. The north face is less steep than the route we climbed, but the drop to the glacier at its base appears to be much further. I walk up towards the peak but decide to leave the highest point untrodden until everyone is here to share it.

After weeks of hauling sleds along glaciers hemmed in by mountains it is strange to have such an expansive view in all directions. I have learnt how difficult it is to judge distances and angles in the mountains but there is no disputing that Mt Minto is the highest peak in sight. Mt Meier and Mt Royalist have lost some of their appeal now that we have climbed their taller neighbour. Thirty kilometres to the east, however, the pyramidal summit of Mt Sabine, which gives the illusion of being higher when seen from the coast, is asking to be climbed. New and unexplored territory surrounds it. I cast my eyes across the rear side of Mt Herschel and the backs of the mountains which flank the eastern side of the Tucker. It seems unbelievable that we dragged ourselves and our portable survival kit in a huge arc around the far side of that range. Apart from Thistlethwayte Pass and Football Saddle our path is all downhill from here. That does not lessen the fact that it is still a very long way back to the ship.

I look across the slightly convex south face to where my line of footsteps leads up beneath the lower eastern summit. No-one is in sight. Carefully I edge towards the lip of the south face and drop to my hands and knees. Wind blasts my face as I lean over the edge. Sixty metres directly below

Greg, Lyle and Chris have roped together for safety because of the steeper ground, unstable snow, and strengthening wind. Glenn and Jonathan follow behind.

me, Greg, Lyle and Chris are still at the snow-covered notch in the rock buttress. I wonder what is delaying them until I see Chris going through the motions of belaying a rope while Greg climbs. The rope itself is invisible from this distance on the shaded snow. The wind must have strengthened down there as well and made them decide to rope up. The extra time it is taking them makes me thankful we did not need to rope together for any other section of the climb. From above I can see, at the top of the gully which runs up the face from the notch, a narrow ledge leading across to where I kneel. The steep headwall can be avoided by a simple traverse.

'Up here!' I shout. 'Up here.'

Greg scans the summit ridge for a few seconds before spotting me. I reach out an arm and wave him up. Another rope will speed progress considerably so I move away from the lip and take the rope out of my pack.

I hammer in an aluminium stake for an anchor but I am still uncoiling the rope when Greg appears over the lip.

'Jesus, I'm cold,' he says. 'Belaying down there for ages. Can you come and take the rope so that I can warm up?'

Not the place to warm up, I think, since inactivity has made me grow steadily colder since I arrived. I suppose warmth is a relative term, and up here we are out of the worst of the wind.

I finish organising the ropes and start to belay Chris up the gully. It is bitterly cold standing in the wind at the lip, so after a few minutes I turn to protect my face. To my surprise, I see Lyle hugging Greg. What is surprising is not the hug but Lyle's presence on the summit. Had he followed the line of my footsteps, I would have seen him, so he must have climbed up a gully between my route and Greg's. Chris reaches me, and with a smile he steps away from the edge and unties.

'How was it?'

'Hard and scary. I've never climbed anything like those lower ice-slopes without a rope before.'

'Shows what you can do when you're in a hurry.'

He squeezes my arm and moves across to the others. With the wind so strong I decide that the only way to get the rope back down for Jonathan and Glenn is to climb down with it. The rope gets hooked on sharp rocks but climbing down is relatively simple. Jonathan is belaying Glenn across to where he stands on the notch.

'Rope here for you!' I shout into the wind.

When Jonathan waves an arm in recognition I climb back up to the summit. Glenn is moving very slowly so there is time for me to go back to where Chris, Greg and Lyle stare out to the north. The four of us clump together in a celebratory hug—the only form of central heating in this part of the world.

Back on the face, Glenn has almost reached Jonathan at the bottom of the rope I left in place. Glenn ties on while Jonathan climbs up unroped. Glenn can manage only a few metres at a time before he has to stop and lean against the snow. After a couple of minutes I shout at him and pull on the rope. He slowly climbs a few more metres and then stops again.

Jonathan climbs up to me and carefully steps around the rope.

'Thanks,' he says, and though his face is completely obscured by a mask I can sense the warmth of his smile. He moves past me and walks across to the others.

'Hurry up!' I shout to Glenn, but he does not move. 'Get your arse up here!' I scream, pulling on the rope.

With this encouragement, he struggles a couple more metres, then stops again. Each time he collapses against the snow I deliberately increase the level of my abuse. If the cold is crippling him then the sooner he is up here in the sun and out of the worst of the wind the better. If the altitude is the problem the summit is the best place for him to have a good rest before heading down. Glenn's predicament aside, I can feel that the cold is starting to chill me more than superficially.

Finally Glenn shuffles across the last of the traverse.

'Step around behind me,' I direct him. 'Then go and stand up there. Don't crampon the rope.' When he is safely over the lip I help him untie.

'How are you?'

'Exhausted.'

'Well, it's all downhill from here.'

He tries to laugh but it comes out as a cough. 'I slipped down there,' he says. 'Slid about 7 metres.' He bends forward to breathe deeply, then straightens up before speaking again. 'I thought I was going to die but the ice-axe stopped me, just like it says it will in the books. I just lay there. I couldn't move until Jonathan threw me a rope.'

'We'll find an easier way down,' I say, and think how close we are to stepping beyond our limits. Glenn is exhausted, Chris and Lyle are not much better off, and I am dangerously cold. Those thoughts temper the elation we deserve to feel now we have all reached the summit ridge.

I put my arm around Glenn and lead him across to where the others huddle. The wind seems to be strengthening up here now, and that makes me even more keen to get moving.

Greg offers me a handmade chocolate.

'Margaret bought these in the Blue Mountains,' he says.

With a clumsy mitten I shove the sweet in my mouth. Even though it is frozen I can taste its mouldiness.

'This is mouldy.'

'So's mine,' says Lyle. 'But we'd better not tell Margaret because she'd blame herself.'

'I always thought they were overpriced,' I say, eating it anyway, in the hope its food value will warm me up. Chris passes me the bag of nuts and dried fruit, and I stuff my mouth with a mitten-full of nuts.

I jump to my feet and start to dance around trying to warm up. 'Any one know the time?'

'Half past five.'

'Shit! No wonder I'm cold.' Two hours standing around in temperatures of $-20°C$ and with a 40-knot wind.

Chris laughs. 'Everyone's cold.'

'Well, let's get out of here then.'

'We'll just go up to the summit and take some photos.'

I turn around to incite our photographer to move, but the scene which greets my eyes leaves me speechless. Jonathan has pulled back his hood, to display huge white eyebrows which make him look as if he has aged 200 years. While he climbed his breath was forced up past his eyes by his face-mask and, when the condensation escaped, it froze on his thick bushy eyebrows. Lyle, his hands bared down to his last pair of inner gloves, attacks these strange icy appendages with the scissors on his Swiss Army knife.

'What the hell are you doing?'

'I can't see,' says Jonathan quietly, obviously not wanting to move his head. Lyle's hands are clumsy from the intense cold. Jonathan winces and groans as Lyle pulls and cuts. It is a grotesque scene, straight from the pages of *King Lear*.

'I don't believe what I'm seeing,' I say. Our presence here is incongruous enough without this bizarre ritual.

I stamp the ground with feet like blocks of wood and keep my fingers shoved under my armpits inside my down suit. I can feel that my body is on the brink of hypothermia—I know the symptoms too well. If I do not start the descent soon, my strength and judgement will begin to deteriorate dangerously.

'I can see!' shouts Jonathan. 'I can see!' He pulls his down hood back over his head and begins to slap his hands together and stamp his feet. 'I've never been so cold in my entire life.'

'Well, bring your cameras up to the summit so we can get out of here.'

High clouds have sprung from nowhere, and the sun's rays have lost most of what little heat they gave. The rest has been blown away by the wind.

The summit is capped by a flat rock which could have been designed for the five of us to sit upon. I huddle between Chris and Glenn.

'So now you're a mountaineer,' I say to Glenn. 'Not bad for a first mountain.'

He starts to reply, but his words dissolve into tears. Our emotions are so raw that the three of us hug and cry together.

'Okay!' shouts Jonathan. 'Get ready.'

Greg and Lyle squeeze onto the rock while Jonathan snaps a series of photos of us holding the banners of the Australian Geographic Society and Sigma Data Corporation.

I begin to shiver uncontrollably.

'Come on!' I shout. Chris hugs me while Glenn rubs me violently on the back, and somehow that combination warms me. Chris pulls out his World Park banner and we hold it while Jonathan takes his last group photos. We jump off the rock and dance around to warm up.

From left: Greg Mortimer, Chris Hilton, Lincoln Hall, Lyle Closs and Glenn Singleman hold up a sponsor's banner on the summit of Mt Minto for Jonathan Chester taking the photograph.

Following page: There is nothing except that which has always been — ice and rocks sculpted into mountains, and frozen valleys full of silence. The view south from high on the mountain during the descent.

Jonathan's face is bared to the elements while he takes photographs. When he lowers his camera I can see his serious expression. Greg is looking anxiously at the sky for signs of weather more dangerous than this chilling wind. Experienced mountaineers know that the most dangerous part of a big climb is the descent, when everyone is tired and cold, and reflexes are sluggish. Chris is busy recording our comments for the film. Lyle and Glenn are the only ones to show any real elation, the rest of us will wait until we are down, and there is real cause to celebrate.

'I have to get out of here,' I say to Greg. 'I'm getting dangerously cold.'

'Before you go,' he begins, reaching into the inside pocket of his down jacket, 'sign this.'

He passes me the piece of paper I gave him last night in the tent. On it is written: '18 February 1988. The first ascent of Mt Minto by the south-west ridge by Greg Mortimer, Lincoln Hall, Lyle Closs, Jonathan Chester, Glenn Singleman and Chris Hilton. As the people making the first ascent of Mt Minto we intend to call the route of ascent the World Park Ridge. As the Australian Bicenntennial Antarctic Expedition we intend that the ascent be used to place Mt Minto as the cornerstone in an Antarctic World Park for the physical and spiritual benefit of all humankind.' Underneath Greg's signature I add my own.

'What are you going to do with it now?'

'Get the others to sign it, and then leave it on top of this rock here inside the chocolate box.'

'I'm too cold to hang around any longer. I've been here two and a half hours.' I glance around at the others who are taking photographs or staring at the view. 'You'll be okay? Glenn seems to have got his wits back.'

'Yeah. We'll be right.'

'I'll go and make some dinner.'

'If you can find anything to cook.'

This mundane conversation seems extraordinary up here on the summit of Mt Minto, the focus of our energies for the last two years. Yet Greg and I have shared too many desperate descents to waste time congratulating ourselves now. The force of superstition influences us again.

I shoulder my pack and move towards the ridge. Then I clamber down the steep rocks to the west of the summit because this appears to be the easiest way down. Be careful, I tell myself, or you'll slip and there'll be no stopping you. I reach a point where I can cut off the ridge and onto the steep slope of snow. After a few minutes of rapid down-climbing the angle eases enough for me to face outwards and virtually run down the snow, which is soft enough for me to stop myself if I fall. Once I pass the small saddle on the ridge, I am on hard ice again so I descend more slowly.

My fingers ache as they come back to life, but I welcome the pain because it dispels my fears of frostbite. My feet are more stubbornly cold, but the rest of my body is warm. That warmth dissolves the fervour which drove me down from the summit; there are still 1000 metres to descend and 3 kilometres to plod across the glacier, but now the prospect no longer worries me. I look up and see one small figure near the top of the snow slope. Maybe Glenn delayed them with more filming. The panorama around me now is certainly worth a few photographs.

I get out my camera and shoot the last four frames in the roll. I think about changing the film, but my aching fingers do not want to face the cold. It is enough to stand still for a few minutes. The softness of the evening light filtering through the high clouds gives an ethereal quality and lessens the distinction between heaven and earth. The long shadows cast across the glaciers give a discrete identity to each of the hundreds of

mountains stretching out before me. There is nothing here except that which has always been—ice and rocks sculptured into mountains, and frozen valleys full of silence. The marks of the few people to have disturbed this vast region will have long been obliterated by the wind and snow. Minutes pass until I begin to feel cold again. I put my camera away and continue the descent.

Fifty metres above our lunch-site I rejoin the rocky ridge and stop to remove my crampons. While on the top, I placed my water-bottle against the back of my pack in the hope that my body heat might help thaw the ice which fills it. I shake the bottle and see even more of the water has frozen. It is too cold for even wishful thinking to work. The cap is so firmly frozen in place, I cannot budge it. A sharp jab with my ice-axe makes a small hole which I suck at eagerly. Maybe a little less than half a mouthful, but worth destroying my bottle for. The cold freezes all the moisture out of the air, which means every breath is another step towards dehydration.

I look up and see that Lyle is only 50 metres above me. I wait while he undoes his crampons, then I offer him my useless water-bottle. He sucks it anyway. Together we continue down the ridge. The wind starts to strengthen again, so we drop off the eastern side of the ridge to escape its blast. Progress is good because, as well as being sheltered, we avoid the rock steps on the crest of the ridge, which are easy to climb up but arduous to descend. After 200 metres of thin lines of rock poking through the ice, the slight spur we have been climbing down finishes at the top of a steep ice slope. We stop and clip our crampons back onto our boots. Both of us have warmed up from our rapid descent, so our situation no longer seems as serious.

'I don't remember climbing up so far,' Lyle says, staring at the glacier still several hundred metres beneath us. He looks tired.

The view from the summit. It is a magical feeling being higher than any of the thousands of peaks around us, as well as being the only humans on any of the land we can see.

'It's always like this,' I explain, 'Because the excitement of climbing towards the summit makes you forget the distance you've covered, but when you come down, you're always exhausted.'

We begin to move again. It is simple to traverse back to the main ridge and take a diagonal line down the huge snowfield which makes up the lower part of the south-west face.

I climb down quickly but cautiously, because this morning I noticed a line of crevasses stretching across the face. From above they are impossible to see. With Lyle dropping back behind me, and with the ropes somewhere up near the summit with the other four, I would have to wait a long time for a rescue if I fell in. Virtually every mountain face has a bergschrund crevasse marking the end of the mountain slope and the start of the slope which feeds the glacier below. This crevasse forms because the mountain snow and the glacier have different rates and directions of slide. Without much of a detour I find a place where the crevasse is hidden beneath a crust of ice and snow thick enough to drive a truck over. Or a skidoo. From below I can see that the bergschrund is dangerous only in a few places.

Crossing the bergschrund is always a moment of relief because it means that the steep slopes of the mountain are above and behind. But now in its place is the deep soft snow filling the huge bowl at the head of the valley. The warmth of the sun, checked up higher by the strong wind, has managed to soften the surface we walked over this morning. I plod slowly through snow that is halfway up my shins. It is better than the neck-deep stuff I have encountered on other glaciers but at the end of a long day it is still hard work. I am worn out by the climb and the cold. At least while I struggle through this interminable soft snow, the cold is not a problem. The wind is almost imperceptible down here, so to stop myself from sweating profusely I undo my leg zips. Damp clothes are dangerous when the temperature is below zero. Even my feet have warmed up, though all my toes are numb. I expect they will be without feeling for months now, as they were after each of my Himalayan climbs. On the way home from Everest I bought shoes in Hong Kong which were too small because my feet were too numb to feel the tightness. They looked good, though. Strange how my mind wanders now that my survival no longer depends on the correct placement of every step.

I stop to rest, and turn to look for the others. The mountain is bathed in bright orange light. A few hundred metres behind me Lyle is walking out of the orange into the shade. Hundreds of metres above him I can make out three tiny dots on the snow. The last person must be over the crest somewhere near where we had lunch. The mountain is so grossly foreshortened that the others appear to be still near the summit. While I stare at the golden slopes of Mt Minto, Lyle, drawing slowly closer to me, is a reminder that time is passing. The wind picks up and freezing air rushes through the open zips of my suit. I shiver, pull up the zips, and start walking again. In Antarctica the cold always overpowers any other feeling.

Ahead of me now, the evening sun highlights the traces of mist which hover on Thistlethwayte Pass. Camp is hidden in the hollows beneath, so I cannot see how far I still have to walk. To the east, cigar-shaped clouds float above Cape Hallett, though the Cape itself is out of sight now. Pink and apricot tinge the coastal mountains. The sky behind the peaks is a much darker grey over there. In a month's time night will come again from that direction. To the west, the granite buttresses of Mt Adam and Mt Royalist shine with pink snow and golden rock. I stop and swing my pack to the ground, so I can capture the beauty of the scene with photographs. Behind me the whole of Mt Minto is visible now. The twists and

turns of the ridge no longer pose questions, but tell of hard ice, shattered rock and the ceaseless wind. Already I have memories of a climb only a few hours old.

By the time I pick up my pack, Lyle has almost caught up to me.

'Unbelievable, isn't it?' I call out.

He just shakes his head, lacking the breath or the words to reply.

Within minutes I plod into the line of the drift-filled steps we made yesterday and this morning. These are easier to follow because the snow beneath has already compacted. The sunset darkens almost imperceptibly.

I crest the last rise and look down at the tents only 30 metres away. It is 9.20 pm, fourteen hours after setting out. At last I can stop moving without growing colder. I crawl inside our tent and rest for a few minutes. Lyle fetches the stoves and pots from the other tent and we begin the long task of melting snow for dinner. We must drink huge amounts tonight or we shall not have the strength to get back over the pass again tomorrow. I pump the stoves, put lids on the pots, then take off my boots and smile. It seems remarkable, but the six of us have done it. The mountain is climbed, which means our journey is half over.

During the next two hours the others arrive in varying states of exhaustion. Glenn had to interrupt his plod across the glacier with long rests. His hands and feet are close to frostbite because he let himself cool down. There is a lining of frost between each of his five layers of clothing. Lyle and Greg help him loosen his clothes in our tent while I continue cooking. Last of all, Jonathan arrives, ecstatic about the sunset, his cameras dangling around his neck. Despite our exhaustion our elation begins to express itself. With our first drink we begin to forget the bad parts—thirsts we could not slake, frozen noses and cheeks, and the perpetual cold of the wind. By the time we reach the ship only the good memories will survive.

The colours of the clouds to the east are reflected by the snows of the Ironside Glacier and the surrounding mountains. This slowly changing sunset is one of the most dramatic sights any of us have seen.

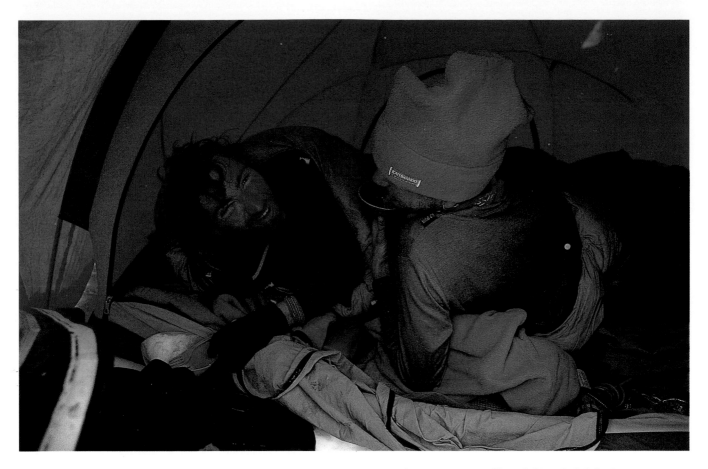

Glenn (left) and Chris back at camp: exhaustion and concern clearly show on Glenn's face.

Friday, 19 February

Lyle sits on his haunches in the snow by the door, making what breakfast he can with the remnants of our supplies. We stretched out two days' food over three. and now he is faced with six very hungry men. He starts well by producing English Breakfast teabags and making me the best bowl of tea since we left the ship. I tell him as much, so a few minutes later he interrupts my writing to hand me back my bowl. It contains an inch of hot water and the same two teabags.

'Great!' I say, lifting the bags out and letting them drip into the bowl. 'In most circumstances I would take this as an insult.'

He chuckles. 'In most circumstances it would be.'

I drink the tea, and it tastes good. I glance at the date on the top of the page in my diary and cannot believe we left the ship only sixteen days ago. We have become a close group, out of touch with the rest of the world and the normal passage of time. Closeness is unavoidable when an experience like this one is shared. What we did not predict is the bond of faith and understanding which has grown between us. The change in attitude this morning is more than relaxed tension. Everyone's mood has changed now that our goal, which so often seemed impossible, has been achieved. First, I found it hard to believe we were in Antarctica — now it is hard to believe we have climbed Mt Minto. I wonder not only at our achievement but at the desire for adventure which brought us here. How can we hope to convey to others back home what drove us on when we ourselves do not understand it?

The activity outside makes me feel guilty, so I put away my diary and quickly stuff my sleeping bag and clothes into their different stuff sacks. Greg crawls back inside the tent.

'One of Glenn's big toes has gone black already,' he says quietly. 'Definitely frostbite.'

'Shit.' After ten years I can still remember the horror of discovering that my fingers and toes felt wooden because they were no longer just cold but frozen.

'Is it painful?'

'Didn't you hear him putting his boots on?'

'Is that what all that noise was? I thought he was abusing his camera again.'

'I told him it'll be all right once he gets moving.'

I nod, then say what both of us are thinking. 'Well, it has to be, doesn't it?'

'That's why I said it.'

Lyle prepares breakfast from leftovers the morning after the climb.

Glenn leaves as soon as he is ready, because he knows he will be slow. The sky is overcast, and the occasional gust of wind warns that an afternoon blizzard may be brewing. Without having to dismantle the big pyramid tent and with no sleds to load, the rest of us pack up the camp quickly. Our sense of urgency returns so, after a perfunctory farewell to the place which saw us almost accept defeat before we were granted success, we shoulder our loads and follow Glenn. Greg, Chris and Jonathan make much better time up the slopes of Thistlethwayte Pass because their skis prevent them from sinking into the deep snow, but Lyle and I soon catch up to Glenn.

'How's it going?'

'Hurts a lot, but I'll get there.'

'Hopefully it'll be easier for you now you've got our footsteps to follow.'

'Yeah. That will help.'

'We'll see you along the way.'

What else can I tell him? I know that the cold has once again damaged what is left of my amputated toes, but for the moment my feet are too numb to feel anything. For Glenn, the pain overpowers the cold.

The climb up from the Ironside Glacier is half the distance we climbed from the Man O'War three days ago. Our packs are a little lighter, because we have no food nor fuel. The contained elation of success gives us new energy. Today's height gain of 200 metres seems insignificant compared to yesterday's ascent of the mountain, and there is the reassurance that once we crest the pass it is all downhill for 120 kilometres until we reach the bottom of Football Saddle. Less than an hour after leaving camp we are on the crest of the pass. Chris waits for Glenn. Ahead of us Greg and Jonathan's ski tracks disappear down the hill in an enviable series of s-bends.

We reach the pyramid tent seventy-six hours after leaving it. Snow has drifted over our footsteps and covered up the other two tent sites, so it looks as though we left here weeks ago. It feels that long ago, too, because our time in the next valley was spent dealing with fears and emotions completely different from the drudgery of manhauling.

From the pyramid I pass out bottles of fuel and bags of food so Jonathan can fill the stoves.

'Tropical down here, isn't it?' says Greg. 'Such an amazingly sheltered valley.'

The sun shines weakly through the clouds and tiny, perfectly formed snowflakes fall on the page as I write. I brush them aside every line or so even though it is too cold for them to melt.

'It's civilised more than tropical,' says Lyle. 'Flexible salami, multiple lenses for the camera buffs,' then he pauses to smile, 'and photos of the kids.'

Jonathan sits by the stoves melting snow as the rest of us watch Glenn stagger slowly towards camp. Chris has gone back to carry his friend's pack; now he skis a short way in front of him. It is heart-wrenching to see Glenn's short, flat-footed steps and the fixed grimace of pain on his face. More than anyone else here, I know what he is going through. The scene prompts bad memories: the throbbing pain of bad frostbite followed by months of incapacitation. All of us are hoping that Glenn's damage appears much worse than it is. We are too far away from help to deal with a serious injury. If we have to pull him on a sled, our chances of reaching the ship before the winter freeze will dwindle almost to zero.

Glenn collapses onto Greg's pack on the snow.

'Well, you guys are sure teaching me about expeditioning the hard way,' he says.

'You're teaching yourself,' I say.

'Ah,' says Greg dismissively, while helping him to sit comfortably. 'This is an easy trip. Wait till we take you on a hard trip.'

'I'm going to Hollywood after this.'

'I've heard that's a hard trip,' I say.

'But it's not cold.'

Then Lyle asks the question: 'How are your feet?'

'I hate to think.'

'Let's have a look,' says Greg.

Glenn undoes his gaiter and boot, and winces. Frostbite is a serious injury in such a cold place so far from help.

Glenn undoes his gaiter and boot, and winces when Greg helps him remove his inner boot. He pulls off his sock, and we gather round to see. His toe is black and hard—obviously frostbitten, but not as bad as I feared. There will be no permanent damage if we can prevent it getting any worse. Glenn pulls on his sock and hops across to the pyramid tent. The obvious thing is to get him busy with the cooking while we pitch the other tents and set up the radio aerial again.

It is an exciting moment when we cluster around the radio at 8 pm.

'Reading you loud and clear, Jonathan,' says Don, although there is obviously some distortion, because it is Greg at the microphone. 'What is your position?'

'At our base camp at the head of the Man O'War. Yesterday—that is, 18 February—all six climbers reached the summit of Mt Minto. Over.'

'Fine,' says Don almost dismissively. 'When will you get back to the ship?'

'Tell him we like it here, and can he give us another month,' I mutter. What about some congratulations, just for being alive, if not for the climb? I glance at Lyle who smiles and shakes his head. Don has other things on his mind.

'The *Greenpeace* is in Edisto Inlet at the moment,' Don continues. 'They must head north in two days' time. Because of the mobile ice-floes and the lateness of the season I have asked them if they would fly you out with their helicopters. They are happy to help. In fact, they are ready to fly tomorrow morning.'

'Copy that Don.' Greg pauses for a moment. 'That option aside, I calculate our arrival at Edisto Inlet to be on 27 February. Repeat 27 February.'

'That is too late for safety, Greg. Will you be ready to fly tomorrow morning?'

'Suggest we sched. tomorrow morning at 8 am. Over.'

'Will you be ready to fly tomorrow morning?' Don asks urgently.

'Suggest we sched. tomorrow morning at 8 am,' Greg repeats. 'Over.'

'Copy that.' The radio is silent. 'By the way, congratulations from all of us here. Ship signing out.'

Greg stands up.

'What about that then?' he asks. 'Bit of a surprise.'

'Don's obviously feeling the pressure,' says Chris.

'We've got no idea what's going on down there,' says Jonathan. 'Mobile ice conditions could mean anything.'

'Could mean a bad case of paranoia.'

'Or it could mean the pack-ice has drifted back in again.'

'Well, let's have dinner and talk about it.'

Inside the pyramid, we are tense. We realise that we have achieved our goal only by making the most of our opportunities. Greenpeace's guarantee of our safe return to the *Allan And Vi Thistlethwayte* is an offer we cannot refuse. Psychologically though, none of us is ready for the social and physical confines of the boat—except Glenn, who is more than ready because of his damaged foot. Greg and Chris feel that to accept Greenpeace's help would detract from what is already an exceptional expedition: a small team managing to pull off an outrageous feat without assistance. Lyle is ambivalent. He is fired up to enjoy the ski down, but he is anxious to get back to his family as soon as he can. Jonathan, as always, sees the practicalities of both options. I am mindful of frostbite. None of us has the right to deprive Glenn of his chance of a painless journey back to the ship. His injury does not cripple him, but if we are forced to travel in bad weather his frostbite could easily worsen and cost him his foot or, if things really go against us, his life. We must never forget how unforgiving Antarctica can be. Though we have differences of opinion, there is no argument. We all see we must accept our chance to escape.

Later, when I curl up in my sleeping bag, my mind races over the implications of the radio message. If the weather is fine tomorrow and the winds are not too strong, this will be my last night on the ice.

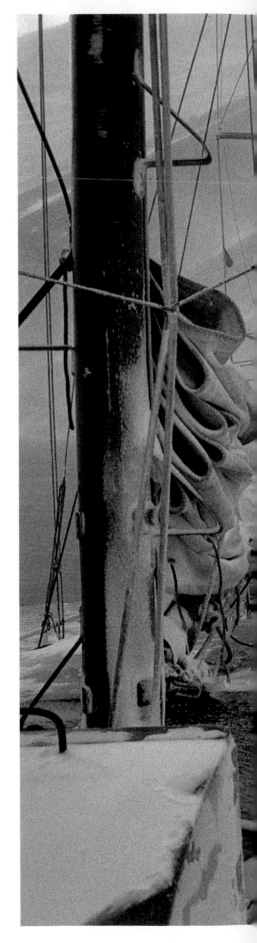

During our absence, life at Cape Hallet has not been all sunshine and penguins.

It's Moments Like These

IT'S MOMENTS LIKE THESE

'I'd let reason lapse a bit so that I could go for the summit, and now I was paying the price. And I felt really guilty and angry with myself, because I knew that I'd become a liability to the expedition if I couldn't walk, if I couldn't ski, if I couldn't get back to the coast.'

GLENN SINGLEMAN

Saturday, 20 February 1988

It is 6.30 am and already there are sounds of great activity outside. Half an hour ago I heard Greg call out to the crunching of feet in the snow, 'What's it like out there?'

'Clear skies…almost windless…and incredibly beautiful.'

'A perfect helicopter day?'

'Yeah.'

And so I sat up, slipped a pen into my sleeping bag so that the ink would be warm enough to flow onto the page, hunted for my gloves, pulled on my jacket and vest, then reached for my diary and began to write.

Beside me Lyle is also scribbling madly. I suppose that like me he is trying to capture impressions of the last few days before we are whisked away from here. After a fitful sleep through the coldest night yet, last night's conversation, and the decision we reached, seems unbelievable. But, like every part of our Antarctic trip, nothing is sure until it is achieved. Although the weather is clear now, by the time the chopper is due to depart it may be cloudy again. Cloud seems to be characteristic of this valley, this haven of soft snow and almost windless skies. We were spellbound by our first view of the cirque of mountains at the head of the Man O'War, but since then we have had only tantalising glimpses through the clouds of magnificent fairy-tale cliffs, the lower ramparts of those unknown peaks.

Greg unzips the door of the tent and passes in bowls of coffee. Behind him the sun shines white on the snowy peaks against an empty blue sky. Soon, perhaps, that emptiness will be filled absurdly enough by the tiny dot of a helicopter.

Outside, Jonathan is banging his boots together to dislodge snow from the treads. Snow flies off them into our tent.

'Jonathan,' I call out, 'if you do that through ninety degrees, the snow won't land in our tent.'

'If you get up it won't be a problem,' says Greg sharply.

'This is a vital moment of the expedition,' I retort, 'to be captured while it happens.'

Jonathan turns sideways and continues smashing his boots together. A moment later he cries. 'Jesus Christ! Look at this!'

He steps forward and pokes a boot through the door. The toe is shattered like an egg shell. These boots are designed for the lowest temperatures

During the coldest night we spent on the continent Jonathan's mountaineering boots froze, becoming brittle enough to crack them when he banged them together to remove some snow.

Previous page: Bad weather makes our retreat down the Tucker Glacier seem endless.

164

The weather is perfect for our first day of skiing back towards the coast. Jonathan and Lincoln head down the Man O'War Glacier towards Mt Achilles — Glenn is no more than a small dot on the glacier.

mountaineers are likely to encounter, and yet last night the plastic became brittle enough to crack.

'I knew it was cold last night. Must have been −30° or −35ᵘC. Imagine if this had happened on the top of the mountain! Instant frostbite, and up there that could've cost me my life.'

'Or at least made you blur the summit photos.'

Minutes later, two bowls of porridge are handed in, followed by Jonathan and Greg.

'What if you go with Glenn?' Greg asks me. 'Might as well look after your feet as well.'

I shrug, but I am excited by the prospect. Only now do I realise how much I have been suppressing the worry that we might be trapped on the continent for the winter. 'My feet will be okay. I'm happy to go, but I'm also happy to stay. What about you, Lyle?'

'I'd rather be last to leave with Greg.'

'What if there's only one flight?' I ask, remembering his concern about being away from his family for the winter.

'Even so, we'll be able to travel much lighter. I reckon we'll get out in time.'

'What about Chris?' I ask. 'Or you, Jonathan?'

'Physically I feel better than when we left the ship, so it makes sense that I stay,' Jonathan says. 'You heard how keen Chris is to ski all the way back to the ship. I'd like to get some shots of the chopper taking off, anyway.'

So I am it. 'Sure,' I say. 'I'll go.'

'Well, you'd better get organised,' Greg says with the hint of a smile. Perhaps this is his way of getting me to put away my diary. Time to finish my porridge and get up, and—how bizarre—time to get ready for the helicopter.

Outside, there appears to be no reason why the helicopter cannot land today, and so we are puzzled during the 8 am radio sched. when Don talks casually about irrelevant matters without mentioning the flight plan. Again we can hear him clearly, but he has difficulty reading our replies. Finally he mentions that the low clouds, fresh snow, and a stiff breeze are unlikely to change, but that he has a sched. with Greenpeace at midday just in case. We deduce that the conditions at Cape Hallett make flying out of the question.

'Why couldn't he bloody well say so?' asks Greg. 'He's meant to be an experienced radio operator. How the hell are we supposed to know what the weather's like down there?'

Greg's reaction is more vehement than the situation calls for. The strain of our journey is beginning to tell on us all. Glenn looks despondent but says nothing. Ahead of him is at least one more day of pain.

Chris slaps him on the back. 'Just take your survival gear. We'll put the rest in one of the pulks.'

'Okay,' he says. 'Thanks.'

'And then get out of here. We'll catch you up.'

Glenn laughs halfheartedly. 'That's for sure.'

The helicopter will be nothing more than a promise until we are deafened by the roar of its strange wings. The world of machines and other people is too far away for us to be really disappointed if it does not arrive. The weather is perfect, and today we face the steepest part of our long run down the glaciers.

Greg sits silently on his pack and pulls his gaiters down over his mountaineering boots. He picks up his pack, clips a rope from his harness to the small pulk and then starts walking along Glenn's ski tracks.

For the first time since leaving the ship we have dismantled the camp and are ready to leave before 9 am. I wait while Jonathan takes a few last

The morning after our return to base camp we wait for a radio message from *Greenpeace*. The idea of a helicopter evacuation, mooted the night before, is a necessary evil, but still hard for us to accept.

photos of this magnificent campsite, and of Lyle and Chris tying the pyramid tent on top of their pulk.

Because the snow is excellent for skiing, Jonathan and I soon overtake Greg. He seems particularly unexcited by the chore of walking and he waves us past without a word. An hour later we catch up to Glenn.

'Still hurts,' he says, obviously in better spirits now that he is making reasonable progress. 'But skiing is a hell of a lot better than walking in my climbing boots.'

We take photographs while Glenn moves ahead and pulls out his movie camera. Behind the small dots of Greg, Chris and Lyle, the mass of Mt Minto rises above the unnamed peak to the north of Thistlethwayte Pass. After only three days of struggling with a vertical landscape, we are again creatures of the vast, gently sloping Antarctic glaciers. Once more our mountain seems to tower above us to unattainable heights.

The skis slide smoothly over the snow, and the pulk is a comfortable weight. It is a formula for contentment. Shortly before noon we stop for another radio sched. with Don, only to hear that the weather is still bad on the coast. Ahead of us, the Man O'War drops suddenly and takes a sharp turn to the south. The beautiful mountains which surround Mt Minto like sentries will disappear behind the smaller snow peaks which are closer to us, as soon as we drop down the slope. This fabulous panorama is worth one last leisurely appreciation over lunch.

Chris and Lyle are irritated because the pyramid tent on top of their load makes the pulk tip over constantly. Spirits rise at the sight of food, though we have the usual problems of fingers going numb from the cold as we attempt to cut cheese, spread jam, and undo the knotted plastic bags of dried fruit. The sun is warm enough to begin drying the sweat from my inner boots, but the slightest breeze is literally freezing. I sit cross-legged with my feet tucked up in my lap to stop the wind whipping through my socks.

Greg sets off straight after lunch while Glenn and Chris film us packing up. We launch ourselves down the slope with gusto, having forgotten what a joy it is to cover ground quickly. Soon we catch up to Greg who breaks through up to his ankles with every step, and finds hauling the small pulk hard work. We attach his pulk behind ours until the snow conditions, which are ideal for us, improve for him as well.

At 3.30 pm we reach the spot where we camped six days before. I want to keep moving but Jonathan suggests we stop for a few minutes' rest. Greg stops with us. In the stillness which replaces our puffing and the slide of our skis, we hear a cry. We look at each other in alarm, but say nothing in case our speech drowns out the message. Another shout drifts through the still air, but we cannot distinguish the words.

'Must be a cry for help,' says Jonathan at last. 'I'll go back and see what's going on.' He unclips from our pulk.

'Signal us if you need us,' says Greg.

We sit on our pulks and watch Jonathan ski back along our tracks until he disappears into the slight hollow we trudged out of, grunting, ten minutes before. We hear another shout but cannot decide if this is a call for assistance or an instruction to stay put. I unclip from the pulk and get ready to ski back. Immediately a figure crests the rise, followed a minute later by another and then by two more.

'That's all of them,' says Greg, getting up and continuing to walk south.

The first person to reach me is Glenn.

'What happened?' I ask as soon as he is close enough to hear me.

Lincoln and Greg find pulling the small pulk slow, hard work.

'Chris wants you to stop so he can record the 4 pm radio sched.'

Jonathan skis up to us, and smiles. 'I should have waited here,' he says, 'But better to be sure.'

'We should catch up with Greg,' I say. 'He's got the radio battery in his pocket.'

We clip onto the pulk and set off again. Greg is almost out of sight but our skis give us the speed to catch up and call out to him to stop. Chris reaches us just in time but the sched. tells us nothing new. Don says it is still windy and heavily overcast at Cape Hallett. I wonder if the others share my fear that the bad weather may soon move inland.

The long downhill run which I had been looking forward to is not as smooth as I had hoped, because the wind has formed irregular patches of ice on the surface of the snow. Jonathan and I draw ahead once again. When the slope begins to ease off, Jonathan convinces me we should stop to refuel. It is still another 10 kilometres to our main depot, and if we are to make the most of tomorrow we must reach that depot tonight. The leftovers of lunch are packed on our pulk, so by the time the others catch up to us we have chocolate, dried fruit, nuts, biscuits and cheese ready. Unfortunately our water-bottles are either empty or the contents have frozen. We shall have to tolerate our thirst until we reach camp. We eat everything which is readily accessible, then Greg and Chris swap places. Greg is tired of walking, and Chris is sick of hauling the pulk with the pyramid tent strapped on top.

Greg skis off with delight, leading a breathless Lyle. Jonathan and I pack away the scraps of our snack and follow. Soon the others disappear into the shade of the peak which rises above the glacier to the west. As Jonathan and I ski towards the shadow I see a lake shimmering across to the left. A few moments of admiration pass before I remember it is far too cold for any expanse of liquid water to exist. It must be a mirage. Jonathan notices it as well, so I am not seeing things.

'I've seen mirages in the desert,' I say. 'But never on ice.'

'It's a first for me, too'.

Our marvel is short lived. When we draw closer to the border between light and shade, I can see that the mirage is no more than the shadow of a summit cast onto the glacier beyond a sunlit ridge in the foreground. From the shadow's edge we can see the darkness stretching down the face of the mountain, over the glacier, and ending at the limits of what was our mirage.

We hurry across the mountain's cold shadow. Ahead of us we can see the layer of cloud that floats above the Tucker, no doubt an extension of the clouds which keep *Greenpeace*'s helicopter shipbound at the coast. The shaded slope drops away beneath us and, as we watch, Chris and Glenn reappear as tiny dots on the sunlit slope below. The cold encourages us to work up a good rhythm, and soon we catch up to them. The four of us reassure each other that camp cannot be more than half an hour further on.

Glenn is managing well, though his gait has become more and more like a shuffle. I can understand why, for my foot is also hurting. Now that the slope has levelled off I imitate his shuffle by keeping my foot flat on the ski. Even so, the binding squeezes my toes every time I ease my weight from the ski to slide it forward.

We reach the top of another steep slope and to our dismay the expanse of snow stretching ahead of us is empty. There is no sign of Greg and Lyle, nor of our camp.

'Maybe half an hour from here, then,' Jonathan mutters.

The tracks of Greg and Lyle, who have skied ahead, appear to vanish in the clouds flowing up the valley of the Tucker Glacier.

The cloud mass which fills the Tucker overflows and slides up the glacier towards us. Soon we are swallowed by it, and so we ski steadily down the slope surrounded by the peculiar formless pink of this sunset cloud. It is impossible to judge our speed or the angle of the terrain ahead of us. The tracks left by Lyle and Greg and their sled are our only reassurance that other beings share this misty existence.

The half-hour passes, and perhaps another one after that, yet still there is no sign nor sound of the camp. We crest a small rise and see dark shapes only a hundred metres in front of us. It is the big wooden sledge, with Lyle and Greg huddled over their pulk as they unlash it and unpack the radio. We ski down to them.

'Sched. time?' I ask, and Greg nods.

Eight o'clock. I unclip my boots from the ski-bindings. The toes of my left foot are burning with pain. All I want to do is crawl into my sleeping bag, but first we have to pitch the tents and guy them together firmly. Jonathan begins tuning the radio.

While my fingers fumble with the tent poles, I turn my thoughts to our progress—anything to take my mind away from this intolerable cold. It has been a long day, but there is the satisfaction of having travelled 30 kilometres. If we can maintain this daily average, and if the weather is kind to us, we shall be back at the ship in another four or five days. The amount of gear we must collect at this depot is horrifying, and I am amazed that we managed to drag it all up here. Maybe we will take a week to reach the coast, which means arriving perilously close to Don's 1 March deadline. With cloud settling around us, it seems that the chances of any helicopter flights are shrinking. We all know the *Greenpeace* has a tight schedule, with a planned visit to the French base at Dumont d'Urville before returning to New Zealand to resupply. Those on board will not be able to wait more than one or two more days at Cape Hallett for good flying weather. After

that we shall be on our own. I smile at my thoughts. We are very much on our own already.

Jonathan stands up from the radio. 'Still stormy at Cape Hallett,' he calls out, then he bends over and disconnects the battery.

Sunday, 21 February

A cold morning on the Man O'War Glacier where it is joined by the Fitch Glacier. The slight breeze blowing down the valley from the mountains makes my long underwear and fibrepile jacket feel useless. As quickly as I can, I rummage in our pulk for my water-bottle so that Jonathan and Glenn can fill it for me. I hurl it unceremoniously through the door of the pyramid then dive back inside the tent I share with Chris. Showers of frost dust me when I bump the tent walls in my hurry to crawl back into my sleeping bag. From the low temperatures of this depot on the glacier, one would not guess we dropped 1200 metres yesterday.

Jonathan tunes up the radio, and we hear Don's voice. Good reception.

'The sea-ice is beginning to freeze,' says Don. 'And soon we'll be frozen into Willett Cove. We'll have to consider moving out of here today. Don't worry though — we'll be able to pick you up, but we have to move into open water. Otherwise we might well be here for the winter.'

Jonathan calls the *Greenpeace* who are also on frequency, and tells them our weather conditions.

In reply comes a question. 'Can you see how thick the cloud layer is, and how high it is above the Tucker?'

Greg takes the mike. 'There is a thin layer of cloud several hundred metres above the Tucker. Repeat. A thin layer of cloud several hundred metres above the Tucker.'

'Copied that. Would one flight be of any use? Repeat, would one flight be of any use? Over.'

'Yes. One flight would be of great assistance. To lift out one man and equipment we no longer need.'

The big sledge moves easily down the hill, a gentle reintroduction to the torture of hauling it. Today Chris, Greg and I share the pain of its weight. For the first time, Lyle gives his skis to someone else and walks with a pulk behind him, but this is not why he looks miserable all day. When we stop for lunch he tells us his feet are numb with cold because his mukluk boots were frozen when he squeezed into them this morning. I suggest he wears his mountaineering boots instead.

'They are too small for comfortable walking,' he says. 'I think they will cripple me.'

'Tight boots is one reason why my toe got frostbitten,' says Glenn. 'They restrict blood circulation. You're much better off wearing your mukluks, even if they are frozen. So long as you can still wriggle your toes.'

'I can wriggle them, but they feel like blocks of ice.'

'They should be all right.'

Glenn is in better spirits today because he is coping much better with the pain of his frostbite. Soft snow slows us down, especially since we are hauling the big sledge again, which means Glenn is able to keep pace with the rest of us.

Our different reactions to our predicament, now that the mountain is climbed and we have only more hard work ahead of us, makes me realise

Left: **We must concentrate on conserving our strength, staying correctly oriented in the mist, and trying to predict the course of the weather.**

171

the cumulative value of my previous expeditions. Jonathan, Greg and I have already served the apprenticeship of adding mental anguish to physical pain. We have learnt that in a crisis mental energy cannot be spared for depression and anger. We must concentrate on conserving our strength, staying correctly orientated in the mist, and trying to predict the course of the weather. Visibility and snow conditions have been worsening as the day progresses, and we have a depot to find somewhere in the white murkiness ahead of us. By late afternoon we are skiing into gently falling snow.

Chris, on the long rope out in front of us, has been steadily running out of energy during the last hour. He has had a difficult job trying to work out the best route without anything visible ahead of him for scale. Several times he has fallen over after losing his balance in small dips hidden by the all-pervasive whiteness. Behind us, Lyle has struggled all day through soft snow without skis, Glenn has managed to tolerate the pain in his foot, and the rest of us are just plain tired. Greg uses the radio sched. as an excuse to stop. None of us complain even though we are a couple of kilometres short of our depot. The snow begins to fall thick and heavy while we pitch the tents. We would not have found the depot in this at any rate.

Greg turns to me and says, 'Maybe you and I should cook tonight.'

There is more to this statement than the meaning of his words. Greg is falling back on the depth of our experience. More than once we have had to struggle for our lives together against hostile conditions, and have proved that we can rely on each other. We may be heading into one more such battle now. Our skills have stood the test, and by taking on the chore of cooking we will let our companions get as much rest as they can.

'I was thinking the same thing,' I say. 'And if a chopper does come, I thought I should stay behind.' My voice is heavy as I speak, because the

The Antarctic summer is very short, and the increased cold warns us of winter's steady approach. At night, to avoid going outside, we pass food from the pyramid kitchen tent on a snow shovel.

pain in my amputated toes makes me wish this particular adventure was over.

'Send Chris out with Glenn, you mean?'

'Yeah.'

He nods. 'They've had enough.'

I laugh. 'Haven't we all?'

As soon as the pyramid is guyed out I shove the cook box inside and begin the laborious process of melting snow. Soon it is cosy and warm, and the walls drip with moisture as my wet clothes begin to dry out. Cooking can be a joy, but not at this pace. It is well after midnight when we fill the last of our water-bottles and switch off the stoves. Five hours remain before we must wake and light them again.

Monday, 22 February

Two days ago the idea of helicopters whisking us back to the ship seemed incredible, and now the prospect has slipped back once more into the realm of fantasy. Outside it is snowing, and because everything is so white, I cannot judge the visibility; it may be a hundred metres or even a kilometre, but certainly the conditions put helicopter flights out of the question. We are as much on our own now as we have ever been. Even more so, because yesterday we did not find our depot of food and fuel, even though it is only 2 kilometres away. Food is important in these low temperatures, but fuel is absolutely vital. Without kerosene to feed our stoves we cannot melt snow—a life-and-death matter in this place where all the water is frozen.

If we cannot find our depot in this white-out we shall be faced with the decision of continuing the hunt, or pushing on and hoping we can find the next one, 19 kilometres further down the valley. It is essential for us to

Bad weather on the Tucker Glacier. We are amazed to think that less than two weeks ago dusk did not exist here. In another month there will be the darkness of night.

find that depot because we do not have enough fuel or food left to reach the one further to the south, and if this weather worsens into a full-scale blizzard, we might be trapped for days or even a week. Whatever the weather, we are in for a long hard day.

I groan inwardly when I pull on my mountaineering boots because I know their coldness will suck the heat out of my feet within minutes and leave them numb. Then I shall spend the rest of the day either waiting for them to thaw or wishing the throbbing in my toes would stop.

Outside, when we are ready to go, Greg makes a statement. 'Listen you guys, I reckon we are getting ourselves into a really serious situation. I've been awake since 5.30, and now it's quarter to ten. That's four hours — too bloody long. This storm could last for days but we can't let it stop us from finding our depots. We haven't got time to stand around, unless we want to spend the winter here. That's the way we're heading. Yet you stand there like stunned mullets.'

Nobody says anything, for we all see the truth in his words. Our energy levels are down after weeks of pushing ourselves onwards. Each morning we lose more of the drive which at first made us jump out of our sleeping bags and rush off up the glacier while half asleep. To avoid being daunted by the size of our undertaking, we have trained our minds to face only the tasks which immediately confront us. I suppose that Greg has crystalised in our minds the shortcomings of that attitude. After yesterday's poor progress in deteriorating weather, we are beginning to allow small tasks to absorb too much of our energies. By not facing up to our situation we risk being overwhelmed by it. Our path is leading us towards a winter on the continent, and only by a combined and determined effort can we avoid that fate.

'Well let's get out of here,' says Chris.

Earlier this morning, when the clouds lifted briefly, visibility down the valley was good enough to allow Greg to walk 100 metres in the right direction. Now the clouds have dropped over us again, and all we can see is whiteness. I walk along the trail of Greg's footsteps. Soon I am overtaken by Greg and Jonathan pulling the other yellow pulk. I follow 50 metres behind them, shouting 'Left!' or 'Right!' to stop Greg deviating from his course. Ahead of us the whiteness is a curtain we are unable to brush aside.

Again walking is hard work because the snow is soft. Glenn overtakes me, proving that he will not let frostbite slow him down. I imagine that his feet are as cold as mine, and he may not be quite so vigorous when they warm up and he begins to feel the pain once more. But by the same token, nor may I.

Through the yellowness of my storm goggles, I get occasional glimpses of the eastern wall of this valley. Nothing firm: only the cracks and squares of crevasses and ice-cliffs giving only random details of the huge snow faces of the mountains flanking us.

'Right! Right!' I shout, but Greg only waves a ski-stock and continues towards the edge of the glacier. He must have decided to head for the depot we left near the junction of the Cache 'n' Carry Glacier. I have difficulty matching the pace of the three on skis in front of me. Behind, Lyle and Chris are not gaining on me, an indication that the sled must still be too heavy.

I crest a small rise and see that Greg has left the others and has skied towards a crevasse. Presumably he is wondering whether this is the site of our depot, but he turns and heads back to Jonathan and Glenn. Ten minutes later the three of them stop, and as I approach I can see that they have found our supplies. The tracks of Greg's skis lead straight to it.

'How's that for a bullseye ?' he shouts back to me.

Now that we have reached the depot we must make some drastic reductions in weight. The extra load here will only slow us down, and we cannot afford to lose any more time. In a plastic barrel we cache extra food, a rope, and some climbing gear, which will be useful to anyone coming this way before the cache is swallowed by the glacier.

While we sort the loads, Lyle and Chris arrive looking annoyed and obviously weary already.

'Bit heavy, is it?'

'More than a bit,' says Lyle. 'Let's dump the whole bloody lot here.'

But rather than that, Lyle and I saw the sledge in two with the ice-saw. It is a simple task except that the teflon runners refuse at first to give way to the large teeth of the saw. We tie the heavy box of film gear onto the shorter of the two pieces and stand the other part above the cache as a marker. As we lift it into place we agree that this piece alone must weigh over 20 kilos. Meanwhile, Greg begins to burn our rubbish in a shallow hole in the snow.

Chris and Glenn, who were filming the remodelling of the sled, turn their attention to Greg.

'How do you feel about doing this?' Chris asks. 'Considering we have carried all our rubbish with us so far, and intended to take it back to the ship and away from Antarctica?'

Greg pours a little more kerosene on the fire, then stands up, 'I'm not happy about it, but we're now in a really serious situation. We're in the middle of a white-out, and we have 19 kilometres to go before reaching our next depot. It's almost noon, but we must make that depot before this storm worsens into a blizzard and we can't move. Burning the rubbish is better than just leaving it here, and we'll still be carrying all our tins and other stuff that won't burn.' He pauses and pokes the fire.

We have a depot to find somewhere in the white murkiness ahead of us.

'It's better than leaving all of us, and everything else', I interject. 'I'm sure you'll agree with that.'

'Yeah,' says Chris, 'I think I do.'

As the person walking, I am the slow link in the chain today, so I leave the others to clean up. I set a course for the dark shape of rock-cliffs high on a peak on the eastern wall of the valley. This section of our route was crevasse-free on our upward journey, which means I am able to plod through the snow without any particular fears. When clouds thicken enough to obscure the buttresses I keep staring at the spot where they disappeared, waiting for another glimpse, while keeping my feet moving mechanically. Nothing interrupts my rhythm. It is strange, plodding into the nothingness of the blizzard, not watching my feet, staring at white clouds yellowed by my goggles in the hope of a landmark appearing somewhere.

The hard work of snow-plodding, hauling a pulk and carrying a pack is enough to make me work up a sweat and a thirst. I stop to have a drink of water. When the others overtake me I let them get a short way ahead so I can enjoy the silence and being alone. I can see how the new shortened sled runs well on the flat and downhill, but Lyle and Chris still struggle to drag it uphill. A long gentle rise makes us all puff and grunt. We need a rest at the top of the slope and it is time for the next radio sched. so we stop for lunch.

'The advantage of this sort of weather is that it keeps you moving,' I remark.

Glenn agrees, but without enthusiasm.

Greg seems in good spirits now that we are making reasonable progress again. He talks about Manly in April when the surf is best. He plots an imaginary route along the Corso there, culminating in the fish and chip shop on the corner, and then a surf at the beach.

When I give rein to my fantasies they head for the dry air of the Blue Mountains of New South Wales, where the warm sun draws oils from the eucalypts and other plants. Or I think of meeting Barbara on the wharf, or being with her anywhere, listening to her talk, learning about the excitements of her pregnancy. All these things could not be further from the middle reaches of the Tucker Glacier.

By using a block of chocolate as a chopping board I am able to cut the cheese into rough slices rather than the crumbling chunks of recent lunchtimes. It is not as cold down here only a few hundred metres above sea level and the cheese is not quite as frozen. We eat everything edible from the supplies I collected from the depot: a bag of pecan nuts, two blocks of chocolate, two packets of biscuits, a block of cheese, a bag of dates and one of dried apples. Our hunger is a frenzy for the essential fuel the cold and the work demand. We do not have enough water to drink because Chris and Glenn's bottles froze solid outside their tent door last night.

We push on quickly. Jonathan spots a dark object, an unusual sight on the endless white glacier. He and Greg make a detour to see what it is and discover Chris's Therm-a-rest mattress which dropped off the sled almost two weeks ago.

'A great omen,' I shout from behind, and we continue our slog.

The visibility has improved a little now, but our pace is slowed by a long, rising traverse around a hill. Several times the ski tracks disintegrate beneath me and I fall into one crevasse after another. None are wide enough to do more than frighten me and make me struggle for firm snow again. The others skied across them all, unaware of their existence. Once past these potential dangers I catch up to the others looking at the map.

The wide junction of the Staircase Glacier opens out before us, and somewhere on its flat expanse is our cache. There is food and fuel there, of course, but most important to Chris and Glenn, the cache contains the exposed film stock. The cloud level has lifted to reveal sunset on the peaks across the Tucker. High above us are bands of blue sky. It looks to me like a sign of clearing weather, but Greg says conditions might stay unchanged for days. We haul our loads for another twenty minutes then stop and look at the map again. I groan inwardly when I see that the pencilled triangle marking our depot is on the far side of the glacier. Although it is almost 7 pm we all agree to push on. If clouds drop down to glacier level or a blizzard blows in the morning it might be impossible to find the cache.

Greg and Jonathan start off, immediately followed by Lyle and Chris. I remain watching them and gathering my strength. I have little energy to spare for anything. The others drop down into a flat-bottomed gully, moving in close single file. In the poor light, I can distinguish only their outlines. Four pairs of arms and ski-stocks move in time to the slow gait of their skis, like a giant caterpillar slowly making its way across the snowfield. The ski-stocks form the tips of its jointed legs; our cache is its destination. The shuffling, creaking noise is strange enough to belong to such a creature.

I sit there for a few minutes longer until their sounds are replaced by silence. The scene is empty of everything except beauty. My sweat begins to freeze, so I stand and move on. Glenn is not visible behind me, and I presume he is still descending the long gentle slope above the gully.

As I sink into the snow up to my ankles with every step I accept that there is no chance of catching up to the others in these conditions. I look from side to side on the chance that the others have missed the depot, but see nothing except the blankness of the glacier and the vague shapes of the mountains beyond. The clouds continue to lift and disperse, but the soft light of dusk is upon us. I am amazed to think that less than two weeks ago

On reaching the depot, we decide we do not have the strength to haul our sledges as well as the extra load. Reluctantly, we cut our wooden sledge (left) in two and leave half of it with a cache of spare food and climbing equipment. Greg sets fire to our burnable rubbish (above).

dusk did not exist here. In another month there will be the darkness of night.

Ironically, I am too tired to devote all my energies to trudging. My mind has had enough and wants to drift off to thoughts of other places. I combat the weariness by counting my steps, a simple mechanism which directs my strength to my muscles. I glance up and see that the others have stopped. The depot, I wonder? But Greg skis across to the left and stares in different directions. I stop counting at 1000, with 100 metres to go. When I reach the sleds, Jonathan is connecting the radio, and Greg and Chris are unrolling the wire for the aerial. Lyle empties his pack and heads off across the Tucker.

'Where's he going?'

'The depot's over there,' says Greg.

'Where?'

He points, using the mountains behind as landmarks, but I can see nothing but white snow, fading in the half-light of evening.

'There's a pile of snow there,' continues Greg. 'I hope it's the depot. Lyle will be mighty pissed off if it isn't.'

'Eight-thirty,' says Jonathan. 'I'll try to make contact.'

Pulling the big sledge proves to be impossibly slow, even when it is lightly laden.

We did not manage to call at 4 pm, even though we postponed lunch to limit ourselves to one break in the afternoon. When we did stop, we were so hungry that everything besides eating seemed irrelevant. Except the cold, of course. The cold is always with us.

Jonathan tunes into *Greenpeace*.

'Mountain party, mountain party, mountain party...

Jonathan gives *Greenpeace* our position. Our reception of them and of Don on the *Thistlethwayte* is good but they have difficulty deciphering our signal.

'Weather clearing,' says Jonathan. 'Weather clearing.'

'Suggest next sched. at 0400 hours. We shall try to fly before the wind picks up again. Do you copy? Over.'

'Roger, roger, roger.'

'Did you get that, Don?' asks the voice of the *Greenpeace* radio operator.

'No, *Greenpeace*.'

'I'll try again. Mountain party, next sched. 0400 hours; 0400 hours next sched. Do you copy? Over.'

'Roger, roger, roger.'

'That was a roger, wasn't it, Don?'

'Affirmative.'

'We shall try to fly tomorrow morning. There is not enough light now, and there won't be appreciably more until 4 am. Do you copy?'

'Roger, roger, roger. You will fly in the morning if conditions are good.'

'Copy you well now, Jonathan,' says Don. 'Do you copy him, *Greenpeace*?'

'Yes, copied that. Suggest we switch to 540 frequency now in case this frequency does not work tomorrow.'

Jonathan battles with tuning the radio, and with the frustration of receiving clear signals while not being received in turn. I continue pitching the tents, my mind buzzing with the news. This morning we were seriously thinking about being forced to spend the winter here, and now we are faced with helicopter flights tomorrow.

Glenn skis into camp. I walk across and hug him. 'Jonathan's just been talking to *Greenpeace*. They're going to fly at 4 am.'

Glenn smiles but says nothing. He knows better than the rest of us the feeling of disappointment.

'Where is Lyle?' he asks suddenly.

I point to the small figure still walking out across the Tucker, before I paraphrase the last words of Scott's companion, Captain Oates: 'He may be some time.'

'Where the hell is he going?'

'The dump's out there.'

'I can't see it.'

'Me neither, but Greg and Jonathan reckon it's there.'

I pick up a pair of skis from beside the sled and use them to guy out the pyramid tent. When the tents are pitched, I hear a shout—Lyle has reached the depot.

Tuesday, 23 February

The alarm bleeps at 3.45 am. I fumble for my watch among the icy gloves and caps on the floor of the tent and switch it off.

'Quarter to four, Jonathan.'

'Okay.' I hear him lighting the stove.

There is a rustle of nylon from the pyramid.

'A perfect day,' announces Chris.

'Yeah?'

'Not a cloud.'

I snuggle into my sleeping bag and try to stop my hopes from rising. There might be a storm blowing on the coast. One flight would make so much difference. Glenn could get out, and we could get rid of all the film gear and most of the climbing equipment. The rest of the Tucker would be a cruise. I stop those thoughts and concentrate on the coziness of my sleeping bag, knowing I shall have to relinquish it soon.

'Five minutes, Jonathan.'

'Okay.' His voice changes tone. 'Mountain party calling *Greenpeace*. Mountain party calling *Greenpeace*. Do you copy? Over.'

There is no reply. Tension increases as Jonathan tries again. Still no reply. Then finally: '*Greenpeace* calling mountain party. Come in please.'

'Mountain party reading you loud and clear. Go ahead.'

'What are the conditions this morning? Over.'

'Perfect visibility,' says Jonathan. 'Perfect visibility.'

'Copy that. Estimated wind speed?'

'Greg?'

Next to me Greg screws up his face. 'Five knots,' he says.

'Five knots,' repeats Jonathan.

Not even that, I think.

'Stand by,' crackles the radio. So much depends on *Greenpeace*'s next words.

'We will fly at 0500 hours. Suggest we sched. again at that time. Over.'

'Copied that. You will fly at 0500 hours and we will come up on this frequency at that time.'

'Affirmative. *Greenpeace* signing out.'

'Mountain party signing off.'

I let out a yelp of delight, which settles into the silence beyond the camp.

'Well,' begins Greg, 'I guess we'd better get up.' Yet we continue to lie in our sleeping bags, soaking up the last of their warmth.

'Chris?' Greg calls out. 'If the chopper can take two people, how about you go with Glenn?'

'I thought Lincoln was going to go.'

'Change of plan.'

'Why?'

Following page left: Lyle stands by our makeshift helipad and holds a tent bag aloft as a wind sock — no wind. The helicopter prepares to land.

Following page right: The helicopter lands at the precise moment the morning sun touches our campsite. As the machine drops slowly over the glacier, clouds of snow are blown over us.

'Just how it is.'

'Want to get rid of the film crew in one hit?'

'That's right.'

A pause...'Okay.'

Greg looks out the door. 'Long time before the sun reaches the camp. Looks bloody cold out there.'

'Bloody cold enough in here,' I mutter.

Greg gets out of his bag and dresses with customary speed. He pulls on his boots and steps outside, then I follow his lead. Already Greg is shovelling snow 30 metres south of the tents. When I go over to help him he suggests we use one of the empty pulks as a grader. This works well, with Greg at one end and me at the other. The effort of dragging the sled through the loose snow is welcome because it warms us in the early morning cold. Greg wears the scowl which has become a familiar expression every morning, but I am still not sure whether he is just waking up or silently cursing everyone else's slowness. I can hear Glenn wailing as he tries to squeeze his sore foot into his frozen inner boots. Lyle, too, is battling with his boots while Chris rushes around packing his gear. Jonathan is inside with the roaring stove: 'Making a hot drink,' he announces. 'And keeping the radio warm.'

By 5 am we have cleared the surface snow away from an area 15 metres square. Greg goes to the radio while I quickly pack my sleeping bag. My hands and feet are cold, and the sun across the glacier is a long way from us. In the clear morning sunlight I can easily make out the snow pyramid which marked the depot, half a kilometre away. I marvel that Jonathan and Greg spotted it in the gloom of last night's clearing storm.

I strain to catch the words of the sched. and hear all that I need to.

'We shall fly from the *Greenpeace* in ten minutes and expect to arrive at your camp at 5.30. Over.'

'Roger,' says Greg casually. 'We have cleared a landing pad for you.'

It seems unbelievable that this can be happening. Even if Greenpeace can manage only one flight, our sleds will be hundreds of kilograms lighter and we will no longer be slowed down by one man walking. Best of all, we shall be able to stop worrying about the condition of Glenn's feet.

Time has returned to our world once more. We have an appointment with a helicopter in twenty minutes. Apart from our radio scheds, this is

Greg and Glenn (right) introduce themselves to Gary Dukes (left), the helipilot.

the first occasion in weeks, even months, when our timetabling depends upon someone else. It is a strange feeling for, though we hurry to pack up everything, the minutes seem to drag.

'There it is!'

I rush for my camera bag before looking up.

The helicopter is a tiny dot high above the Tucker. Except for clouds and the avalanche ten days ago, this is the first moving object we have seen since crossing Football Saddle. We are accustomed to changes happening slowly, which makes the helicopter's arrival feel rushed. It sweeps around us in a broad circle, silhouetted first against the shaded walls of the peaks to the east and then against the sky.

The 'whoop-whoop-whoop' of its rotors slicing the air is precisely the sound we expect to hear, yet the noise seems an intrusion. How much more appropriate to this peaceful continent if the machine were to land and depart without a sound. But the helicopter is an envoy from a different world, one with less room for ideals and dreams than this empty land.

The machine hovers above our tiny campsite, as if to give us a moment to accept its sudden, noisy presence, then drops slowly to the ground in clouds of snow swept up by its rotors. The pilot steps out and walks towards us. We introduce ourselves over the roar of the engine. 'Gary Dukes,' he says, and we shake hands. After the trials and dangers we have endured, it is strange to share this moment of salvation with someone we have never met before.

We lash the dismantled sled and the pyramid tent to the skids, load the rear half of the cabin with boxes of film gear and bags of rubbish, hug Chris and Glenn goodbye, then turn our backs to the clouds of snow blown at us when Gary raises the machine into the air. Within seconds the machine is hundreds of metres away, and half a minute later it is gone.

'Lightweight expedition now, isn't it?' says Lyle, looking at the small mound of gear next to our two dome tents.

'Let's make it even more lightweight by drinking this Milo.' I pour the steaming liquid into our mugs and turn out the stove.

'Thank God we've got rid of the big sled and those film boxes,' says Lyle.

'Not to mention the film crew,' I say, but jokes at their expense lose all value now they have gone.

'We'll be able to sprint down the glacier if the chopper can't make it back,' says Jonathan, passing mugs to Lyle and Greg. 'But I expect that we'll all get out. Conditions are perfect.'

Somehow, the arrival and departure of the helicopter has intensified the silence, and the Tucker Glacier seems more enormous now only four of us remain. What makes me feel most alone is the realisation that our adventure is nearly over.

We load the helicopter as quickly as possible so that Gary will have time to come back for the rest of us.

AGAINST THE WIND

AGAINST THE WIND

'...through the toss'd ranks of mirth and crying,
Hungers, and pains, and each dull passionate mood, —
Quite lost, and all but all forgot, undying,
Comes back the ecstasy of your quietude.'

RUPERT BROOKE, *Hauntings*

Tuesday, 23 February 1988

The glacier slips past beneath us with unbelievable speed. Jonathan reaches across in front of me and snaps a photograph of the crevasse field below. The cockpit is jammed so full of gear that it is difficult for us to move without getting in Gary's way.

The landscape appears make-believe from up here. The Tucker Glacier looks every bit as immense as it felt when we trudged slowly along it. The long parallel lines of hidden crevasses which furrow the surface at the edge of the glacier are occasionally split into dark fissures. From the air, the middle of the glacier is the same flat and featureless expanse it seemed to be when we were manhauling.

Tight-fitting headphones muffle the noise of the engine, but nothing can reduce the helicopter's vibration. I look at the dials covering the front of the cockpit but I cannot work out which one indicates our altitude. The mountain peaks still rise above us, yet we are flying about 2 kilometres above the ice. This new perspective only reinforces my impression of the enormous scale of the continent.

We fly into thin cloud when we round Trigon Bluff and start heading east. The sky above is grey, and gravid with storm clouds. The world beneath turns monochromatic in the diffuse light; details and distances become much harder to judge. This is an instant lesson in how vital good flying conditions are in Antarctica. Back at our campsite, under clear skies and surrounded by sunlit peaks, it seemed inevitable that the chopper would return to take all six of us. Now I can see how a slight deterioration of the weather could mean Greg and Lyle must be left behind. It would be a long and lonely ski, but with minimal loads they could make the journey in three days. Yet the chopper is drawing close to Football Saddle only fifteen minutes after leaving camp. Gary takes the machine across the top of Football Mountain, too far from the saddle for me to spot our cache of gear.

Beyond the saddle, Edisto Inlet is completely free of ice, which has altered the mood of the small bay. The place seems much wilder now, but perhaps this is because the helicopter has broken our connection with wilderness. Already that rapport, which came from having to bend before the wind and the cold, is beginning to disintegrate.

After the long voyage south in our 21-metre schooner, and then our isolated and spartan three week journey inland, the *Greenpeace* seems huge and its array of facilities overwhelming.

Previous page: The jib remains furled as we steer the ship into relentless contrary winds.

The *Greenpeace* with its V-like wake is steaming directly towards us. Gary banks the chopper in a wide turn so that we circle the ship and approach it from the stern. We land on the helipad. Orange-suited figures run to the doors and unlatch them. Hands reach for my seatbelt, unclip it, and help me out of the cockpit. The deck is swaying slightly and the smell of sea air and diesel flood my nostrils. Everything is happening too fast. The man who guides me across to the barrier separating the aft deck from the helipad does not attempt to say anything above the roar of the helicopter. Chris and Glenn are waiting, pointing their microphone and camera at me. I wonder if I look as bewildered as I feel. There appear to be dozens of people on deck, including another film crew. The only familiar face is Peter Malcolm, the second helipilot, whom we met in Sydney many months earlier.

'Culture shock, isn't it?' says Chris, pushing the microphone towards me and no doubt hoping I will reply. It is all I can do to nod.

'Wait till you go below,' says Glenn.

Jonathan joins us and breaks into a huge smile. He glances around. 'I'm going to stow away on this.'

I expect to be directed somewhere, but everyone leaves the four of us alone. While the chopper is being refuelled, Gary swaps places with Peter. Then the fuel hose is put away and everyone stands back. The engine roars more loudly, the helicopter rises slowly into the air then accelerates up and away.

Below decks, the ship is like a floating hotel. We meet the captain, Jim Cottier, who leads me up a series of staircases to the bridge which is almost the size of the entire cabin area of the *Allan And Vi Thistlethwayte*. I talk to Don on the radio, who suggests that I do not wallow too deeply in the

Our equipment, collected from the various caches with the aid of the helicopter, litters the aft deck of the *Greenpeace*. It is difficult to comprehend that three weeks earlier we skied for a day and a half over sea-ice to reach the point where the *Greenpeace* now floats.

Above: **Chris keeps his tape-recorder running as the rest of us arrive.**

Left: **Lyle takes advantage of the radio telephone to ring his wife.**

luxury of the *Greenpeace*. Instead of heeding Don's advice, I wallow as deeply as possible, beginning with a shower — my first for the year — followed by hot pancakes and fresh fruit eaten at a table which has plenty of elbow room.

Then it is back on deck to watch the helicopter land with Lyle and Greg. Lyle in particular looks lost, like a wild animal who has woken up from drugged sleep to find itself inside a cage. I suppose that for him the sea is a prison first and a route back home second.

To our list of simple indulgences, Lyle adds a press release and a call to his wife Camille on the radio phone. Meanwhile Jonathan leaves with Gary to retrieve the gear from Football Saddle. Under Greg's guidance, Peter Malcolm was able to land and load each of our caches along the Tucker, but he had no room for the gear at the saddle.

I am overwhelmed by the changes taking place, not only the sudden translocation but the different attitudes demanded of us. When we set out from the ship three weeks ago, Antarctica soon dictated the terms of our relationship with the environment. Once we accepted our limits we began to feel comfortable in our isolation. But now that we are afloat again, we are no longer driven by the need to escape the continent before the winter. Instead we are faced with new people, and despite our relief at being here, it takes a short time to remember that we are once more social animals in a society numbering more than six. The others seem to be coping well enough, chatting and telling tales which must sound exaggerated. The thirty-two people on board *Greenpeace* have spent several weeks in Antarctic waters, and yet I feel distant from them.

I go up on deck to escape the oppressive heat and to be alone with Antarctica. I am moved by Captain Jim Cottier's willingness to wait at Cape Hallett for the opportunity to fly us out, and by the warmth of our reception when we reached ship. Nevertheless, I am not ready to be the focus of other people's attention because, just for the moment, I cannot find the resources to reciprocate.

The sea of Edisto Inlet is slightly ruffled by the wind. The *Greenpeace* feels huge and totally secure. I look around the shore and see a few pieces of

Above: Viewed from the decks of the *Greenpeace*, the *Allan And Vi Thistlethwayte* appears small and fragile.

Left: Now that we know that we will not be stranded on the continent for the winter, we feel free to celebrate the first ascent of Mt Minto. Moments after the helicopter deposits Greg and Lyle we huddle together for a group photo.

pack-ice still nestled in against the glacier. The storm clouds are darker to the east, which suggests that the weather is worse in that direction. Probably the sun is still shining brightly on the Tucker Glacier. I wonder how long it will be before someone's eyes are there again to appreciate its beauty.

I spot the helicopter before I hear it. Peace and solitude must be taken in small doses now. Gary swoops low over the ship then circles back to land on the helipad. Jonathan is bright-eyed from the excitement of landing in a difficult spot and digging out our gear from the snow which had drifted around it. Now that all the gear is assembled in one place again, I am astonished to see how much we managed to pack into our sled-train when we started out from Cape Hallett. No wonder our poor skidoo made such hard work of hauling it.

We are called to lunch, and I am torn between saving room for the feast I know Margaret will have prepared for us, and taking advantage of *Greenpeace*'s limitless generosity. A bird in the hand, I decide. We are still eating when word comes that the *Allan And Vi Thistlethwayte* is standing off the starboard stern. We rush upstairs to see our small ship lying to 250 metres away. The *Greenpeace* crew have already begun ferrying our gear across. From the decks of the 950-tonne *Greenpeace*, our 40-tonne schooner looks small indeed. We wave, and the figures on board wave back. A Zodiac motors towards the ship and, as it draws closer, we see Ken and Don, with Pete at the rudder. They tie the boat to a mooring line then clamber up the ladder. We shake hands and hug each other, but with so much to do there is no time for more than cursory greetings. Ken and Don take off in the chopper with Jim Cottier so that the two skippers can find the best route through the ice ahead. Meanwhile Pete helps us and the *Greenpeace* crew to lower our gear into our Zodiac and *Greenpeace*'s inflatable. I can see the distinctive silhouette of Margaret over on the *Thistlethwayte*. Even from here I can sense her impatience to be with us again.

When Pete steers our loaded Zodiac gently against our ship's battered red hull, Margaret's smile almost splits her face in two. I throw her the bowline then swing over the rails and embrace her. Colin, as always, is busy with

Above: Homecoming! Margaret welcomes Greg aboard.

Left: Glenn climbs down to join Lincoln in the Zodiac leaving Greenpeace's hospitality behind.

some adjustment or other, this time in the wheelhouse.

'Congratulations,' he says, extending his hand. 'How was the climb?'

'Straightforward,' I say, then think of how misleading this must sound. 'At least compared to what we expected from below. The biggest problems were the cold and the wind.'

'Like here,' he said. 'At least your mountain didn't get blown around the place, I suppose, unlike these bloody icebergs.'

In one sentence, Colin summed up and dismissed the dangers they had faced while we were away.

Pete heads back to collect more people. The *Greenpeace* looks enormous from our cluttered deck, so I take some photographs before getting down to the job of stowing our gear. Scarcely any of the deck is visible under the barrels, packs, skis, pulks, jerrycans and boxes of film gear, stoves and food. Glenn helps me lift the hatch cover off the hold. As soon as everyone is on board, Margaret ducks into the galley and reappears minutes later with a plate of jam-covered scones. There is no doubt about it now, we are back where we belong. Our few hours on the *Greenpeace* was an interlude of unreality. We have gone without comfort and absolute security since leaving Sydney so, despite its battered appearance, engine troubles, and cramped quarters, the *Thistlethwayte* feels like home.

Don starts motoring north even before everything is properly stowed. Lyle is busy lashing jerrycans to the base of the foremast; Pete and Ken lift the Zodiac out of the water and lash it back on the aft deck; Chris ties jerrycans aft of the wheelhouse; Glenn and Jonathan pass our packs and the film gear down into the Fish Cabin; I sort food for Greg to stow in the hold. I end up with a large pile of delicacies which I think should be kept accessible in the galley.

Margaret looks dubiously at every packet or tin which I hand to her.

Pete delivers Chris and Lyle from the
Greenpeace to the cramped but familiar
quarters of the *Allan And Vi Thistlethwayte*.

'There's no room,' she says. 'We restocked when we brought the winter
supplies back on board the other day.'

I insist, knowing that she has little experience with post-expedition
appetites. We reach a compromise which leaves me happy and Margaret
only moderately distressed. Plentiful food and Margaret's cooking and
company are the most cheering aspects of the three-week voyage ahead.

For the six of us, the euphoria of starting our homewards journey is
quickly replaced by deep-seated weariness. As soon as we push through
the broken ice-floes into the open waters of Moubray Bay the seas begin to
roughen. I feel too tired to resist the rising queasiness in my stomach, so I
retire below and lie in my bunk where I fall asleep instantly.

Hours later I am woken for dinner, a timely prelude to going on watch. I
learn that Chris and Glenn have changed places on the roster so that I am
now to stand watch with Colin and Chris. Lyle and Ken do not appear for
dinner. The suffering has begun for them already.

Our sched. with *Greenpeace* is disheartening because they are not only
20 nautical miles ahead of us but are motoring into a Force Nine gale. It
appears that Antarctica is not going to let us escape easily. Our hopes of an
easy passage to Australia are being dashed almost as soon as they are
raised.

By the end of our watch the seas have begun to roughen markedly.
Colin stays on to take Ken's watch with Glenn, while Chris and I stumble
down to the Fish Cabin and collapse into our bunks. After a month in
these latitudes the cold no longer seems ferocious, even though the rigging
is coated with ice and the temperature continues to drop with the onset of
winter. It is my weariness which is destroying me. During the weeks of
effort onshore, the dangers of frostbite, crevasses and sudden storms meant
that my mind could never rest. At night we shared our sleeping bags with

water-bottles and boot liners to prevent them from freezing, and kept one ear awake for the coming of a blizzard. Beyond the continual silence we could hear the slow trickle of the hourglass as the days before winter slipped past. Now I find there is nothing to keep my mind tuned in to what is happening around me. Every other concern is secondary to my need for sleep, and I happily leave the decision making to the sailors.

Wednesday, 24 February

The day passes in a blur of sleep and storminess. Waves pound our tiny ship, crashing against the hull and washing over the deck. It is dangerous to go outside without a harness, but even more dangerous to crouch on deck near the Fish Cabin attempting to clip the harness to the cable running the length of the deck. Instead we peer out of the door then make a dash for the wheelhouse. Though we are carrying no sail, the 50-knot wind has the ship leaning dramatically to port. The motion in the galley is too violent to make it a refuge from anything. No-one wants to eat so Margaret is spared the battle of trying to cook in impossible conditions. The water is frozen in the pipes, so we drink from a barrel of water lashed inside the starboard door of the wheelhouse.

Outside on deck, buckets, barrels and jerrycans are coming loose and disappearing over the side. The ice which coats the deck and the rigging makes it too dangerous to venture out and secure the objects which remain. Since we are hove to, with the wheel lashed in place, standing watch is a matter of hanging onto the handles on the walls of the wheelhouse and looking out for icebergs. Time passes quickly as I put my energy into keeping upright and regularly peering at the radar screen or out the window. There are no decisions to be made, just the storm to be weathered.

The air in the Fish Cabin is foul because the doors must be closed to keep the water out. Even so, when the biggest waves come over the deck, water manages to squirt through the door seal. Lyle has not moved from his bunk since we left Moubray Bay yesterday, apart from dashes up the stairs to vomit out the door. The floor is a metre deep in film boxes and backpacks: it has been too rough to stow anything properly, but at least everything is jammed tight. The snow on our packs has melted so that everything is sodden. Waves inevitably break across the deck when someone is entering or leaving the cabin. Chris and Lyle catch the water in their bunks because they are directly at the bottom of the stairs. The rest of us stay dry, and our bunks are real havens. It must be two or three degrees above freezing when we are all inside, and this feels tropical after the perpetual iciness of the continent. We do not care about the miserable state of the cabin because our bunks are the only places we want to be.

The soft dusk of midnight is lost above the heavy storm clouds. Beneath their mantle, amongst the huge black waves of the Southern Ocean, it is indisputably night. It is almost dark in the Fish Cabin, and all of us lie deep in sleep. I have wedged bags full of clothing tightly around me so that I do not slide up and down my bunk, despite the bucking of the ship. Inside the cabin the noises of the gale are muffled, except for the constant clanging of the halyards against the mast. I am adrift on another ocean, the endless waters of dreamless sleep.

Suddenly a huge wave slams into the starboard side of the boat. I am thrown into a sitting position. The ship has tipped on its side. A burst of adrenalin wakes me completely, but I fall back down on my bunk as the ship rights itself. It is too dark for me to see the others, but a series of

THE VOYAGE HOME

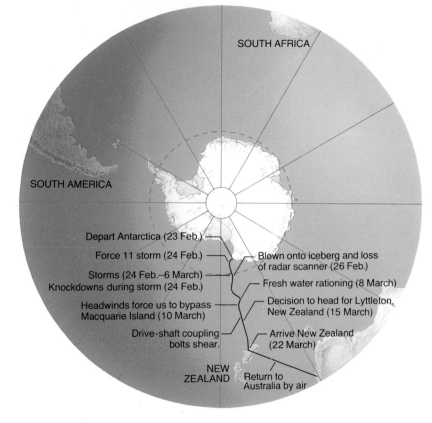

SOUTH AFRICA

SOUTH AMERICA

Depart Antarctica (23 Feb.)
Force 11 storm (24 Feb.)
Blown onto iceberg and loss
of radar scanner (26 Feb.)
Storms (24 Feb.–6 March)
Knockdowns during storm (24 Feb.)
Fresh water rationing (8 March)
Headwinds force us to bypass
Macquarie Island (10 March)
Decision to head for Lyttleton,
New Zealand (15 March)
Drive-shaft coupling
bolts shear.
Arrive New Zealand
(22 March)
NEW
ZEALAND
Return to
Australia by air

curses from around the Fish Cabin tell me they shared my fright.

'That was a big one,' says Lyle, who is more awake than the rest of us because he has been in his bunk for the last thirty hours. 'Hope there's not going to be too many more of them.'

I lie there and wonder if any damage has been done. The motor still throbs steadily in neutral, ready to head us away from an iceberg or to operate the bilge pumps. I try to remember who is on watch, then I look across and see that Jonathan is not in his bunk. Within minutes I am asleep again.

Hours pass, but it seems only minutes later when another breaking wave smashes against the ship, this time with even more dramatic results. Again I am thrown upright, instantly alert. Instinctively, I reach out to grab Glenn who is falling to the floor after bouncing off the roof. He lands on Chris who has been thrown almost into Lyle's bunk. Water pours through the closed door onto all three of them. A terrible grinding noise comes from beneath the floor. My immediate fear is that the tailshaft has been knocked out of skew and is drilling a hole through the hull, and with the horror of this thought I fail to realise that the ship has righted itself. Greg rolls out of his bunk beneath me and throws the packs and film boxes out of the way. Glenn dives for the lightswitch. When the floor is cleared the noise is even worse. Greg rips up the floor cover and we see cans jammed around the tailshaft. Without hesitating he reaches down and works the cans loose. The mangled containers join the other debris on the floor. He and Glenn replace the panel and drag the film boxes back in place. If the boat is going to continue these antics it is better to keep our packs as the top layer because they are not as heavy and have no sharp edges.

The ship must have rolled through more than 90° because the floor had to lift before the cans stored in the bilge could fall over the divider which

isolates the tailshaft. The cabin doors must have been beneath the water. How much more would it have taken to capsize us? Can this boat take any more before it begins to fall apart? I lie there listening to the blood thumping through my veins. It is much longer before I drop off to sleep this time, and twice during the night minor knocks slap the hull and wake me with the fear that the inconceivable is happening. The only sounds in the darkness are those of the engine and the relentless gale.

Left: **Day after day gales batter the ship until we begin to wonder whether we will survive.**

Thursday, 25 February

In the morning the storm still rages. Concern about our situation begins to force sleepiness aside, even though last night's ferocious waves have vanished. For the first time I sense Don and Pete's worry. 'At its worst it was Force 11,' says Pete. They obviously believe our predicament is very serious, in contradiction to Don's radio message last night that all was well. Colin finds plenty of scope for his negativity, but I sense that he relishes our struggle. As long as he has confidence in the boat I shall be able to keep my own fears under control. He knows better than anyone what this vessel is able to handle. The engine now has an oil leak, which is disturbing because the seas are far too rough to be able to hunt for the cause.

The crippling edge of our exhaustion has worn off, despite the desperate conditions. That everything was very wet seemed irrelevant in the beginning, but now that the worst of the gale seems to have passed we are getting impatient to reorganise the boat. Everything in the Fish Cabin and Pleasure Dome is exactly as it was when we left Cape Hallett, only wetter and more battered. The galley is an indescribable mess. The floor is greasy from spilt food and kerosene; the tea towels are so sodden and dirty that they are worse than useless; everything not actually frozen is damp; the sink refuses to drain because we are on a permanent port tack; the stoves have water in them now so that they die with a splutter then fill the galley and the wheelhouse with fumes.

Despite all this, most of us jam ourselves around the table at lunchtime and eat biscuits with cheese and pickles. Margaret manages to heat and serve some tinned soup. Her constant good humour, after being up all night repacking the shelves and cupboards, reminds us that the eleven of us are in this together and should find strength in each other. From the trajectory of the tools which flew from the engine room bench and smashed into the panel of switches and fuses on the port side, Colin estimates that the ship tipped through 110°. He seems pleased to have found some way of measuring the angle precisely. The tops of the masts would have been under the water. We will not be able to assess the damage to the engine and rigging until the storm abates.

Friday, 26 February

The door to the Fish Cabin is unlashed and Pete's voice shouts, 'Can anyone come on deck? There's a rope wrapped around the prop, an iceberg closing in, and we need to get the storm jib up.'

Greg and Jonathan roll out of their bunks immediately. Chris follows. I hesitate because I am not anxious to go back outside into the storm. My feet have only just started to warm up after my two-hour stint on watch. When Glenn and Chris prepare to film the operation, I decide to stay in my bunk. There will be plenty of helping hands.

Everyone hurries with their waterproofs, fumbles amongst the dozen green gumboots on the floor, and scrambles for the ladder, with Greg leading the way. I wriggle out of my sleeping bag and scamper up the stairs to shut the door after Glenn because the outside latch is broken, then I lie in my bunk and listen to the busy noises on deck. Through the skylight I can see Pete struggling with a frozen halyard, bashing it against the mast to break off the ice. Footsteps hurry along the deck, rigging clangs, the wind whistles, and waves smash against the hull.

I sense the urgency above me and wonder whether I should go up. An overcrowded deck will only make things more dangerous, I tell myself, glad to find a reason for staying in my warm, dry sleeping bag.

There is more bashing of frozen ropes, shouted words I cannot catch, and then the familiar flap of a sail. I can feel the different movement of the boat, the vessel pulling like a dog on a leash. Then silence except for the noises of the storm. The crisis must be over.

Fifteen minutes later Jonathan comes below decks.

'Bit of an epic?' I ask.

'More than a bit.' He shakes his head with disbelief. 'The rope around the prop was one of the stern halyards, and it was also wrapped around the radar. They freed one end, so the prop turned, but it wound up the halyard and wrenched the radar dome off the mast. It went flying through the air like a giant frisbee. We now have no radar, and still another few days or a week of iceberg territory to sail through.' He pauses and reconsiders the scene. 'Would've been funny to watch if we weren't in such a desperate situation. We came so close to getting smashed into the iceberg. That would have been the end of us. No more Bicentennial Antarctic Expedition. Might still be the case. Icebergs move fast in these conditions and we've got no bloody radar now. Be great fun tonight, peering into the darkness. I don't think I'll be sleeping much.'

I say nothing. No part of this journey is going to be easy.

During the rare calm spells we are kept busy maintaining the sails and the rigging. Greg works astride the boom.

Sunday, 6 March

More than a week has gone by since I last opened the pages of my diary. Somehow I have lost the inspiration to write. Or maybe I just want to forget about what is happening. But of course, it is impossible to forget. The big gale passed after four or five days and, though it blew us north, it brought us directly into the path of another storm, followed by still another, and although conditions are better today, I do not dare hope that this is more than the lull before the next storm.

I curb my impatience, because it is the first step on a short path to depression. Jonathan and Lyle are already heavily infected with that mood. This journey back across the roughest ocean in the world is the final stage of our adventure, and I should be learning from it. This is easier to write than to practice.

Looking out for icebergs from the bow has become a regular part of watch duty since the loss of the radar. This forced contact with the elements during the storms is exhilarating, and it literally washes away preoccupations and dreams of other places. The purging of all that is irrelevant to the present is always an expedition's *raison d'être*, whatever the professed goal.

On the ship, being harnessed to the safety cable takes the edge off the danger, but the all-absorbing quality of the experience is the same as being on a big mountain during a storm. Yet in the mountains each climber is alone with his own strengths and weaknesses; failure means we have only ourselves or our gods to blame. At sea, the ship sets the bounds of our universe. It is much easier to have faith in metal and canvas than in the need for harmony with the environment, even though the best moments of sailing are when the wind, the boat and the sea work together.

Like all other sailors, our faith must lie in the vessel. Jonathan heads the ranks of the unbelievers and, after the events of the last week, I may join him.

Chris and Pete spent a few days repairing the jib, which was ripped during the gale. Chris is always resourceful and eager to keep his hands and his mind busy. All our sails have suffered from being frozen and whipped by the wind, even though they were lashed to the booms. Obviously, the sails should have been stowed below decks during the month the boat was at Cape Hallett, especially since the engine has been so troublesome.

For the last few days the Satnav has been giving erratic readings. A red light shows that it is receiving satellite signals, but they are rarely processed to give a fix of our latitude and longitude. It is hard to know whether the irregular fixes are recent enough to indicate anything worthwhile. There is a chance they are totally inaccurate. The device seems to be working properly again today. Perhaps it senses the threat of the sextant now the sun is shining weakly.

Glenn and Chris discuss filming the evening radio sched. before stepping into the wheelhouse.

The winds today are more gentle and, though the waves are still large from the storms, the choppiness has eased. Ken detects a grating noise from the engine. He and Colin and Don discuss the different possibilities, run the engine with the prop disconnected, and then decide that Ken should slip into the hold. With the help of a torch he is able to find the problem.

'Looks like the fan-belt to the oil pump.'

We start the engine again and his diagnosis is confirmed. Colin tells him where the spare should be, but it has vanished. After a short deliberation Ken cuts the belt and heaves it overboard.

'The motor only uses enough oil to need the pump during tight ma-noeuvring,' explains Colin. He starts the engine and everything sounds normal. 'The only manoeuvring we'll be doing is when we come into harbour.'

Fate seems very easily tempted during this expedition, so I hope we do not regret this short-term solution.

Tuesday, 8 March

I wake up, read for a while, then slowly dress. Life is much more bearable in the Fish Cabin without the constant throbbing of the engine, even if it means we are getting nowhere. The succession of storms has meant we have been getting nowhere for days now, so a change in the speed seems to make little difference. Yesterday Colin shut down the motor until he can establish the cause of the oil leak. Through the skylight I see that Glenn and Jonathan are struggling with the mainsail. The wind must be stronger than the sounds down here suggest.

In the galley, I greet Margaret and sit next to Greg.

'Hey, guess what?' he says.

'I don't know. What?'

'There's a 10-metre rip in the mainsail.'

I am not sure whether to believe him. 'Really?'

'Yep. Right down the side next to the mast.'

The mainsail is now out of action, as well. The craziness of our predicament makes me laugh. Greg laughs too.

Glenn and Jonathan join us at the table, but they are past seeing the humour of the situation. Colin appears and sits next to Glenn.

'The first thing to do,' he begins, very business like, 'is to start water rationing. The next thing is to get all available hands repairing the sail. I can demonstrate the sailmakers darn...

Greg interrupts. 'Surely the first thing to do is check out how much water we've got left before deciding whether we need to ration it?'

'We must do that as well.'

I leave them to it. Hours later Greg declares that the starboard water tank, which we thought was full, is in fact empty. Immediate blame goes to the knock down in the storm: somehow the pipes were split. Whatever the cause, water rationing is to begin henceforth. Without going short, we have sufficient water for another four weeks.

A month seems like plenty of time until I calculate that after two weeks at sea we have sailed and motored only 14° north of Cape Hallett to a latitude of 58°S. A month will give us barely enough time to reach Australia if we continue at this rate, provided we can make some ground to the west. It had always been our plan to call in at Macquarie Island on the way home, simply to break our voyage, but now that diversion has become a necessity. Don has daily radio contact with the Australian research station on the island, and we are only 4° to the south of it, but still 12° to the east. Colin is wary of anchoring there after the recent sinking of the *Nella Dan* supply ship on the rocks in the poorly protected harbour.

Thursday, 10 March

When Don rises an hour before his radio sched. he is unsure of his movements and his actions—symptoms of feeling at a loss with our situation. He has what he considers conflicting responsibilities, apparent in his evasive radio discussion with his colleagues of the Oceanic Research

Foundation last night. He wants the ship to reach Sydney in time for a refit before the ORF's proposed circumnavigation of Australia. Few of us on board consider that a reasonable expectation, not only because of the timing but because of the extensive refit the ship will require. In almost three weeks at sea, we have not made any progress at all to the west, and our logical destination now should be New Zealand. We have no option except to tolerate our predicament, but it would be madness to prolong the voyage past the first safe landfall.

We are almost at the same latitude as Macquarie Island but still impossibly far to the east. There is mail for us on this tiny and remote outpost of Australia, as well as freshly-baked bread and beers ready to be lined up on the bar. The generous inhabitants of Macquarie will have to eat the bread themselves and return the mail on the next supply boat. Once again we feel the limitations of our craft and the power of the forces of the ocean.

Don asks Greg and me what information he could ask for from Macquarie Island. Greg suggests contact times and frequencies for the New Zealand base on Campbell Island, some distance to the north-east of us. Don thinks the idea is a sensible one. I am pleased, because I see such contact as a definite push towards New Zealand. At sea, it appears that many decisions are dictated by the weather, so a sit-and-wait attitude develops in response.

With nothing else to do Jonathan spends hours attempting to take the perfect albatross photograph.

Chris and I are to start watch at midnight. Rather than going to bed for two or three hours after dinner, we do our best to keep Margaret, Jonathan and Glenn awake by playing dice. Greg and Pete are on watch, but Greg joins us while he is not at the wheel. At 11.40, Pete calls us out to look at the aurora.

An amazing sight greets us when we step outside. Every other display of these charged cosmic rays lighting up the night sky has been a half-hearted shimmer of green close to the horizon, but tonight the aurora is a brilliant green brush-stroke across the full width of the sky. We stand out on deck and crane our necks in wonder. The green band shimmers and changes shape like a borderless veil shaken by unseen hands. As we watch, directly above us the veil changes to mauve and pulses brightly before fading back to green. It has all the majesty of a heavenly vision, and when the green fades in turn to blackness we are left with a feeling of awe.

Sunday, 13 March

Today was just another rough day on the Southern Ocean—until the tailshaft broke. The torsional vibration caused by the engine running on only two of its three cylinders for weeks on end has finally proved too much for a tailshaft coupling. Perhaps it would have lasted the voyage had we been spared the continual battering by big seas and contrary winds. The temporary repairs Colin made to the universal joint on the voyage south are proving more than temporary, because it looks as if he will not be able to dismantle the pieces to weld the break. The only possible solution is to braze the coupling together again in situ, and then reserve the motor for coming into port. Even that option must be deferred because working in the Fish Cabin bilge is impossible in these rough seas. Though Campbell Island is almost on our course, we shall not be able to collect fresh water there because we need a motor to approach land.

Our sail repairs will be tested properly now. Let us hope our stitches are stronger than the wind because these sails are our only tickets home. Everyone on board, apart from Colin and Don, is wondering why we attempted such a long and hard voyage with this tiny ship. Perhaps even

Colin and Don are wondering, too. Of course, the answer is that passages to Antarctica are extremely difficult and expensive to organise, and none of us—not even Pete, who has made the same journey in an even smaller vessel—knew how tough the Southern Ocean could be on a ship as old and fragile as this one. The Oceanic Research Foundation agreed to the charter, and they did mention that there was much maintenance to be done. Not until we were at sea did we appreciate the significance of that qualification. The hull has proved itself virtually unsinkable, and the masts have proved their strength, but almost everything else has failed: the engine, the radar, the generator, the Satnav, the sails, the water tank. The kerosene stoves continue to function only because of Margaret's patience and Colin's ingenuity. What surprises me most is that Jonathan decided to make a second voyage south on this ship after his journey to Commonwealth Bay in 1985. I suppose it is proof of his love of Antarctica and his appreciation of Mt Minto as a worthy goal.

It is easy to lie here in my bunk and think negative thoughts, yet I know that afterwards the precarious nature of each sector of this expedition will add to its stature. Others might regard our expedition as foolish, but the eleven of us feel that we have achieved a real pioneering feat. The odds have been against us at every stage of our adventure, from our engine troubles and the fire at sea, to the ship being stuck in the pack-ice, from the six of us left skidoo-less on the continent, to battling the wind on the slopes of Mt Minto—and now for three weeks the Southern Ocean has refused to let us escape. Only during the struggle to regain control do we make any progress.

Wednesday, 16 March

Yesterday we set our course for Lyttleton, the harbour which services Christchurch. At lunchtime, while I sat restitching the top of the mainsail in the wheelhouse, Greg delivered a clear, realistic outline of the options before us. Little doubt remained that it would be foolish to head anywhere except the east coast of New Zealand's South Island. All that was needed was for our captain to accept the fact; and within hours of Don and Colin concurring with Greg's polite pronouncement, the wind came from behind and filled our sails. Once again it seems as though Antarctica governs our destiny by driving us to this traditional port of departure and return for polar expeditions.

Today everyone is in high spirits. There is a great feeling on board now that the crew, which has gone through so much, is again united by the one idea. Only now that the vital decision has been made do I realise the destructive nature of indecisiveness.

It is ten years since I last visited New Zealand to climb in the Southern Alps. Margaret, Lyle and Glenn have not been there at all. It will be interesting to see how my perceptions of Christchurch have changed after a decade of travelling to more exotic countries in search of the ultimate mountain. I have learnt there is no ultimate mountain, only an ultimate moment which can be repeated anywhere if the circumstances are right. It is my fate that I can find those moments most easily amongst the cold and danger of high peaks. The timeless quality of Antarctica stretches those magical seconds into an infinite mood of peace and beauty.

The motion of the boat is many times more comfortable now that we are under sail with a favourable wind. The southerly breeze allows us to head directly towards our destination, and with good speed. Last night on watch

we sailed through waters which glistened phosphorescent with every wave against the bow. I stood alone by the rails and enjoyed my own private light show. It seemed as if the ocean was celebrating our speed and the approach of our new destination.

Colin and Ken take advantage of a calm morning to braze the tailshaft back together. The operation is successful but Colin suggests that the motor be reserved for coming into port.

Monday, 21 March

I sit secure and content with my feet up on the rails and my back wedged against the wheelhouse. There is no danger of getting pitched overboard because the breeze is pushing the ship smoothly through the water. I revel in the joy of sailing with the wind. When a strong gust tilts us further to port, water laps over the deck but I stay dry and sheltered. The gentle music of Ry Cooder floating out of the wheelhouse drowns the conversation inside, so I feel comfortably alone. It seems appropriate that the silence of the ocean is replaced by man-made noises, because soon such sounds will be all that we shall hear.

I stare west to the sunset. Night is coming early because the sun is dropping behind the dark mass of the Banks Peninsula. A crescent moon, which common sense tells me should be rising at this time of day, nevertheless follows the sun's example by sinking towards the rugged skyline.

The sunset colours are richer and brighter than the soft, familiar tones of the ocean and Antarctica. Because of the difference, I am captivated by the beauty of this land rising out of the sea even more than I was by our first sight of the frozen continent. On that day, almost two months ago, my excitement was tinged with fear. The world's most inhospitable environment awaited us, and I wondered how I would cope with the challenges ahead.

Now, at our adventure's end, there are no obstacles between me and the future. I feel as though the purpose of our journey was to give me this serenity.

The orange of the western sky fades through yellow into grey. The silhouette of a solid, snowless land is etched by a bright golden line, and then seconds later the light is gone. Endless Antarctic sunsets are a long way behind us now. The transition from timelessness to the ephemeral passed unnoticed behind weeks of stormcloud-ridden skies.

Two lighthouses begin to blink their silent warning, not only of rocky headlands and reefs, but of the human life on this land we sighted this morning. The sky has darkened enough for me to spot a planet shining brightly. Inside the wheelhouse, the cassette finishes playing. As the darkness closes in I am left with only the moon, the illusion of three stars—two of them erratic—and the rhythmic slap of the sea against the hull. It is the simplest formula for happiness I have known.

Tuesday, 22 March

The fresh smell of pine fills my nostrils, though the nearest trees are still more than a mile away. The steep grassy hillsides which flank the long approach to Lyttleton Port dwarf our yacht. A huge container ship chugs past while we wait for the pilot boat to come out and guide us to a mooring. As I stare up at the container ship, which has sailed the world, our achievement begins to take scale.

For three months we have kept our own company and devoted ourselves to achieving our private ambition. The nature of our goal has meant we

Beside the wharf at Lyttleton, New Zealand, (from left) Lincoln, Glenn (standing on the rails), Jonathan, Don, Margaret, Colin, Ken, Pete, Greg, Chris and Lyle line up for a last group photo on board our battered vessel.

have lived apart from the rest of humanity, and in such circumstances it is easy to feel self-important. But now, when there are other boats approaching the harbour, cars travelling the roads across the hillsides, and houses scattered over the headlands, I no longer feel quite so special. The people in all these places lead their own lives, and no doubt attach the same importance to their goals as we attach to ours.

Our expedition feels like a major achievement, but the presence of other people—a whole nation of them—makes me see our trip in a different light. The snows of Antarctica have already obliterated every sign of our passage, except for the small depot of food and equipment we left on the Tucker when we desperately tried to lighten our loads. I expect the penguins and the seals have already forgotten our brief intrusion. The Southern Ocean is as wild and empty as it ever was, and the albatrosses are left with only each other to follow now. Only in the human world does our expedition have any relevance: it can be catalogued as another adventure, another mountain climbed.

Of course, the journey to Mt Minto means much more than that to the eleven of us. Our friendship is cemented by the terror and the joy we shared, and Antarctica has changed our perception of the world.

I look across at two boys changing the tack of their sailing dinghy. As they wait for the wind to fill the sail, their voices float easily over the water. The varnished wood of the hull reflects the morning sun, and the new sail shines brilliantly white as it billows and then loses its wind. To me, theirs is just another boat, but to them it may be the ticket to adventure.

Epilogue

Sydney Harbour Bridge, 5 August 1988

'Think invisible,' says Greg softly, then he begins to sprint up the shallow steps leading up the huge girder.

Margaret and I huddle behind the barbed-wire fence in the shadows of the sandstone pylon. To us, Greg is as obvious as the Opera House across the harbour, but late on this mid-winter night there is no-one walking the foreshores to see him. Ten minutes earlier, a police car cruised through the carpark on a routine patrol, so hopefully it will be some time before they return. Soon we will be high enough above the water to be less conspicuous from the ground. We watch Greg disappear inside a rectangular column of metal at its junction with the curving lower span of the bridge.

'Your turn, Margaret.'

She bites her bottom lip and glances across at the carpark and the plaza. All we can hear is the hum of the traffic above our heads. She smiles at me weakly then dashes up the stairs. I wait until she is halfway before following her. The floodlights are dazzling, and they make me feel as vulnerable as a rotating metal duck in a carnival sharpshooting stall. I run out of breath well before the inviting darkness of the vertical girders where Greg and Margaret crouch and wait. I collapse next to them, gasping.

'We can take things more slowly after this next bit,' says Greg.

Again Margaret and I follow him. The angle of the span eases a little as it bends out over the water. We rest before tackling the difficult job of getting above the roadway without being seen. The others go ahead but before I reach the shelter of the next girder a train comes thundering along beside me. It travels past too quickly for me to be spotted, but the whoosh of its silver carriages only metres away is frightening.

The rest of the climb is straightforward, a simple matter of being careful not to slip on the smooth metal, and of keeping a firm grip on the rungs of the ladders which link one level to the next.

When we reach the top of the Bridge we share it with a giant flashing red light, a flag pole and a stupendous view of Sydney Harbour. Although there is no moon, the reflections from the city lights reveal the details of the buildings along the shores. The mesh of streets is alive with the red-amber-green dance of traffic lights and the pairs of headlights and tail-lights which stop and start and form queues around them. The harbour is quiet except for a brightly lit floating restaurant a kilometre up the harbour. Even at this distance the sounds of its disco music float easily across the water.

'There's Walsh Bay,' says Margaret. 'In fact... Look! There's the boat!'

At first it is difficult to distinguish the dark shape of the hull against the black water, but the three red masts are distinctive. After four months back in Australia, it already seems unbelievable that eleven of us sailed to

Left: Colin and the crew he gathered together in New Zealand bring the boat into Walsh Bay, after sailing the refitted vessel across the Tasman Sea. Waiting at our departure point for Antarctica, I feel a mixture of satisfaction and disbelief when I see how small our boat looks even here in the enclosed waters of Sydney Harbour.

Antarctica on board the tiny vessel. The *Allan And Vi Thistlethwayte* appears so small and insignificant next to the wharves and the buildings behind.

I had the same impression of the yacht when I watched it motor under the Harbour Bridge—now beneath our feet—on the day of its return to Sydney. Everyone except Colin had flown home from Christchurch within a week of our landfall. After a month in New Zealand supervising the refit, Colin gathered a crew together and sailed up the east coast of the North Island, and then across the Tasman Sea. Tales of good winds and a trouble-free passage proved that the ship had broken the spell cast by Antarctica.

As I stood on the wharf with the other expeditioners and waited to welcome the ship, I thought about how quickly the ten of us had adapted to being back in Australia. We were soon living our lives much as we had before we left, despite the dramatic effect Antarctica had upon our view of the world. I was busy transcribing my diaries; Greg was back in his geologist's office building up a data base; Margaret was again at the helm of The Baytree Tea Shop; Jonathan was already planning a trip to India to research a book; Lyle, while working his way through the reports to our sponsors, had slipped back into his suit, his public relations job, and family life; Glenn's toe had recovered, and he and Chris were working hard on the documentary; Pete had been away on the north coast of New South Wales recording the songs of whales; Don had stepped back into retirement and the world of amateur radio operators. Most telling of all, Ken sold the boat he had been building expressly to sail to Antarctica, and bought land in Queensland. Each of us were living our separate lives again. I had more than that: my world with Barbara had expanded to include our son.

'Unbelievable, isn't it?' I say.

'What?' asks Greg, then continues mischievously, 'That we climbed Mt Minto before climbing the bridge?'

Margaret laughs, but I pretend not to hear.

'That it's all over. That Antarctica is so untouched, that Sydney has been totally transformed in two hundred years. That two places so different from each other exist together on the same planet.'

Margaret shivers in the freshening wind. 'And people only think about *here*,' she says, 'because this is what they know.'

'It's also a damn sight more comfortable,' says Greg.

We stare in silence at the view until the breeze makes us recall that there is winter even in these latitudes.

'Let's go home and get some sleep.'

'Okay,' I reply, but I look down at the boat. 'Remember when we landed at Cape Hallett?' I say after a moment. 'Middle of the night but bright as day? And so cold...'

When I turn around to finish the sentence, Margaret and Greg have already gone. Greg never was a person to live in the past. He reminds me that the future promises so much that it does not need to be crowded by memories.

Appendices

ORGANISING ANTARCTIC EXPEDITIONS

Greg Mortimer

'GREAT God it's a beautiful place.'

Standing on the summit of Mt Minto was a deeply satisfying and emotional moment for all of us. To the west there was an endless sea of mountains and to the east, the endless cold sea. We were so vulnerable and so far from home. We had lived the expedition for twelve months. Overall it had taken two years to organise – twelve times longer than it had taken to execute. Yet, in Antarctic terms, this had been a quick expedition to get underway. The British 'Transglobe Expedition' had taken ten years, while another British expedition, the 'Footsteps of Scott Expedition', had taken five years. Our experience was that organising a journey to Antarctica was something of a logistical nightmare. But don't let that put you off because the sight of the first iceberg is more than adequate repayment.

Organising such an expedition makes it necessary to confront a unique set of circumstances that are obviously found nowhere else in the world. This land of paradoxes, the greatest wilderness in the world, is startling in its beauty, overwhelming in its size and, often enough, in its ferocity. Antarctica features the most extreme climate on the planet and therefore does not allow the luxury of mistakes.

For whatever purpose there is in mounting an expedition to Antarctica, there is but one simple starting point. Everything, absolutely everything, that you need to survive must be taken with you. Traditionally Antarctic expeditions have been elaborate affairs involving heavily constructed ships and requiring large and complex logistical support systems. Recent expeditions, however, have shown that this is not always necessary. It *is* feasible for a small, well equipped group to penetrate well into Antarctica.

In order to understand the complexity of organising an Antarctic expedition it is important to first apprehend the political framework of the continent. The scientific programs of all countries involved in Antarctica are strictly administered at government level. At the time of writing very few countries have a formal policy towards private expeditions. The stance taken by governments, however, is that no logistical support is given to expeditions that are not under direct government control, particularly if the expeditions are non-scientific.

Initially, we approached the Australian government for support. We developed cordial relationships with the Australian Antarctic Division and established our credentials. However, Antarctic Division funds are largely used for scientific work so, because our expedition was largely for pure adventure and our destination was outside the scope of Antarctic Division activities, it was made clear to us from the outset that we were on our own.

Therefore we had to start from scratch and establish a complete logistical framework for the expedition. At least two thirds of the time, money and effort spent in any Antarctic expedition will be devoted to transport. In our preparations we investigated every possible option. We looked at the possibility of flying to Mt Minto! It would be possible using a small plane from South America but the costs would be astronomical. Legal tender in Antarctica is fuel – black gold. Before you can fly from South America, or Australia for that matter, you need to establish large fuel caches on the continent. Such an option was simply cost prohibitive. Our next move was to attempt to charter space on any private ships going into the area. Greenpeace was unable to help because they were heavily committed to maintaining their own base on Ross Island. We approached a private Norwegian expedition which planned to be operating a small ice-strengthened vessel in the Ross Sea. The cost for us to charter the vessel would have been US$600,000! A little beyond our budget. The next line of attack was to find a suitably equipped yacht. This was really the bottom line because the Ross Sea is notorious for bad ice conditions. Once we decided on the *Allan And Vi Thistlethwayte* (then called the *Dick Smith Explorer*) we set the tone of the expedition: we had to become extremely concious of weight, time and safety.

The chances of success were not great but I firmly believe that if you have the right people with the right spirit you can do anything. And perhaps therein lies the secret of organising an Antarctic expedition or any expedition for that matter. But I believe it is particularly true for Antarctica.

Such an expedition needs people with Antarctic experience and in our ship's crew we had perhaps the best. Every one of the eleven people on the team was critical to the success of the expedition. Every person had more than one job at which he or she was very talented. Without that secret ingredient the venture would have failed. To gather such a group takes time. We started with a spark of an idea and it then took two years for the group to gravitate together. When the right person came along it was obvious. So I stress that if you want to have a happy and successful expedition take the time to select exactly the right people.

From the outset we were not sure whether our little yacht would even reach the Ross Sea. So in the event of the expedition being trapped or delayed in ice we had to take sufficient supplies to support eleven people for one year.

At the same time as gathering crew members and logistical planning we were involved in generating the $160,000 needed to finance the expedition. We also felt some responsibility to demonstrate to government bodies that private expeditions can operate professionally and efficiently in Antarctica. Our planning needed to be meticulous and we developed an expedition that was totally independent and self-reliant.

What of the future? I think we are on the verge of a significant change in direction for private involvement in Antarctica. The use of private aircraft is likely to have a major impact over the next decade. It is now possible to fly with a private company (Adventure Network International) to almost any destination on the continent. From any part of the globe you can be at the base of Antarctica's highest mountain, Vinson Massif, in a matter of days. The flying costs are of the order of US$100 per minute once you are deep within the continent, but the important point is that the logistical framework has now been established.

But I recommend that if you really want to fully experience what Antarctica has to offer, organise an expedition with an absolute minimum of machinery. Investigate the possibilities of harnessing the wind and the sun to provide you with power. That would be a bold new direction for our involvement in the world's greatest wilderness.

EQUIPMENT
Lincoln Hall

AFTER a month spent crammed into the *Allan And Vi Thistlethwayte,* we welcomed the freedom offered by Antarctica, but remained in awe of its vastness and its reputation as the coldest place on earth. When we left Cape Hallet our skidoo hauled three sledges, all were overloaded because of the trepidation we felt. The six of us were heading out into the unknown and, as is the wont of humankind, we tried to take with us as much of our own familiar world as we could. The loss of the skidoo forced us to be more realistic, and made us cut down our loads to what we really needed: blizzard-proof shelter, reliable stoves and a generous fuel supply, plenty of food, and adequate clothing. Our medical kit became little more than a first aid kit, and our pile of film gear looked less like the stocktake for a shoot of *Gone With the Wind* and more like the equipment to film a short version of *Chris and Glenn go on Holidays.* Even Jonathan toted only two of his

seven cameras, and I cut down to two slim paperback books.

Greg and Jonathan's previous experiences in Antarctica were invaluable for planning what to take. Polar pyramid tents made by Wilderness Equipment were deemed essential because, despite their weight, they were close to indestructible and could be erected in a blizzard; and we decided that dome tents with double aluminium alloy wands and a few extra guys would be strong enough for nearly all conditions. Both the pyramid and dome tents had snow valences, so when it was necessary blocks of ice were cut with Whitco snow shovels and snow saws and placed on the flaps around the tents' perimeters. Snow pickets were used to anchor the main guys in softer conditions and ice-screws were used when there was blue ice. Although we took shovels and saws to dig in with in case our tents were blown away, there was rarely snow that was soft enough to enable us to dig a cave or trench.

It was fortunate therefore that we did not have to improvise accommodation.

We chose kerosene stoves (both MSR and Optimus) because they burned with greater heat than gas, and the fuel was much safer than petrol. Cooking took many hours each day because all water had to come from melted snow or ice, so it was important to have the most efficient stoves. At the coldest times, priming the stoves was difficult because both methylated spirits and alcohol paste were reluctant to ignite. We used a wooden cook box to store most of the cooking gear during the day and to keep the wind out and some of the heat in when we were cooking.

The biggest problem with mountaineering in extreme conditions is to keep one's hands and feet warm while still retaining the freedom of movement necessary to hold onto the mountain, the rope, and one's climbing tools. We were lucky to encounter relatively straightforward terrain on Mt Minto otherwise we would not have been able to climb the peak on such a bitterly cold and windy day. We all wore Damart Thermalactyl gloves as a bottom layer on our hands, then woollen gloves followed by mittens and/or overmits. While manhauling, the Damart gloves alone were often sufficient, but the constant rubbing of the ski-stocks soon wore holes in them. We had three pairs each of these gloves, but we would not have been over-equipped with twice as many. They were necessary for all the fiddly tasks like lighting the stoves, or lashing and unlashing the loads on the sledges.

Most of us had two sets of long underwear – a lightweight polypropylene set made by Alp Sports, and a more heavy-duty set made by Damart. We lived in them, so each day it was simply a matter of deciding how many layers to wear on top. Kathmandu Clothing made us a selection of brightly coloured (synchilla) clothing, including a jacket, bib-and-brace, bala-clava, a peaked cap, and a beanie-style hat, all of which we found very good. In windy conditions most of us wore Kathmandu Gore-tex trousers and jackets. Jonathan used a one-piece Helley Hansen fibrepile suit and J & H Everest bib-and-brace over trousers and jacket. For colder conditions we had down-filled vests and duvet jackets made by J & H. These were very cozy, although I would have preferred longer sleeves on the jacket to enable me to retract my hands inside the sleeves to warm them up. I also had a down-filled suit made by Mountain Designs which was a real security blanket. I was cold while wearing it on the summit of Mt Minto but only because I had not worn my fibrepile bib-and-brace underneath. These pants, combined with the down suit, would have been too warm for anything except waiting around on the summit. I left the bib-and-brace at camp because I knew that if it was cold enough for me to need it, I would die of exposure while stripping off my down suit and putting on the extra layer.

We had an assortment of sleeping bags. Greg and I used the bags made especially to my specifications by Mountain Designs for our climbs of Annapurna II and Mt Everest. Chris and Glenn used these bags as well, borrowed from the Everest expedition members. The bags were cut large enough for us to wear down suits inside, and long enough to keep water bottles and boot-liners at the bag's foot to prevent them freezing overnight. The sleeping bags were slightly underfilled with high quality down, but extra warmth came from the use of a lightweight, removable Gore-tex shell. The total weight was 2.4 kilograms. Jonathan and Lyle used J & H snow bags.

I slept on two full-length karrimats, but everyone else used one Thermarest and one karrimat. For me, the extra comfort and increased insulation of a Thermarest is not worth the extra weight and bulkiness, nor the time spent waiting for it to inflate and deflate. Also, karrimats do not lose their insulating properties when jabbed by ice-axes or holed by the flaming heads of matches as a Thermarest can.

By the time we reached the mountain, we had depoted most of our climbing hardware, and were left with only two 50-metre lengths of rope, a shorter length of 8-millimetre cord, a few 'nuts' and 'friends' (climbing hardware) for protection, two snow-stakes and three ice-screws. Between us we had three northwall hammers, and we each had an ice-axe. We were all equipped with Footfang crampons, apart from Greg who wore an old and trusted pair of Grivels. My personal experiences with frostbite, as well as those of my climbing partners, have convinced me that snap-on crampons are a much wiser alternative to crampons attached by straps. Jonathan and I wore Berghaus Yeti gaiters which were excellent, and permitted the use of snap-on crampons (some overboots preclude the use of these). The others wore Supergaiters or ankle gaiters, the latter being barely adequate. Our climbing boots were plastic Koflach Ultra Extremes worn with felt inner boots, except by Greg and me. We used aveolite inners. We all had cold feet during the climb, but this was an indication of the temperature rather than a failing in the boots. That the plastic of Jonathan's boot shattered, however, did demonstrate a failing. I believe that the technology is available to make boots better suited to extreme cold. Perhaps they already exist but, as with any equipment, field tests are the only way to make sure. On a multi-day climb in Antarctica the best possible footwear is essential. Frostbite to the feet is a particularly dangerous injury in Antarctica because help is a long way away, especially for small, private expeditions in remote ranges like the Admiralty or Victory Mountains. Although these mountains are close to the coast, they are hundreds of kilometres from the nearest inhabited bases.

For most of our time on the continent we wore one of two types of Sorrel boots. Both have flexible rubber soles and thick felt liners, but Cariboos have leather uppers while Snow Cats have uppers of proofed nylon. The Cariboos were probably warmer until sweat and melted snow soaked into the leather, which then froze. The temperature was never high enough for long enough to thaw and dry the boots properly. We all had problems with frozen inner boots. The boots, socks and gloves hanging above the stove from the roof of the cook-tent every night made the tent look like a laundry. I frequently wore my inner boots to bed to help dry them out.

Our Sorrels fitted into cable bindings on our skis. This system was functional but did not allow much control over the skis. On the long, flat Antarctic glaciers, however, this did not pose a problem. Our skis were metal-edged Asnes. Waxes alone did not give enough grip against the weight of the sledges, so for extra traction we used synthetic skins. Both the skis and the skins worked well.

Our experiences with the reconditioned skidoo were frustrating rather than anything else. Chris and Lyle had a good working knowledge of its mechanics and they made sure we had many spare parts. A brand new machine with ice-studs in its tracks would have been more powerful, as well as providing better traction on slippery ice. Although we were not given the opportunity to run a field test, the Tucker Glacier proved to be the equivalent of a skidoo freeway. On the right kind of snow it is very easy to cover large distances with a skidoo and therefore to put oneself dangerously far from the nearest supply point. We were lucky to have lost the skidoo while still in a position to consider whether to continue or to return to the boat. The big danger of skidoos in Antarctica is that they tempt expeditions to over-extend themselves.

We regretted the loss of the skidoo for practical reasons, but we were also annoyed that we had unwittingly added its bulk to the pollution of antarctic waters. In retrospect, we were all glad to experience the continent without the intrusion of machines. Had we planned a manhaul from the outset, we would have taken a much lighter wooden sledge designed specifically for manhauling, rather than the big cargo one, then the manhauling would not have been quite so great an effort. Our fibreglass pulks worked well. We decided the best

design was that of the 2-metre waisted pulks, which each had two runners about 10 centimetres wide. This design reduced the friction on the snow, was easier to turn, and seemed less likely to meander out of our ski tracks than the shorter, trackless pulk.

On every major expedition we have been forced to improvise something, whether it be a way of coping with the loss of gear or fixed rope in avalanches, or the need to find some form of shelter in the most unlikely places. The lesson is to be always adaptable and aware, because the environment is invariably more powerful than we are, no matter how many gadgets are taken along. Of course, one cannot always expect to win. In Antarctica success is marked by survival and escape before the long, dark winter. Every other achievement is a bonus.

FOOD

Greg Mortimer

It was a sad, sad day when we said goodbye to Margaret's cooking and headed into the cold unknown of Edisto Inlet! No more scones for afternoon tea. Goodbye fresh eggs for breakfast. Arivaderci fresh coffee and cream.

The days that followed were an interesting experiment into the psychology of food. There seemed to be a direct correlation between the distance from the last home cooked meal and the amount of time we spent thinking about food. By the time we had covered the 150 kilometres to Mt Minto we thought about food 150 times a day more than usual.

At the same time, the further we got away from the coast the more critical a good balanced diet became. Each day's food was the next day's energy and to climb up mountains you need mountains of food.

Experience on previous expeditions had shown us that good, tasty food is a huge advantage in an extreme climate. The thought of having to face yet another night of packet cardboard stew soon becomes depressing. I had done my apprenticeship in Antarctica in previous years, living on government issue stews and canned food; I didn't want to go through it again on this expedition. So a great deal of effort was put into developing the menu for this expedition and, in hindsight, it was well worth it.

At the outset I found four different menus in old books about Antarctic and Himalayan expeditions, and by averaging the quantities from the four menus I arrived at some guideline figures. The shore menu had to fulfil three different needs: food to be left at the coast in case of an emergency; food for travelling inland if we used a skidoo; and food suitable for manhauling and for consumption on the mountain. To check the overall quantities I used a rule of thumb: 1 kilogram of food per person per day. It would have been a real nuisance to get stuck for the winter and slowly starve to death.

Once the basic quantities were established it was a matter of letting the imagination run wild. Obviously there were different requirements for each aspect of the menu. The emergency shore food could be bulky and without weight restriction, whereas the manhauling and mountain food needed to be much lighter. I didn't worry too much about expense not only because diet is such a critical consideration for a happy expedition but because the overall food bill is only a small percentage of the total expedition budget.

The basic philosophy behind our choice of food was to provide a high carbohydrate, high fibre, strong tasting diet with as much variety as possible while we were inland. We expected to consume as many as 6000 calories per day while manhauling or climbing but somewhat less if using a skidoo or if stranded on the shore. There was a mixture of vegetarian and carnivore food habits amongst the six of us but the menu was very largely vegetarian. Some meat was taken in the form of salami and tinned fish.

Our food sponsers were generous and very helpful. For manhauling and climbing, Sanitarium in particular produces wonderful food such as muesli bars, nuts, dried fruit and whole grains.

Attention was paid to how heavy all the inland food would be, but without being obsessive. It is possible to have a good mountain diet without relying on those light but ghastly dehydrated stews. Our only dried food was fruit and vegetables. Care was also given to devising main meals that were relatively easy to prepare in the confines of a tent, hence a reliance on rice and pasta with strong accompanying tastes from herbs and spices. As it turned out the evening meal would take two to three hours from the time of first lighting the stove to the final licking of the bottom of the pot.

By the time we were seven days away from the ship we were obsessed by food. Lunches had been designed to be quick and easy without having to cook anything, but they became disgusting affairs. Our table manners all but forgotten, we sat around the sledges partaking of a two-fisted feeding frenzy, consuming obscene quantities of food. By the time we were ten days away from the ship, the sugar cravings were overwhelming. You see, the problem with being well-fed and western is that we develop sugar addictions. Try it some time. Try not eating sugar for a week! Consequently the chocolate and lolly supply needs to be plentiful.

Back on the shore we had left a pile of food about 4 metres long by 4 metres wide by 2 metres high. This was our calculated requirement for six people for one year. A lot less care was taken with this menu. We ordered large quantities of tinned food, bulk grains, flour, biscuits, dried milk, cheese, soups, tinned fish, tinned fruit and beverages. It was, after all, only to be used in the unlikely event of an emergency and we would have presumably had a lot more time available in those circumstances for concocting something edible. A typical day's menu whilst manhauling and climbing was something like this:

Breakfast:
Tea/Coffee
Porridge i.e. Rolled Oats with sugar and milk
Omelette or scrambled egg made from egg powder
Biscuits and spreads

Lunch:
Biscuits (Ryvita, Vitawheat, Cabin bread)
Cheese (all sorts – Camembert, Stilton, Ambrosia, Brie, Cheddar, Jarlesberg)
Salami
Dried fruit (apricot, pears, apples, peaches, mangoes, pineapple, sultanas)
Spreads (jam, honey, peanut butter, vegemite)
Nuts (macadamias, Brazil nuts, cashews, almonds, pecans, peanuts)
Fruit juice
Chutneys, pickles, olives
Oysters
Margarine
Chocolate, sweets
Hot Drink

Dinner:
Soup and dry biscuits
Pasta or rice based dish with a rich sauce or curry
Fresh herbs and spices
Chutneys, pickles, onions, packet vegetables
Tinned fish
Hot drink (coffee, tea, milo)
Chocolate

The menu was a success. While we were inland, each person lost a small amount of weight but our stomachs and minds were well nourished. There is no doubt that every ounce of effort put into developing the food supplies is handsomely rewarded at the end of the day.

FOOD SUPPLIES FOR THE BICENTENNIAL ANTARCTIC EXPEDITION

Allan And Vi Thistlethwayte (to feed 11 people)

Drinks
Coffee:
  ground
  instant (6 kg)
Tea:
  bags (1500 i.e. 2 kg)
  leaves (8 kg)
Milk:
  longlife (40 l)
  powdered (50 kg)
  coffee/milk (24 tins)
  sweetened condensed (72 tins)
  cream (96 tins)
Cocoa (6 kg)
Instant malted milk (6 tins)
Milo (12 kg)

Quick (16 tins)
Soy milk powder (3 kg)
Cordial (24 bottles)
Tang (36 x 500 gm i.e. 18 kg)
Tinned fruit juices (72 x 800 ml)
Dried legume soup mix (12 kg)
Soup powder (20 kg)
Tinned soups (108 tins)

Dairy
Butter: tinned (100 x 454 gm i.e. 50 kg)
Camembert (2 cases)
Cheddar cheese (200 x 500 gm i.e. 100 kg)
Other cheeses (100 kg)
Dried Parmesan cheese (20 tubes)
Custard powder (9 kg)
Yoghurt: powdered culture (20 kg)

Red Meat
Bacon }
Chops } (assorted quantities)
Steak }
Ham: small tins (40 tins)
Meat: tinned (96 tins)
Salami (14 kg)

Poultry
Chicken pieces
Eggs:
  fresh (80 doz.)
  powdered (20 kg)

Fish
Salmon (36 x 440 gm i.e. 15.84 kg)
Sardines (6 cases)
Smoked mussels (48 x 100 gm i.e. 4.8 kg)

Smoked oysters
Tuna: tinned (8 cases)
Paté

Nuts

Macadamias (10 kg)
Hazelnuts (10 kg)
Brazil nuts (10 kg)
Pecans (14 kg)
Almonds (12.5 kg)
Peanuts (12.5 kg)
Roasted nuts (10 kg)

Vegetable Proteins

Dried coconut cream (500 gm)
Dried coconut
Tinned coconut milk (3 tins i.e. 450 g)
Borlotti/lima beans (1 kg)
Chick peas (1 kg)
Lentils (1 kg)
Soy beans (1 kg)
Split peas (1 kg)
Dried tofu (3 kg)
TVP (15.5kg)

Vegetables

Fresh:
  butternut pumpkins (30 kg)
  garlic (4 kg)
  ginger
  onions (20 kg)
  potatoes (150 kg)
  salad vegetables (assorted quantities)
sprouts
Dried:
  capsicum (2 kg)
  carrots (10 kg)
  green peas (7.5 kg)
  mashed potato
  peas & corn (10 kg)
Tinned:
  asparagus (36 tins)
  baked beans (120 tins)
  beans (96 tins)
  beetroot (24 tins)
  mushrooms in butter (2 cases)
  potatoes (50 tins)
  ratatouille (48 tins)
  sweet corn (36 tins)
  tomato (60 tins)
  various stews (96 tins)

Fruit

Fresh:
  apples
  lemons
  mangoes   } (assorted quantities)
  oranges
Dried:
  apples (25 kg)
  apricots (12.5 kg)
  currants (12.5 kg)
  dates (22.5 kg)
  mango/pawpaw (10 kg)
  mixed fruit (10 kg)

  pears (12.5 kg)
  prunes (12.5 kg)
  raisins (12.5 kg)
  sultanas (30 kg)
Tinned:
  apricots (60 tins)
  peaches (60 tins)
  peaches in mango jelly (48 tins)
  pears (60 tins)
  pineapple pieces (48 tins)

Cereals

Bran (24 pkts)
Oats (6 of 9 days) (50 kg)
Cerola (48 x 500 gm i.e. 24 kg)
Muesli (2 of 9 days) (20 kg)
Weet-Bix/Good Start (1 of 9 days) (8 kg)
Rice cakes (240)

Carbohydrates

Flour (150 kg)
Pasta & Noodles (35 kg)
Brown rice (70 kg)
Continental savoury rice (72 pkts)
Long grain white rice (50 kg)
Vesta rice (144 pkts)
Yeast (50 x 35 gm i.e. 1.75 kg)

Biscuits

Family Assorted (not cream) (10 pkts)
Ryvita/Sao (160 pkts)
Shortbread (40 pkts)
Vita Weet (48 pkts)

Cakes

Afternoon tea roll: tinned (80)
Fruit cakes in foil (12)
Pavlova mix (12 pkts)
Snack Pack puddings (2 cartons)

Condiments

Black peppercorns (1 kg)
Salt: organic (2 kg)
Brown vinegar (3 bottles)
Cooking oil: olive (1 tin)
Raw sugar (25 kg)
Icing sugar (6 pkts)
Chilli sauce (12 bottles)
Mayonnaise (8 jars)
Mustard:
  French (3 jars)
  English (3 jars)
Soy sauce (6 bottles)
Tomato paste (24 jars)
Tomato sauce (3 bottles)
Worcester sauce (3 bottles)
Black olives (2 tins)
Chutneys (12 jars)
Gherkins (12 jars)
Pickles (10 jars)
Pickled onions (10 jars)
Golden syrup (20 kg)
Honey (1 bucket i.e. 10 kg)
Maple syrup (2 bottles)
Marmalade & jam (40 jars)
Peanut Butter (40 jars i.e. 10 kg)

Tahini (1 bucket)
Vegemite/Promite (24 jars)

Herbs & Spices

Basil
Bay leaves
Cardamon pods
Chilli powder
Cinnamon Sticks
Creamed coconut
Garam masala
Ground coriander
Ground cumin & seeds
Ground fenugreek
Lemon grass
Oregano
Rosemary
Star anise
Stock cubes (20 x **24 cubes**)
Thyme
Turmeric
Whole cloves

Scroggin

Barley sugar (20 kg)
Bounty (100)
Snickers (100)
Chocolate (300 x 200 gm i.e. 60 kg)
Health bars (500)
M & Ms:
  plain (200 pkts)
  peanut (200 pkts)
Mars Bars (1000)
Milky Way (100)
Minties/Kit Kat

Ship Stores

Dishwashing liquid (12 l)
Shampoo
Soap
Toothpaste (4 tubes)
Woolmix clotheswash (3 bottles)
Paper towelling (60 rolls)
Tissues (6 boxes)
Toilet paper (60 rolls)
Clothes pegs (30–40)

Galley Stores

Dish brushes (5)
Scouring pads (30)
Rubber gloves (3)
Sponges (30)
Weetex/Chux
Tea-towels (6)
Peppermill (2)
Measuring flask (1)
Scales (1)
Can-openers (6)
Garlic press (1)
Cutting board (1)
Wooden spoons (3)
Soup ladel (2)
Tongs (2)
Spatulas (2)
Sharp knives, steel & stone (2)

Grater (1)
Potato peelers (6)
Baking pans:
  bread (3)
  biscuit (1)

Flour sifter (1)
Pressure cookers (2)
Oven mitts (2)
Pyramid toaster (1)
Aluminium foil (2 rolls)

Gladwrap (2 rolls)
Cookery books (various)
Spare cups (various)
Tea pot (1)
Coffee percolator (large) (1)

Mountain Party (to feed 6 people for 35 days)

Drinks
Coffee: instant (1 large tin i.e. 525 gm)
Tea: leaves (2 kg)
Milk:
  powdered (12 kg)
  sweetened condensed (1 kg)
Milo (3 kg)
Soy milk powder (1 kg)
Soup powder (5.25 kg)
Tang (8 kg)

Cereals
Muesli (5 kg)
Oats (5.25 kg)

Carbohydrates
Pasta (8.4 kg)
White rice (8.4 kg)

Biscuits
Dry biscuits (25 kg)
Sweet biscuits (4 kg)

Cakes
Fruit cakes in foil (8 kg)

Condiments
Black peppercorns (200 gm)
Raw sugar (10.5 kg)
Brown vinegar (1 bottle i.e. 1 kg)
Chilli sauce (1 bottle i.e. 500 g)

Soy sauce (1 bottle i.e. 1 kg)
Miso (500 gm)
Tahini (2 kg)
Pickles (1 jar)
Chutneys (1 jar i.e. 440g)
Honey (3 kg)
Marmalade & jam (3 kg)
Peanut Butter (3 kg)
Vegemite/Promite (750 gm)

Red Meat
Salami (6 kg)

Poultry
Eggs: powdered (5 kg)

Fish
Sardines (1 kg)
Tuna: tinned (7 kg)

Dairy
Butter: tinned (10 kg)
Custard powder (1.5 kg)
Dried parmesan cheese (3 tubes i.e. 450 g)
Fresh cheddar cheese (8.4 kg)

Vegetable Proteins
Dried coconut cream (500 gm)
Tinned coconut milk (3 tins i.e. 450 g)
Borlotti/lima beans (1 kg)
Chick peas (1 kg)

Dried tofu (3 kg)
Lentils (1 kg)
Soy beans (1 kg)
Split peas (1 kg)
Tinned beans (4 kg)
TVP (15.5kg)

Vegetables
Dried:
  capsicum (1 kg)
  carrot (1 kg)
  green peas (1 kg)

Fruit
Dried:
  apples
  apricots
  mango/pawpaw   (11 kg total)
  peaches
  pears   3⌡

Scroggin
Barley sugar (5 kg)
Chocolate (10.5 kg)
Health bars (10 kg)
Nuts (10 kg)

MEDICAL CONSIDERATIONS
Glenn Singleman

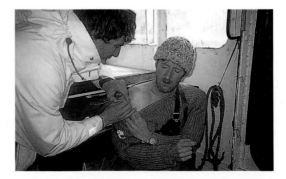

'WE'RE carrying too much weight; cut the medical supplies in half again.'

For the fourth time I reduced the equipment that had *all* seemed so important to me when we started out. I added a small sack of supplies to the depot in the middle of the Tucker Glacier, aware that in doing so the number of conditions that I could treat was decreasing. I was torn between the desire to reach the mountain and the need to be safe and medically prepared for any emergency. We were 100 kilometres from our ship and about 400 kilometres from the nearest Antarctic base with medical facilities. We all had to adopt a 'prevent-ative' approach to injury and illness – the small effort required to prevent an accident overwhelmingly outweighed the effort of a rescue or radical treatment.

I had spent six months before we left planning and preparing for the worst medical disasters imaginable. Each member of the expedition underwent a physical examination and had blood taken for a full blood count, multiple biochemical analysis, hepatitis and AIDS antibody status, and blood grouping. Fortunately the expeditioners fell into two blood groups – O and B – which meant that everybody on the expedition had someone else who could donate the same blood type should transfusion become necessary.

I had to consider the usual medical problems which can befall any group of eleven individuals aged between twenty-six and sixty-five in a given three month period, as well as special precautions needed to approach the Antarctic environ-ment.

The average summer temperature of the North Victoria Land coast varies between 0°C and −30°C, and the added wind-chill factor of an Antarctic blizzard contributes to the 'ideal' setting for cold injury. Chilblains, trenchfoot and classic frostbite are not separate entities but rather a clinical con-tinuum of the same pathological process: the result of constriction of small arteries leading to tissue oxygen star-vation as well as the disruption of cells caused by their water content freezing and expanding. Frostbite results from cold exposure to the periphery. Should cold exposure be severe, a person's core body temperature may fall and hypothermia could result – a rapidly fatal condition. The low Antarctic temperatures mean that the absolute humidity is always low, making dry skin and dehydration very real problems, as well as exacerbating asthmatic tendencies. Twenty-four hour daylight and vast expanses of white increase the risk of sunburn and snowblindness. But an unexpected 'benefit' of the cold environment is that away from the coast (and penguin/bird droppings) the Antarctic environment is almost sterile. While there are less organisms around to cause infection, however, host debilitation and respiratory cilia paralysis (from cold) mean that infections quickly become serious.

Whether in Antarctica, the Himalaya or the backyard, mountain climbing is a hazardous occupation. Falling off a mountain or being caught by an avalanch can result in death or major trauma (a caved-in head, chest or abdomen, multiple fractures and massive blood loss). If a summit is more than 3500 metres high then the possibility of altitude sickness is encountered. (i.e. high altitude pulmonary oedema or cerebral oedema). The danger increases with the altitude but was not a significant problem on the 4163-metre-high Mt Minto.

No less hazardous is sailing the Southern Ocean in a small boat. Motion sickness and the possibility of drowning were added to the cold environment difficulties (themselves exacer-bated by perpetual dampness). Lyle's sea-sickness and his resistance to every known treatment became legendary. In total we tried six different strategies (anticholinergics, antihistamines, two drugs affecting vestibular circulation, Maxolon and accupressure) with minimal success. He lost about 5 kilograms during the four weeks it took to sail Antarctica, but seemed to draw strength from his surround-ings once we arrived. We all admired Lyle's spirit in the face of a chronically debilitating condition.

The psychological stresses of spending three months in an extreme environment with a small group of people cannot be underestimated. Fortunately nobody developed any of the neuroses or psychoses historically associated with such ex-peditions. I suppose we had too many other things to worry about.

In considering the medical requirements before we left, my first instinct was to take a hospital – but we couldn't fit one into our 21-metre schooner! Greg told me I could only take what would fit into five tackle boxes. In consultation with Dr John Roberts (Acting Director of the Royal Prince Alfred Hospital Accident and Emergency Department) I wrote a six-page report listing the expedition's medical requirements. It reflected likely problems, available space and my own capabilities. I sent a copy of this report to relevant pharmaceu-tical companies and requested free samples of the necessary products. Fortunately the response was excellent and I thank all those companies who are mentioned in the list of sponsors.

The medical supplies were prepared so that they could be easily subdivided into kits (although I did not anticipate the degree to which this was to happen). A kit had to be taken up to the mountain, a kit left with the *Allan And Vi Thistlethwayte* and a kit left in the Cape Hallett 'winter over' refuge. We had enough surgical hardware to perform most emergency oper-ations; this was left at Cape Hallett, which would become our base in an emergency. I tried to take enough equipment on our overland journey to keep an injured person alive until definitive treatment could be provided at Cape Hallett, or until an evacuation could be organised from there. This approach became more difficult as we drew near to the mountain, shedding our supplies behind us. By the time we reached advance base camp I had a mere pocketful of equipment, all of which was frozen. It was at this stage that a 'preventative' approach and providence became our best medicines.

Despite recent advances in frostbite management, which help to limit its spread, there is no cure for 'dead' tissue. So it is with some irony that I admit to developing superficial frostbite to my right great toe. This resulted from using new, overtight boots on the day of the actual climb. Though it led to a great deal of pain and trepidation at the time, it has not resulted in permanent tissue loss. Because of the long distance to be covered on foot our choice of footwear was most important. As well as our Mukluk boots, we modified the 'vapour barrier' concept used during 'The Footsteps of Scott' expedition. This system dealt with the problem of sweating feet. Under normal circumstances, socks absorb this sweat, but in the Antarctic cold the sweat turns to ice when the day's effort has ceased (and the heat generated by the working muscles has sub-sided). Thus the chances of frostbite are greatly increased. By using a vapour barrier (like plastic) and roll-on antiperspirants, the 'Footsteps of Scott' expedition had been able to prevent the vicious cycle of frozen sweat in the expeditioners' socks. We used a more potent powdered antiperspirant (Diphemanil methylsulphate 2%) and com-bined it with a fungicidal powder (to stop the footrot that so plagued the members of the 'Footsteps' expedition). The results were good, despite inconsistent implementation by those in our party.

Considering what could have gone wrong during the expedition (medically), remarkably little did; a fact that reflects experience, careful planning, preventative awareness from everybody – and lots of luck.

STILLS PHOTOGRAPHY
Jonathan Chester

DOCUMENTING the Bicentennial Antarctic Expedition was the most challenging photographic assignment I have ever undertaken. The remoteness of our objective and the harsh environmental conditions not only placed great limitations on my ability to photograph, but tested preparations and equipment to the limit.

With the adventurous nature of the trip, and the spectacular scenery and wildlife en route, most of the team took photographs as a personal record. There were exceptions. To save weight whilst sledging on the continent, the film crew, Chris Hilton and Glenn Singleman, left their stills cameras aboard the ship. Greg Mortimer, on the other hand, did have a camera, but was so completely focused on the problems of getting us to and from Antarctica and Mt Minto that he did not expose a single frame during the entire three months.

Greg, I believe, also felt that his restraint was more than compensated for by my excesses. With so much at stake — a book and magazine contracts to fulfil, as well as images to supply to sponsors — and no chance of reshooting, I exposed over 200 rolls. Of the other serious photographers in the team, Lincoln Hall exposed some fifty rolls, while Peter Gill shot twenty rolls.

How much film do you need for such a venture? Everyone had their own preferences as to type and quantity. I estimated my needs on the basis of three rolls of colour transparency and one roll of black and white film per day. An additional 100 rolls were added to the total as a token amount to cover the possibility of being stuck at Cape Hallet for the winter.

Kodachrome was the expedition's preferred film stock and thanks to sponsorship from Kodak Australasia we were supplied with generous quantities of professional 35 mm and 120 mm roll film. The 35 mm colour films used were (in order of popularity) 64 ASA, 25 ASA and 200 ASA Professional Kodachrome, and in monochrome, T Max 400 ASA and T Max 100 ASA. Vision Graphics of Sydney donated the cost of the K14 and E6 colour processing.

Not everyone was comfortable in front of my ever-present camera, but to properly document the expedition co-operation of the other team members was vital. My preferred shooting style was to avoid interrupting the flow of events by trying to record them as they happened. This occasionally meant being subjected to black looks if I was photographing rather than pulling my weight on a halyard.

In several situations, while things were out of control when we were being blown onto an iceburg in a force 11 gale, for example, I was too scared to think about taking photos, but in most circumstances my documentary instincts did not fail me. In fast breaking situations like the fire in the engine room, the heat of the moment and poor light led me to grab my autofocus camera. With its in-built flash I was able to shoot a few frames that captured the anguish of the moment. Having my equipment readily at hand at sea and on the continent meant that it was subject to more than an average amount of physical abuse, extremes of temperature and corrosion. It is, of course, essential for such an undertaking to be well prepared with proven and reliable equipment.

Pete Gill, Lincoln Hall and I were the most experienced and serious photographers and we all happen to use Nikon cameras. This had many advantages, not the least of which was being able to borrow lenses and use each other's cameras with ease. Maxwell Optical Industries, the agent for Nikon in Australia, assisted with the loan of a camera body and several lenses that we were able to share around.

No matter how reliable a camera is, backups are essential for such a risky venture. Lincoln and I took multiple camera bodies. Lincoln had an FE2 body and an FM2 body. This rugged mechanical model is the workhorse of many outdoor photographers for even if the batteries fail, the shutter still works at all speeds. Lincoln's lenses included a 35 mm f1.2, a 35 to 105 mm f4.5 zoom, and a 200 mm f4. Pete Gill used an FM2 body with a short-range zoom and a 200 mm f4.5. My Nikon kit comprised as follows: F3P body plus MD4 motor drive, FE2 body plus MD12 motor drive, FM2 body plus MD12 motor drive, FM body, and an all-weather autofocus L35AW AD. The following Nikkor lenses were included: a 20 mm f2.8, a 28 mm f3.5, a 35 mm f2, a 50 mm E series, a 55 mm f2.8 Micro, a 35 to 70 mm f3.5 zoom, an 85 mm f1.4, a 180 mm f2.8, and a 300 mm f4.5 IF ED. All lenses had skylight filters attached. The only other filters used were polarisers to accentuate clouds and blue sky in some landscape shots.

I had also been lent a Hasselblad CM from Hugo the Foto Surgeon and a Makina Plaubel 6 x 7 cm format camera from Gunz Photographic Pty Ltd for landscape shooting, but they barely came out of their cases on the journeys to and from the Antarctic because of the likelihood of salt damage. And once we were on the continent lack of time as well as their weight prevented me from taking full advantage of these larger format cameras.

Keeping the photographic gear dry aboard the ship was a continual problem, especially when shooting in rough weather, but Pelican camera cases proved ideal for storing it. In milder weather I would regularly keep a case containing camera and lenses strapped on top of the Fish Cabin hatchway for quick access for photographing wildlife. Made of very strong plastic, these cases are completely water-proof but it is necessary to include a sachet of a desiccating agent such as activated silica gel in case any moisture should find its way in while the case is open. The silica gel turns pink from blue when it is fully absorbed, and this happened early in the voyage. Heating the silica gel in a slow oven for several hours will make it reusable, but our 240 volt generator, which powered our convection oven, failed at about the same time.

Storage of delicate camera equipment was not the only ship-board problem however. On a number of occasions when photographing hourglass dolphins in heavy weather, my cameras and I were drenched by unseen waves slamming up against the side of the ship. This would then mean spending the next ten minutes cleaning and drying everything. First, the surface water would be wiped off with tissues, then the camera components and lens would be separated and dried, and finally all surfaces wiped over with a cloth soaked in alcohol to remove the salt. With this careful treatment all the gear seemed to survive such dunkings unscathed. When a wide-angle lens was needed in rough seas, my all-weather autofocus L35 AW AD came into its own.

Once we reached the continent the shooting began in earnest, and at last the larger format cameras and a Gitzo tripod, sponsored by L&P Photographic Supplies, came into use. With daylight around the clock, and so much to do by way of preparation of the skidoo, rations, our personal kits and photographic gear, it was hard to find time to sleep as well as work and photograph.

By the start of the sledging journey my gear had been rationalised to the Makina Plaubel, the F3P with MD4 and the FM2 with MD12 camera bodies, and the 20 mm, 28 mm, 35 to 70 mm, 85 mm and 180 mm lenses, plus the L35 AW AD. When the skidoo went to the bottom of the ocean, with it went my FM2 and 35 to 70 mm zoom amongst other things.

To have any chance of manhauling to and from the mountain we also had to be ruthless in reducing our loads. My two longer lenses, the 85 mm and 180 mm, were too heavy to take and so had to be cached along with the Makina Plaubel at Football Saddle. For the remainder of the sledging journey and climb I was limited to shooting with just the 20 mm and 28 mm lenses on the F3P body, and the L35 AW AD with its 35 mm lens. Fortunately Lincoln still had his 35 to 105 mm zoom and the 200 mm lens, both of which I was able to borrow.

The cold and the extremely varied lighting conditions were the main technical problems I encountered when photographing on the glacier and during the climb. Our deadline to return to the coast before the ship was due to depart at the end of February meant we had to sled at least 15 kilometres each day, so there were few concessions to the needs of still and movie photography. If I stopped to shoot I was usually left behind. It was not uncommon for me to lose sight of the rest of the party, arrive at the lunch spot half an hour after the others, leave before them to get some action shots as they skied by, and then not to arrive at camp until long after the tents had been set up. None of this concerned me greatly, however, for Antarctica is a photographer's paradise.

I knew from experience that the extremely bright and high-contrast lighting caused by all the snow and ice would make it necessary to bracket exposures, opening up half to one and a half stops more than that a light metre reading shown in the camera, or take a reading off the back of my hand. This helps avoid badly underexposed shots that result from just following the camera's meter. If wearing mittens I would take a meter reading off blue sky as well as bracketing. While this method was not foolproof, the percentages were acceptable, and having plenty of film helped.

At that time of year, which was over a month after the summer solstice, sunset and sunrise flow into each other. From about 9 pm until 4 am it was necessary to use a tripod but, to cut down our loads even more, this also had to be cached not very far up the Tucker Glacier. From then on I had to make do with 200 ASA Kodachrome film and take shots hand held. Shooting in the twilight was bitterly cold. Temperatures of $-10°C$ took their toll on fingers, noses, film and especially batteries.

Duracell generously supplied the expedition with a small mountain of AA, C, D and camera batteries, but there was a limit to how many we could carry, so battery hungry accessories such as motor drives and flash guns had to be left behind. None of the cameras were specially prepared for the cold, but a remote Nikon Anti-cold Battery Holder (DB 2) that took two AA batteries and could be kept warm inside my jacket was a saving grace.

In any case, motor drives are not advisable in extremely cold conditions as they can cause static sparks from the film to be quickly transported in the dry air; these sparks show up on transparencies as little blue specks. In extreme cold the film also becomes very brittle and has a tendency to tear at the sprocket holes.

This problem was only encountered in the $-60°C$ wind chill conditions on the summit of Mt Minto. When I had to change film it was so brittle that it snapped off several times as the leader was crimped over to push into the take-up spool. Trying to tear a new leader wearing three pairs of gloves was impossible. Rather than remove a glove and risk frostbite, I had to tear a leader with my teeth. In order to minimise the static discharges and damage to the film in such very cold conditions, I wound the film on and rewound it very slowly. Even so, during the descent, the film jammed and I did not reload until I could remove the precious summit roll in the safety of a make-shift dark bag at the bottom of my sleeping bag.

Fortunately enough of the summit shots were successful, so I don't have to go back and do it all again! If I had my time over, however, I would take an even more simple and standardised set of gear with additional backups. My kit in future might include up to five FM2 bodies but with a similar range of lenses and film as I had on the Bicentennial Antarctic Expedition. Yet will there ever be another shoot quite like Mt Minto? I doubt it!

CINEMATOGRAPHY

CAMERA EQUIPMENT

Glenn Singleman

'IN the severe cold, filming becomes almost impossible. Power leads break, film snaps, and batteries run flat in seconds.' These words from the film version of *The Loneliest Mountain,* summarise the insults to our tormented equipment. When we left Sydney we had three 16 mm cameras, four Super-8 cameras and three sound recorders (see end of appendix for full details).

By the time we reached advance base camp this had been reduced to two Super-8 cameras and a Sony Walkman. On the climb, the flexible power lead from the batteries (kept warm inside my jacket) to the main Super-8 became brittle and snapped. We had to rely on the backup. This camera did not have an external power source; it was powered by two AA batteries inside the camera. At low temperatures, however, batteries give less power than normal. This meant that instead of running the camera for twelve minutes (as they did in Sydney), the two batteries only worked for twenty seconds! Unfortunately we were carrying only six batteries — so we shot a mere sixty seconds of film on the summit. After that our *only* opportunity to experience the location was in the same way as the others — without the bias and pressure of a camera lens. It was our special, unobstructed moment enjoying the most spectacular vista in the world. I was sorry that I was unable to film it, yet glad that I was freed from the necessity of having to.

Chris and I spent six hectic months buying equipment (with no money), researching the problems of cold environment filming and designing systems to protect the delicate instruments. The problems started from the moment we left Walsh Bay wharf. A single dousing from a wave would have ruined whatever it touched and, as did happen, the salt air corrodes the most resilient and cared for items in a matter of weeks. Waterproof housings are expensive, heavy and clumsy, so Tom Williams from High Tops Equipment made us splash-proof cordura covers for all the cameras and sound gear. These were excellent for keeping out the ubiquitous Antarctic drift snow as well as the spray of the Southern Ocean. We stored everything not in use in waterproof Pelican cases.

An iron shoulder is certainly an asset while filming on a small boat in big waves because a tripod is useless — an extra set of arms to hold on with would also help. Large lumps of metal, like cameras, become heat-sinks in a cold environment and I have heard stories about cameramen's eyeballs freezing onto eyepieces and fingers cold-welding onto focus rings. Fortunately, Tom's cordura covers prevented these gruesome possibilities. On many occasions, however, I had to put the camera down quickly, or give it to sombody else, because my fingers were freezing (despite multiple layers of gloves).

Ordinary grease freezes at − 15°C, so, where possible, we applied special low-viscosity grease. Unfortunately we could not apply it to the Super-8 cameras, so I had a lot of problems with the zoom, focus and aperture jamming. Chris also had problems with the Walkman jamming — at times he had to heat it over the stove to make it work. Chris's gas soldering-iron worked overtime in the difficult conditions as nearly every day a 'flexible' lead or an 'unbreakable' connection would become brittle in the cold and snap.

As we filmed we could often hear the camera motors straining and slowing down. This resulted in loss of synchronisation between the film image and the sound (which were being recorded separately). Upon our return to Australia we had to use sophisticated machinery to re-synchronise the sound and image. Condensation inside the lenses was also a big problem. I found the only way to minimise it was to keep the cameras at environmental temperature all the time — if they were kept inside the tents or next to my body, they fogged quickly and the condensation would take hours to dissipate.

After one month at sea, Chris and I had pared down our vast amounts of equipment to a couple of manageable armfuls. We had also evolved our unusual working relationship. When we set out from Cape Hallett we felt completely prepared for the worst Antarctica had to offer, but it only took three days before the skidoo and skis, Chris's best microphone and the wolf-hair windshield were lost. We soon discovered that the backup microphone was large and unwieldy and had to be covered with one of our socks to keep the wind noise down.

When the decision was made to manhaul we had to cache all the 16 mm camera equipment, our only tripod (generously donated by Universal Fluid Heads) and what little backup gear we had. The remainder of the film was shot on a hand-held Super-8 and recorded on a Sony Pro-Walkman. We swapped our Pelican cases for canvas camera carry bags made by Dave Murphy of Summit Gear. These proved to be light, efficient and comfortable assets that accompanied us all the way to the summit.

As we walked away from the Football Saddle equipment cache, we wondered if we would ever see the $20,000 worth of film gear again. We were not prepared to take such a risk with our exposed footage — if we lost it or could not retrieve it, there would be no documentary. Three days later we were instructed by Greg to cache the exposed stock as well, in an effort to cut back the load we were hauling. The bag containing the film stock measured 50 cm by 50 cm — this amounted to a miniscule dot on a glacier measuring 25 km by 120 km. We were doubtful of returning the same way or of finding the cache, so argued strongly that we should not leave the stock behind. The memorable high point of the exchange was when Lyle asked, 'What is more important — getting to the top of the mountain or making the film?' He was completely bewildered when Chris and I replied in unison. 'Making the film!' We had fledgling careers at stake and were responsible for thousands of dollars of somebody else's money in equipment. Television executives in Sydney would not understand excuses — no matter how valid. But it was Antarctica that made the final decision — if we did not cut down on weight, we would probably have to spend the winter at Cape Hallett. As a compromise we left half the precious stock.

As well as coping the weight obsession we had to deal with time-obsessed individuals. The push to get to the mountain meant that nobody wanted to stop and be filmed or talk about what they were doing — they just wanted to get on and do it. Getting the shots meant getting behind, and we were offered no other alternative than to catch up. Our filmic 'raison d'être' was an irritation for the others, but as individuals we were all galvanised by the same special spirit that Antarctica engenders. How pale plastic images and printed words seem in comparison to the reality of that place!

We dedicate our film to The Antarctica World Wilderness Park.

SOUND RECORDING EQUIPMENT

Chris Hilton

FROM the time I first met Glenn Singleman almost two years before the beginning of our Antarctic expedition, we talked enthusiastically about one day making a film in Antarctica. We saw it as a wonderful metaphor for the plight of the planet — could humankind join to protect Antarctica or would it one day become just another oilfield or coalmine? In moments of fanciful imagining, the dream I concocted was of a $20 million epic drama.

Instead Glenn and I became involved in another vision — an audacious and anarchistic scheme — to make a documentary about climbing the tallest man-made structure in the southern hemisphere, the Sydney Tower. It was through this project that we met Greg and Lincoln, who just at that time happened to be looking for a film-crew that also climbed mountains, sailed yachts and enjoyed putting their lives on the line. Coincidences as strong as this one don't come along all that often. And so began a magical mystery tour that led us to the top of the 'Loneliest Mountain' (and back again). To communicate about Antarctica through the film was our first priority and not just a secondary excuse that we used to be part of a great adventure. Glenn and I have developed together as a filmmaking team. In general he takes care of the visuals and I look after the sound. In terms of what gets filmed and how, we make decisions about it together by a kind of arguing consensus approach — when there is time to do so. On this expedition, especially on land, there was precious little time for anything, so we just did what we could.

For recording sound on board the ship I used a Nagra 4.2 quarter-inch tape-recorder with an AKG-CK8 microphone with an elaborate wolf-hair windshield. This tape-recorder weighs about as much as four bricks and is therefore not ideal for manoeuvring around on the slippery decks.

For marking each take with a synch point I used an electronic slate which automatically advances to the next take. A number on the electronic slate lights up at exactly the same time as it fires an internal tone generator within the Nagra, which functions exactly the same as the 'clap' of the clapper board. The beauty of this system for a documentary sound recordist is that you always have one hand free for your microphone.

Once on land I abandoned the yoke of the Nagra and used a Sony Pro-Walkman that was adapted for synchronous recordings. To combat the cold I kept the Walkman inside my jacket whilst recording and it always operated at close to the correct speed. Towards the end of the trip, though, when the weather became particularly cold I had to heat it over the stove to make it work because the grease had become frozen.

For the whole expedition I used an AKG stereo microphone for recording stereo atmosphere tracks. These were recorded on metal cassette tape on the Pro-Walkman. In terms of television broadcasts in stereo, Australia is the most advanced country in the world, and as we had pre-sold the film to a commercial network who particularly favoured stereo, it was worth making this extra effort. Natural sound is very important in making a documentary in order to convey the atmosphere of what it was really like to be there, although most audiences receive this aural information without being aware of it. Good stereo recordings help to 'thicken' the soundtrack and give it texture. Antarctica is one of the best places in the world for recording the sound of activity because there is absolutely no background noise.

After losing my most convenient microphone (the AKG-CK8) when the skidoo disappeared, I had to use the wieldy Sennheiser 815 with its archaic windshield. I carried it all the way to advance base camp on the mountain. From there I used a Sony omnidirectional neck microphone to record the actual climb. The recorded sounds of panting and crunching on the ice and rock came in very handy in constructing the film. The microphone also recorded Greg's moving speech on the summit of the mountain. The words of my own that I managed to record on the top were very ineloquent — 'I'm absolutely stuffed' or words to that effect.

We used the following camera and sound equipment:

AKG-CK8 Microphone

AKG-522 ENG Stereo Microphone (generously donated by AKG)

Bell & Howell 70DR 16 mm

Braun Nizo 6080 Super-8 with crystal synch

Canon 814 Super-8

Canon 814-XLS Super-8

Canon Scoopic 16 mm

Eclair ACL 16 mm

Eumig Nautica Super-8 (waterproof)

Nagra 4.2 quarter-inch tape-recorder

Senheisser 815 Microphone

Senheisser Neck Microphones (2)

Sony Pro-Walkman and metal tapes

Sony Pro-Walkman with crystal speed control (prepared by Mike Moore at BRIG electronics)

Full assistant's kit with light meters, gas soldering-iron, multimeter etc.

SAILING THE SOUTHERN OCEAN

Colin Putt

ANTARCTIC waters, that is, those waters south of the iceberg line, are difficult or even dangerous for small vessels not only because they are so remote and extensive, but because they are influenced by the most violent weather in the world, and because of the presence of icebergs and pack-ice. Despite these hazards the low temperatures are not a major problem during the sailing season, and Antarctic navigation poses few special difficulties.

Many small ships have reached Antarctica in its northernmost part, the Antarctic Peninsula; a few have penetrated to its coasts south of the Antarctic circle; and at least three have entered the Ross Sea, the southernmost sea in the world.

While the Peninsula is not far from inhabited land, supplies, ports and help, the rest of the Antarctic coast is a thousand nautical miles or more from such facilities, and the voyage there and back is a long one. Any very small vessel is inherently limited in her range under power by her capacity to carry fuel, and even if she can carry enough fuel to motor all the way she will be able then to carry little else. You need

plenty of stores and water for such a voyage, as well as equipment and stores for use ashore, and it is prudent to carry enough extra supplies to last a year in case you are frozen in. Your ship must therefore be able to cover most of the distance under sail, although a reliable engine with high thrust is essential for use in the pack-ice. Even without excessive fuel you will still be carrying a very heavy load, and conventional yachts are not designed to do this. Overloading is dangerous in the great winds and seas of the Antarctic, and so is the way in which a yacht hull can accelerate to high speed on a wave. Either factor or both together can lead to the ship broaching and capsizing, to damage on deck, and the loss of deck cargo and even crew. The ideal hull for such a voyage is that used on small, working sailing vessels, such as fishing boats, pilot cutters and so on.

Antarctic weather is ferocious — storms with extremely strong winds are frequent, and they last long enough with unimpeded fetch to build up very large seas. In early or late summer in the higher latitudes icing of the hull and rigging can be a serious problem. To successfully meet the conditions at sea your ship must be well and strongly built, buoyant and sea-kindly, with a short sturdy rig of low windage and simple design. Racing rigs are completely unsuitable, and I seriously suggest that masts only half the height of those that would be fitted to a fast cruising yacht are adequate in the Antarctic. These shorter masts are also, of course, about four times as strong.

Any very small vessel that ventures frequently into Antarctic waters is reasonably certain to be knocked down, capsized or pitch-poled sooner or later, and during certain conditions in a storm she may suffer this kind of treatment more than once within a few hours. In fact, the smaller the ship, the more likely this sort of thing is to happen. Since these accidents cannot be avoided with any degree of certainty, the vessel should be built and fitted out specifically to survive them. The decks, superstructure, ports, hatches and ventilators should be strong and watertight, the cargo and stores must be stowed immoveably, the masts and standing rigging should be short and powerful, and a steering position should be located inside the superstructure. Any centreboard or moveable keel must be secured against upward motion as well as downward motion.

In the higher latitudes, beyond the region of the great westerly winds, there is a reduction in the frequency and duration of major storms during the short summer season which lasts from mid-December to mid-February. This co-incides with the time of minimum incidence of pack-ice, and consequently is the time when it is practicable for a small vessel to venture into the far south. Storms, however, do still occur and you must be properly prepared to meet them. If you find yourself beyond 65° S outside this period, beware.

As you approach the coast of Antarctica, you will probably fall in with large fields of pack-ice. The popular idea of a ship breaking and thrusting her way through this sea-ice is simply inapplicable to a very small vessel, which is too small to push the floes aside, let alone break them. The ice, on the other hand, can easily inflict fatal damage to the ship, for she is too small and light to carry a construction strong enough to withstand heavy impact or the pressure of encroaching ice. In principle a small ship should never touch ice; when the route is blocked she should only enter the pack if a broad, open lead can clearly be seen to extend right through to open water on the other side, and if the weather is calm, clear and settled. Should such a lead not exist, or if the weather is unsuitable, you must wait for conditions to change or look elsewhere for a way through. 'Water sky' (dark streaks on the undersides of low clouds which indicate open water in the vicinity of sea-ice) and 'ice blink' (a whitish glare on low cloud above an accumulation of distant ice) on the clouds are useful indications of where to go and where not to go in search of a clear path. Even if there are only a few bits of ice about it is essential to go slowly to avoid damaging collisions, and you will find that it is impossible to make ground to windward while dodging floating ice under sail. Unless you have square sails which can be backed, you will have to use your motor to achieve sudden stops even when conditions allow sailing in the ice.

If you push into pack-ice without a clear lead through, in the hope of forcing or finding a path, you will almost certainly be stopped and beset. You are very likely to be close-nipped and damaged, and it is entirely possible that you may even be crushed and sunk. Trying to force a way through pack-ice wastes more time than waiting or looking elsewhere.

Much has been written about Archer and Nansen's principle, whereby a hull is built with saucer-shaped sections and without protruberances so that heavy ice pressure will push it upward instead of crushing it. Many small hulls approximate to the correct cross-section and, although they are usually well supplied with protruberances, they may be safely frozen into a sheltered harbour where there is no great pressure or height of ice. At sea, however, many of the great ice-floes are higher than the deck of a very small ship and can push her down and crush her regardless of her shape.

Icebergs are present in large numbers in Antarctic waters, accompanied by growlers, debris and brash which result from their disintegration. To actually come into contact with an iceberg at sea can be fatal to a ship of any size or strength; the larger pieces of debris can also destroy a small ship — and they are much harder to see than a berg. Once in Antarctic waters you must always watch carefully for bergs and pieces, looking for waves that break repeatedly in the same place. In poor visibility you must either stop or proceed to dead slow speed and use the ship's radar. It is unwise to go close to an iceberg as they are likely to shed pieces weighing millions of tonnes, or even to capsize at any time, and the resulting splash could easily overwhelm you. There is commonly a trail of debris stretching for miles in the lee of a berg. If you must pass through this area travel at dead slow, with a lookout at the bow.

During a storm in iceberg waters it would be an act of lunacy to use the often-advocated technique of running before wind and sea under sail or bare poles, because you could easily run into icebergs by giving the ship her head. If you try riding to a sea anchor and find yourself drifting on a collision course with a berg, you will probably have to cut the cable and lose the sea-anchor. The only practicable ways of riding out a storm among icebergs seem to be to heave to or, if the wind is too strong, to lie a-hull. While thus riding out the gale you must keep a good lookout all round because, propelled by deep currents, icebergs can move in any direction at surprising speeds, and, however violent the conditions, you and the ship must be ready and able to make sail or use the engine if any piece of ice comes too close.

With a good small ship and the right crew, and with unremitting care and patience, you will not only be able to sail into Antarctic waters and survive, but you are likely (although by no means certain) to reach your chosen destination. But to attempt, despite poor ice and weather conditions, to force your way to your objective because you are over-committed to sponsors, passengers, the media, or to your own ego, is a recipe for disaster.

RADIO COMMUNICATIONS

SHIP BOARD COMMUNICATIONS

Don Richards

RADIO COMMUNICATIONS during the Bicentennial Antarctic Expedition was conducted on both commercial maritime frequencies and amateur radio frequencies.

The communications equipment consisted of two Stingray ship-to-shore transceivers, Kenwood transceivers (models TS-430S and TS-680S) and Codan field transceivers. With the exception of some experimental work on the 6M amateur band (discussed further below), all antennae were single wires.

Communication on commercial frequencies was carried out, with a few exceptions, over distances of up to 600 nautical miles. This range included contact with Australian coastal stations during the voyage south from Australia and the equivalent New Zealand stations on the return journey; the Australian bases at Macquarie Island and at Casey Station on the Antarctic continent; the New Zealand and American bases at McMurdo Sound; the Italian base at Terra Nova Bay; the *Greenpeaces's* base in McMurdo Sound; and with our mountain party during their climb. Communication with the Australian base on Macquarie Island on both the southward and return voyages was of great assistance as we were able to receive relevant weather forecasts prepared by the Bureau of Meteorology in Melbourne. Our main source of information and support, however, came from the *Greenpeace*, which was in almost daily communication with us from the time we were making our approach to the Ross Sea in late January until we were off Banks Peninsular and about to enter the New Zealand port of Lyttelton on 22 March on the return voyage. *Greenpeace* was well fitted with communciation and weather equipment and the skipper, Jim Cottier, provided reliable weather forecasts, while their radio operator, David, relayed ice reports from the USSR or the USA sources whenever they were available.

Contact with McMurdo, the American base, was interesting, but complicated. They used different frequencies, depending on the subject being discussed or the information requested. This necessitated quick changes of operating frequency, so for this sort of work the Kenwood TS-430S was more useful than the Stingrays as the available frequencies

of the latter were limited by the crystals fitted. The male radio operators at McMurdo were formal and rather distant; but the women were more friendly and relaxed. They would give us a weather forecast and then qualify it by saying that it was prepared from the best data available and no guarantee would be given as to its accuracy and no responsibility taken for any damage that may occur as a result! However, they were concerned for our safety, particularly when we were held in the ice for several days on our final approach to Cape Hallett.

A most important use of commercial radio frequencies was in communication between the ship and the mountain party during their approach to Minto along the glaciers, and then during their return to the ship. Scheds (scheduled transmissions) were set up for daily contact in the evenings, with alternate times and frequencies established in the event of contact not being made on the primary sched. Greenpeace also listened to these scheds and was ready to relay messages if necessary.

Reception at the ship was generally poor due to the necessarily low transmission power of the shore party's portable equipment, but the mountaineers enjoyed better reception as the transmission power available on board the ship was relatively higher. However, by listening hard and with patience communication was maintained daily until the last few days of the climb, when the final ascent was made without a radio. Communication was re-established immediately after the ascent, and the news of the success was passed on to Sydney straight away by amateur radio.

Greenpeace were standing by and radio contact was made with the mountaineers as soon as the weather cleared, in order to make arrangements to locate the party as they returned down the glacier and to bring them back to our ship by helicopter. This strategy saved days of walking by the shore party and ensured that we were clear of the Ross Sea before the winter ice could freeze us in. Reliable radio contact was essential during this critical part of the expedition once the mountaineers had left the ship.

From the time we left Sydney Harbour we were, by prior

arrangement, in daily contact with an amateur station, VK2LW, in the Blue Mountains, just out of Sydney. Only on a handful of occasions was communication impossible or so poor that we had to give up after passing a position report. Thus during the entire expedition the latitude and longitude of our position was known each day by friends in Sydney. In this respect communication by amateur radio was as reliable as on our previous expeditions to the Antarctic. The frequencies used were in the 20M amateur band.

Each night at about 8 pm local time, whether at sea or waiting for the mountaineers at Cape Hallett, contact was made between the ship and VK2LW, giving the ship's position and a situation report. After the conclusion of 'official' business personal messages were sent from those on board to relations and friends at home. The messages were then telephoned to the people concerned. Some of the families had

short-wave receivers and would listen for an account of the day's happenings, or at times they would visit VK2LW or a local amateur radio operator and speak directly with those on the ship. Distances were too great and the power of our equipment insufficient to enable us to use the telephone services normally available to ships at sea.

Experimental transmissions were made from the ship on the 6M (50 mega Hertz) band, as well as from the Antarctic continent using special antennae. This resulted in several contacts from the ship with amateurs in Australia and New Zealand during the voyage south, but no contacts were made from the continent.

Our thanks to Kenwood (Australia), Australian Electronics Monthly, Codan, VK2VC and the Antarctic Division for lending us equipment.

FIELD COMMUNICATIONS

Jonathan Chester

THE mountain party began the traverse with two Codan HF portable radios. The main unit was a 6924 Mark II SSB transceiver, which was used with a dipole antenna that had been cut to suit the crystal frequencies we had specially installed in the unit. The commercial frequencies were chosen not only to give a range of options as we moved further away from the ship base, but to be compatible with the New Zealand, Scott Base and Australian National Antarctic Research Expedition (ANARE) primary working frequencies. We also had several marine distress frequencies so that we could communicate with passing ships should the need have arisen.

The main radio power supply was initially a 12-volt sealed car battery that we planned to recharge from the snow machine (skidoo). A military specification Phillips Elcoma solar panel, charging a 4 amp hour, 12-volt Nicad movie camera battery pack was carried as backup.

Once the skidoo was lost, the car battery and Nicad system had to be cached along with most of our other gear to save weight. Fortunately the film crew had two spare Expedition Batteries that we were able to use to run the 6801. These were lightweight (approximately 400 gm), 12-volt, 7 amp hour, lithium batteries purchased from Automated Media Services, Denver, Colorado, USA. Though very expensive ($150) because the lithium battery's performance is independent of the temperature, they were the best backup we possibly could have asked for. In future they could be considered as the first resort for a similar operation.

The radio worked well although we had to keep it warm during the night and were forced to warm it over the stove to try and improve performance in the very cold conditions: −10° C was not uncommon. Condensation forming on the radio proved to be a problem when cooking inside the tent.

Before evening or morning transmissions, the dipole aerial was strung up and kept aloft on ski poles and skis. We tried to orient it as best we could forming a broad V, with the open end

pointing towards the ship.

To save battery power, scheds were only made once a day and transmissions were kept as brief as possible. The primary sched. time was 8.30 pm in the evening, with a secondary sched. at 9.30 pm if we had been unable to make contact at first. Sometimes we were still sledging at 8.30 pm. We had a primary frequency that we would call on for five minutes at each sched., and if there was no contact we would switch to a pre-arranged secondary frequency. If both evening scheds were unsuccessful for reasons of poor propagation or any other cause, we followed the same primary and secondary sched. programme at 7.30 am and 8.30 am the next morning.

During our return trek to the coast, regular three-hour scheds with the 6801 were instituted to keep the helicopter evacuation party informed of our position and the local weather. These communications were instrumental in assisting the *Greenpeace* helicopter to pick us up and so avoid spending an unplanned winter in the Antarctic.

The second field radio was a very compact 1-watt, HF Codan 8332 hand-held transceiver that had both whip and dipole antennae. This unit had capacity for only two frequencies, which we made compatible with frequencies in the 6801. Because of the very low power (6 AA alkaline cells), we found the unit operated only in line of sight up to about 20 kilometres. The radio was, however, instrumental in saving Chris Hilton's life and mine. When we were caught in the break-out of the pack-ice in Moubray Bay, the Codan 8332 enabled us to call the ship for help. When we needed to cut down our weight, however, this hand-held unit also had to be cached.

Any party contemplating a similar undertaking would be well advised to investigate using a compact amateur HF transceiver as a field radio, providing a licensed operator was part of the team and snow machine transport was being used.

NATURAL SCIENCE

Peter Gill

ALTHOUGH governments tend to regard Antarctica and Antarctic science as their special domain, private expeditions have made valuable contributions to our knowledge of the region and its natural history since the early days of the continent's exploration. In recent years this knowledge has increased enormously but there are still large gaps in our understanding. The Antarctic ecosystem is probably extremely dynamic, but certain fundamental aspects of it, such as the distribution and abundance of species, are still poorly understood and can only be studied by observation over time.

When I was asked to join the expedition I began to consider what sort of scientific program would suit our other activities. I didn't have to think too hard: a vessel the size of the *Allan And Vi Thistlethwayte,* with its small and busy crew, does not lend itself to the types of research – often highly specialised work requiring sophisticated technology – carried out on larger ships. Our program was very modest, being based on simple observations of vertebrate fauna during passage and at Cape Hallett, as well as recording prevailing conditions such as sea state and temperature, and weather and ice conditions. I also wanted the others to become interested in the wildlife of the south, and to participate in my observations whenever possible.

We had hoped, after depositing the climbers at Cape Hallett, to pursue my special interest in whales by returning to the Ross Sea to look for them, to observe their feeding behaviours and record their underwater sounds. Ice conditions dictated otherwise, however, and the penguins, skuas and seals of Seabee Hook came under scrutiny instead. Due to 'pre-departure overload' I hadn't prepared for this eventuality, and was unable to seek answers to specific questions which specialists could have provided me with. The observations at Hallett are thus those of a naturalist, enthusiastic but perhaps not quite well enough informed.

Observations at Sea

SEABIRDS: A daily log was kept of sightings. Oceanic birds are difficult for novices to identify, but several of the crew became keen observers: in the lonely expanses of the Southern Ocean they are companionable viewing, from the powerful soaring of albatrosses to the delicate mothlike fluttering of storm petrels. As we motored south the predictable changes in species occurred, and it's always a thrill to record the first sightings of the more polar species, confirming our approach to the world of ice. Over thirty species were sighted during the voyage – too long a list to include here.

MARINE MAMMALS: As marine mammals are notoriously difficult to identify at sea, I asked to be informed of any sightings. Our most common sighting, however, was of one of the most distinctive small cetaceans in the world – the beautiful, exuberant and little-known hourglass dolphin *(Lagenorhynchus cruciger)* – which accompanied us on six occasions between 52° 28' S and 65° 25' S latitude.

Fur seals were sighted on two occasions: the first, at 45° 40'S was probably either an Australian fur seal *(Arctocephalus pusillus doriferus)* or a New Zealand fur seal *(A. forsteri)*; and the second, off the New Zealand coast, was almost certainly the New Zealand species. These creatures are often found well away from land, and the first one sighted accompanied us for several hours. Crabeater seals *(Lobodon carcinophagus)*, a krill-eating denizen of open sea pack-ice, were seen when the *Allan And Vi Thistlethwayte* was beset in close pack at the mouth of the Ross Sea.

Baleen whales winter in warm tropical waters and feed in the Antarctic in summer. None were sighted until we approached Cape Hallett, when we were treated to the sight of fifty or more fin whales *(Balaenoptera physalus)*, which, at a maximum length of 24 metres, is the second largest after the blue whale *(B. musculus)*. The whales were spread out and feeding in pods (groups) of up to twenty, their tall blows golden in the evening light. Unfortunately we were unable to approach the feeding action and so could not identify the prey, which was probably a species of krill *(Euphausia* sp.) Several Minke whales *(B. acutorostrata)* were also in the area.

Underwater vocalisations were recorded by hydrophone while a pod of fin whales swam nearby, and these sounds appear to be particularly interesting: preliminary analysis indicates that they are hitherto unrecorded, and may possibly be specific to feeding situations in the Antarctic. Very little work has been done on whale vocalisations in Antarctic waters, not least because the ships used by national expeditions are expensive to operate, and very noisy underwater; yachts, being cheap to operate and quiet, are ideal for this type of research.

Observations at Cape Hallett

BIRDS: When we arrived on 1 February 1988, there were, at a conservative estimate, some 20,000 Adelie penguins (*Pygoscelis adeliae*) in the rookery on Seabee Hook. Recent surveys indicate that Adelie numbers at Hallett have returned to the levels which existed prior to human settlement in 1957. The effect of human habitation in the decade or so from 1957 was a reduction by a third in Adelie numbers: the station was abandoned for this reason in 1973. At the peak of the breeding season there would be close to 250,000 penguins in the rookery, so my estimate may have been very conservative.

Most birds seemed fat and healthy, and adults were frequently seen feeding two chicks, an indication of a good season. In a poor season one of the two chicks produced by Adelies often dies. The presence of feeding whales in close proximity to the Cape indicated a food source within easy reach, at least for a time. The numbers of penguins declined dramatically over the weeks of our stay, as juvenile birds fledged and adults completed their post-breeding moult before heading out to sea for the winter. By the time we left there were fewer than 200 birds in the rookery.

On 16 February 1988, two freshly moulted Chinstrap penguins (*Pygoscelis antarctica*) were seen on Seabee Hook, mingling quietly with the Adelies. They were presumably from the colony in the Balleny Islands, several hundred kilometres to the north.

South polar skuas (*Catharacta maccormicki*) are very sensitive to human disturbance and have been declining in numbers at Cape Hallett. They are very determined defenders of their nests and young, and we gave them right of way whenever possible. Frequently we observed skua chicks brought into the rookery by their parents to be closer to their food supply as they grew. Predation by skuas on weak or abandoned penguin chicks is constant, obvious and brutal, but the oft-maligned skua is merely struggling to raise its own brood before the brief summer ends. A dead banded skua was found and the band sent to the Dominion Museum, Wellington: the bird was twenty years old.

We also noted the presence of different species of petrels at Cape Hallett. Wilson's storm petrels (*Oceanites oceanicus*) were commonly seen, and were possibly nesting in the cliffs of Cape Hallett. Others included Southern giant petrels (*Macronectes giganteau*), which were seen twice; Snow petrels (*Pagodroma nivea*), which were also seen twice; and a flight of Antarctic petrels (*Thalassoica antarctica*) which were seen winging inland at high altitude.

MAMMALS: Weddell seals (*Leptonychotes weddelli*) were common visitors to Willett Cove, resting on ice-floes and beaches during the day, where they are easily approached. The largest number present at a given time during our stay was thirty. The breeding season had finished before our arrival, and we saw many weaned juveniles. Weddell seals feed at night, diving as deep as 400 metres to catch fish and squid.

Of great interest were the underwater calls of these animals, which could be heard at night through the hull of the boat, and which I recorded on several occasions using a hydro-phone. Dr Jeanette Thomas of Hawaii, an authority on Weddell sounds, has told me that the recordings are significant because, except for this case, there are no other existing recordings made when subadults are present; and because there are few recordings made outside the breeding season. The Hallett sounds may also be a regional 'dialect', distinct from those in other parts of Antarctica.

Leopard seals (*Hydrurga leptonys*) were seen in Willett Cove on two occasions, in an area where juvenile Adelies learn to swim. Although the leopard seal preys on young penguins during the breeding season, and has also been known to prey on young Crabeater seals, it is primarily a krill eater.

A mature bull elephant seal (*Mirounga leonina*) was hauled out on Seabee Hook on 10 February 1988. While immature and female animals remain in subantarctic waters, where breeding occurs, adult males are known to moult on Antarctic beaches in summer, although their activities in far southern waters are otherwise a mystery.

Three Minke whales were sighted in Edisto Inlet, two of them while the ice was breaking out during 6-7 February 1988. It may be that these animals were moving into the area just made available for feeding by the egress of the ice. These sightings were very brief.

It is difficult to study the wildlife of Antarctica without becoming aware of the threats which face it. This expedition reinforced in me the wonder that I had felt on a previous visit, as I considered the toughness of such creatures as the Adelie penguin, which is totally at home in conditions hostile to our frail human forms. They have adapted to their permanent ice age over tens of thousands of years, as have the other Antarctic fauna. Yet in the short history of human incursions into the region we have managed to grossly disturb the existing balance by such endeavours as the massacre of the baleen whales and, more currently, the destruction of Antarctic finfish stocks, which is still in progress.

The longterm effects of these disturbances are not yet known, but the new threats which loom − notably the exploitation of krill and of mineral resources − promise no more restraint than was shown to the whales and fish. In fact, these developments directly threaten the most essential requisites of animals such as Adelies − their food supply and their breeding sites. We may be witnessing the beginning of the end for the Antarctic marine ecosystem. The destruction of finfish persists despite sound scientific advice against continued fishing, and the way toward mineral exploitation has been cleared by the creation of the Antarctic Minerals Regime, although its proponents claim that it is primarily a conservation document.

There is no shortage of scientific research being carried out by governments in Antarctica, and yet the ultimate hypocrisy is to justify their presence under the banner of science while manoeuvring for economic and political advantage, to the ultimate detriment of the Antarctic environment. Private organisations without vested interests, such as Greenpeace and our own expedition, seem to bear the responsibility of informing the public about these issues. While I doubt that the scientific results of our expedition will raise much dust, hopefully they may have increased your awareness of some unique and beautiful animals, and of the problems which confront their immediate future.

A WORD FROM THE SHIP'S COOK

Margaret Werner

My occupation is cooking, and the food I prepared at my tea shop in Mt Victoria, NSW, must have pleased my rockclimbing friends because they invited me to be cook and quartermistress on their expedition to Antarctica. I had no hesitation about the adventurous nature of the voyage, but I was unsure about cooking at sea. I had never sailed anywhere before, so I resolved not to get sick — luckily my resolution worked! I had visions of being able to bake lots of cakes and biscuits for the crew to enjoy but a rocking kitchen made everything more strenuous and time-consuming than I imagined. The motion of the *Allan And Vi Thistlethwayte* was unpredictable, so I needed to hold on and brace myself in order to complete even the simplest manoeuvre. I quickly learned how difficult it was to pour tea — and get it in the cup — while trying to hold onto the cup, the teapot and something firmly attached to the floor or walls of the ship!

Rather than working out a menu for three months, I roughly calculated the quantities of various food-stuffs which could be stowed in relatively accessible places. After that, I rarely planned our meals more than one or two days in advance. I did prepare about a week's worth of meals in Sydney, which I intended to keep in the ship's refrigerator for the first week at sea, but because of our late departure we ate most of these meals before we left Sydney Harbour.

The weather had a marked effect on the menu. If it was very rough I prepared an easy meal like scrambled eggs and baked beans, followed by tinned peaches and custard. Also, rough weather dampened people's appetites, so I did not need to prepare as much food. When conditions were good I was able to produce more elaborate meals: for example, soup, followed by potato curry or gnocci, with steamed pudding or pancakes for dessert. Lunch was usually a do-it-yourself affair once I had cut up cheese and pulled out packets of biscuits and jars of pickles and olives from storage, but sometimes I would cook chappatis or pikelets. Much of the food generously donated to the expedition was easy to use, such as nuts, powdered milk and tinned food.

Boxes and boxes of rice cakes and snap-frozen dinners (reserved as emergency rations for the winter) created storage problems because they were bulky and their cardboard containers tended to disintegrate when stowed near water. They were continually moved from place to place while I rummaged for supplies to use immediately.

Tinned food was stored in the bilges under the floors of the cabins. The bilges filled with water and, though the water was pumped out, the labels had to be removed so that the sodden paper did not clog the pumps. The contents of each can was written on the can with marking pen, then the whereabouts of every can was recorded in a book. Of course, this procedure took lots of time, but our provisions would have been impossible to locate otherwise. Close to the kitchen area and easily accessible were lockers in which we stored food for immediate use, and shelves where plastic jars were secured behind rubber cords to prevent them jumping around. All containers were plastic, as glass is a dangerous commodity on board — a factor we were glad we had remembered when our boat tipped over in the gale and containers went flying all around the galley. Rather than broken glass to clean up, we only had banana chips, custard powder, peppermint tea, and dozens of containers and utensils. The amount of food stored on board was huge because we had enough to keep eleven people fed for one year in case we were frozen into the sea-ice for the winter.

Storing perishables was another problem, the main obstacles being space and refrigeration. We stored apples and oranges under Chris's bunk and they kept perfectly — we were even eating them two months after leaving. The potatoes managed to find a dry place in the Fish Cabin. My biggest grouch, though, was the storage of my onions in mesh bags on the aft deck which consequently meant they froze when we reached 60° S.

Fuel was another consideration. Gas would have been convenient and clean, but dangerous on board a ship carrying diesel fuel. The alternative was kerosene or electricity, and for the first week or so we had both. Initially we had 240-volt power and a small fan-forced oven to bake bread. I was able to make scones and cakes if enough cake-mix remained in the baking dish. Judging by their short life when presented to the crew these were all very successful. We also had an electric jug to heat water for drinks — very convenient, especially for those standing watch during the night.

When the generator broke down, however, everything had to be cooked on three rather derelict primus-style stoves. Eventually I became proficient at operating them, but there was a constant leakage of unburnt kerosene fumes which brought oaths from the boys on watch in the wheelhouse. Life would have been much easier with new, good-quality stoves of the same design. Another problem we had was that of seawater leaking into the kerosene jerry cans, which was not detected until it was transferred into the stoves. As a result, the stoves frequently went out, sending black smoke pouring up into the wheelhouse each time. The primuses themselves were fitted into a custom-made Kelly stove-housing, where they could be set perpendicular so that the pots remained reasonably full even when boat was leaning through 40°. This arrangement proved satisfactory except when we were in very choppy conditions and I had overfilled the saucepans. Refilling the primus stoves in rough weather halfway through cooking a meal was a frustrating chore, and sometimes the kerosene spilled, causing the floor to become very slippery.

Under the stoves was a compartment for the gash (nautical for rubbish bucket) which had a long rope on it. While out on the open ocean the gash was handed up to the boys in the wheelhouse who emptied the rubbish overboard. The empty bucket was trailed by the rope in the ocean to rinse it. All plastic bags and containers were kept on board to be disposed of when we returned to Australia, filter-feeding whales can choke on plastic bags, and we did not want to make even the smallest contribution to the extinction of these species. In Antarctic waters, we were careful not to throw anything overboard because we were aware of the delicate marine ecosystem there.

Another interesting aspect of cooking at sea in a small boat was how we had to *think* about using water. Hot and cold taps in a normal household kitchen are taken for granted, but in a yacht the size of the *Allan And Vi Thistlethwayte* pumps for cold fresh water and cold seawater were all that we had. Water storage was aft in the galley, at floor level and under the bench seats. As we progressed south, our feet were always cold because of the metal tanks full of water. From the time we reached the pack-ice until we crossed that latitude again five weeks later, the water froze in the pipes overnight when they were not in use. It was necessary to heat seawater on the primus, then soak rags to wrap around the valves in an attempt to get the fresh water pump working. This was a horrible job so, when we were moored, Pete, Ken and I collected water from the melt-off at the foot of a nearby glacier and stored it in a plastic barrel lashed to the wall in the wheelhouse. Obtaining water for cooking therefore meant climbing the stairs up to the wheelhouse to fill the kettle or pan with cups of water from the barrel.

While at sea, washing-up was an entertaining affair, and the procedure changed with our different tacks. On the starboard tack, our sink remained continually full of water, unless the sea-cock was shut, and all the water was ladled into a saucepan to be thrown overboard. On a port tack, the sink drained. It wasn't unusual for the person doing the washing-up to have their clothes drenched or their gumboots filled by water leaping from the sink when the boat was hit by a larger than average wave. The person drying up had to be quick to catch the bowls sliding backwards and forwards on the bench before they fell to the perpetually wet and slimy floor. Since returning to Australia I have discovered a woven rubber mat which would have been wonderful for stopping dishes sliding about during drying up or when I was serving food. (Of course, in rough seas food even jumps out of hand-held bowls.) Our fresh water was precious, so dishes and washing-up had to be done in seawater, which does not hold a lather even if one uses a whole bottle of detergent. All hot water had to be heated on the primuses.

Even with these difficulties we managed to eat very well. The best approach was to see the funny side of all the catastrophes — which meant we had a hilarious time in the galley.

SPONSORSHIP

Lyle Closs

In 1988, Australia's Bicentennial year, most Australian companies were involved in some form of sponsorship. In return for it they gained media exposure, strong marketing vehicles, the best seats for their executives and guests at various functions and events, as well as many other benefits that gave a quantifiable return on their investment.

Few sponsors, however, were told that they could not watch the event they were sponsoring. Few were told that there were major dangers associated with the event for which they were putting up money. But no other sponsors were offered an event that encapsulated the challenge of true exploration, the spirit of the frontier, and the danger and excitement of going where no humans had ever gone before.

All we needed was a ship and enough fuel, food and equipment for eleven people to sail 4000 nautical miles, survive for up to eighteen months in the most inhospitable climate in the world, as well as for six of the team to travel 300 kilometres overland across unknown glaciers and through passes, in order to scale a massive unclimbed peak.

We were an endorsed Bicentennial event, but were given no funding by the Australian Bicentennial Authority or any other Government department. So we offered a wide range of promotional benefits tailored to the requirements of each company we approached and to the level of sponsorship they wished to provide.

The task of organising the expedition and acquiring sponsorship consumed us for fifteen months, leaving our families and friends bewildered and too often alone. It was a long and arduous task. Again and again we received letters of rejection, politely wishing us well in our venture.

We attended meetings in company boardrooms, in advertising and public relations agencies. We showed photos, talked enthusiastically, presented proposals, made endless follow-up phone calls. But still polite rejection pursued us across the numerous corporate reception rooms—and so on we went to the next.

Computer Sciences of Australia lent us a personal computer on which I wrote letters during every night of 1987. By October, however, we were getting desperate.

Then Sigma Data Corporation came in as our first large sponsor. This enabled us to pay for the skidoo and sledge that were so crucial to our plans. We had ordered the equipment with no idea whether we would be able to pay — and our suppliers had been pushing for their payment.

Australian Geographic also came in as a large sponsor, and things seemed to be on the move at last. Companies agreed to supply us with their food and equipment in return for photos of their products in the extreme conditions of Antarctica and for credits in the expedition documentary and book. Some went further — Rosella-Lipton supplied us with a range of foodstuffs, and helped us purchase a second-hand Zodiac rubber raft: we had a Continental Cup-a-Soup sign painted on its side.

With only weeks to go we were still far short of our target. Sam Chisholm, the managing director of the television network, TCN Channel 9, decided to back our film, thus providing much needed funds, but still we could not afford to charter the boat. It was mid-December, and we were due to sail on Christmas Day.

Greg Mortimer and I agreed to borrow the extra money and somehow try to make it up in whatever way possible on our return. Then Allan Thistlethwayte stepped in and saved us from this desperate measure.

A mining entrepreneur who had once just missed out on a position as a base leader with the Australian National Antarctic Research Expeditions, Allan wanted to travel with us. With regret we explained that he could not come. The conditions were likely to be too extreme. Despite this, his enthusiasm for our venture carried the day. It was a fantastic moment for all of us. We could leave Sydney with a balanced budget, saving all our energies for the task ahead.

The members of the Bicentennial Antarctic Expedition would like to thank the following sponsors without whose help we would never have succeeded:

Abbott Laboratories
Air New Zealand Ltd
AKG Accoustics
Alex Boden
All Graphics
Alpine Accoutrements
Astra
Attiki Pty Ltd
Australian Geographic Society
Hugo Bandelie
Bayer Australia Ltd
Beecham Research
  Laboratories
Best Foods
Bioglan Laboratories (Aust.)
J. Blackwood and Son Ltd
Boehringer Ingelheim Pty Ltd
Bollé (Dick Blass Optical)
Boots Company (Aust.) Pty Ltd
Campbell's Soups (Aust.)
  Pty Ltd
Cerebos (Aust.) Ltd
Ciba-Geigy Australia Ltd
CIG Medishield
Codan Pty Ltd
Colgate-Palmolive Pty Ltd
Computer Sciences of Australia
  Pty Ltd
Cottee's Foods
CSL-NOVO
David Bull and Associates
D. B. Briggs Pty Ltd (Norski)

De Costi Bros Seafoods
Demeter Food Products
Dulux Australia
Duracell Batteries
ETA Foods Ltd
F. H. Faulding Pty Ltd
Fawns and McAllan Pty Ltd
Film Australia
George Kinnear and Sons
Glaxo Australia Pty Ltd
Greens General Foods Pty Ltd
Gunz Photographics Pty Ltd
High Tops Equipment
ICI Australia Ltd
J & H Agencies
Janssen-Cilag Pty Ltd
John Danks and Son Pty Ltd
Kathmandu
Ken Brown's Inflatable Boats
Kenwood Electronics Australia
  Pty Ltd
King Gee Clothing
  Company Ltd
King Wyatt and Co. Pty Ltd
K Mart (Aust.) Ltd
Kodak (Australasia) Pty Ltd
L & P Photographic Supplies
  Pty Ltd
Lederle Laboratories Division
  (Cyanamid Australia Pty Ltd)
Letona Foods
Maritime Services Board of NSW

Master Foods of Australia
Maxwell Optical Industries
  Pty Ltd (Agent Nikon)
May and Baker
Meadow Lea Foods
Mountain Design Australia
Nestlé Australia Ltd
Nixdorf Computer Pty Ltd
NSW Egg Corporation
Ocean Oil
Outboard Marine Australia
  Pty Ltd (Johnson)
Paddy Pallin Pty Ltd
Pan Books (Aust.) Pty Ltd
Parke Davis Pty Ltd
Pergamon Press (Aust.) Pty Ltd
Philips Electronic Components
  Pty Ltd
Plumrose (Aust.) Ltd
Project Blizzard
Queensland Butter Marketing
  Board
Ricegrowers' Co-op. Mills Ltd
Roche Products Pty Ltd
Rosella Lipton Pty Ltd
Rosken/Fisons
  Pharmaceuticals
Rowntree Hoadley Ltd
Safcol Holdings Ltd
Samuel Taylor
Sanitarium Health Food Co.
Schering Corp. USA

Searle Australia Pty Ltd
Sigma Data Corporation
  Pty Ltd
Summit Gear
Superscan Pty Ltd
Taubert Systems Pty Ltd
Allan Thistlethwayte
Thrifty Link (Burwood)
TCN Channel 9
Toshiba (Aust.) Pty Ltd
Universal Fluid Heads (Aust.)
  Pty Ltd
University of Technology
  (Sydney) Media Centre
Upjohn Pty Ltd
Verglas
Vision Graphics
Wellcome Australia Ltd
The Weston Biscuit Co.
Wilderness Equipment
Winthrop Laboratories
Wyeth Pharmaceuticals Pty Ltd
Youngs Flour Mills

ACKNOWLEDGEMENTS

THE members of the Bicentennial Antarctic Expedition would like to thank the following people without whose enthusiastic energy the preparation of the boat, the preparation and stowing of stores, and therefore the expedition, would not have been possible:

Quentin Blades, Florence Bondu, Ian Brokenshire, Camille Closs, Ian Collins, Phil Cushing, Simon Disney, Heather Dutton, Libby Eyre, FIMA team, Les Gaborits, Ron Gaher, Pete Giles, Elaine Gromovsky, Norma Harrington, Adam Hartley, Mary Hartley, Andy Henderson, Warren Jacobs, Chief Petty Officer Rory Jobbins, Celia Jones, Phil Kelly, Ralph Lindsay, Joe Lorincz, Roddy MacKenzie, Helen McMahon, Robin Miller, Geoff Mills, Vicki Mortimer, Jenny Pitty, Jane Putt, Michael Ragg, Keith Ralfs, Geoff Richards, Barbara Ryman, Barbara Scanlon, Ilona Schmidt, Alister Sim, Ron Sim, Walter Slamer, Arthur Sorenson, Adrian Teague, Alex Theakston, Margot Turner, Tim Watson, Kathie Werner, Tanya Werner, Jenny Young, and those whose names have somehow been omitted.

Before we departed for the Antarctic, we received invaluable advice from the Antarctic Division, and we are particularly grateful to Ian Allison, Rod Ledingham and Robin Graham. We would also like to thank all the amateur radio operators who, evening after evening, listened into our radio scheds and went out of their way to relay messages for us. The Expedition also wishes to express their deepest thanks to the crew of the MV *Greenpeace* and, in particular, Jim Cottier, Peter Wilkinson, Peter Malcolm and Garry Dukes. Finally, the people who made one of the most important contributions to the success of the expedition but, sadly, who often receive no credit – our families, partners and close friends: without you all we could never have done it.

ADDITIONAL PICTURE CREDITS

The video, *The Loneliest Mountain*, is available from Film Australia.

Index